Ilchester Almshouse Deeds. From the time of King John to the reign of James the First, A.D. 1200 to 1625. With appendix: containing some brief topographical notices of ancient Ivelcester.

William Rector Buckler

Ilchester Almshouse Deeds. From the time of King John to the reign of James the First, A.D. 1200 to 1625. With appendix: containing some brief topographical notices of ancient Ivelcester.
Buckler, William Rector
British Library, Historical Print Editions
British Library
1866
204 p. ; 8°.
10368.f.16.

The BiblioLife Network

This project was made possible in part by the BiblioLife Network (BLN), a project aimed at addressing some of the huge challenges facing book preservationists around the world. The BLN includes libraries, library networks, archives, subject matter experts, online communities and library service providers. We believe every book ever published should be available as a high-quality print reproduction; printed on- demand anywhere in the world. This insures the ongoing accessibility of the content and helps generate sustainable revenue for the libraries and organizations that work to preserve these important materials.

The following book is in the "public domain" and represents an authentic reproduction of the text as printed by the original publisher. While we have attempted to accurately maintain the integrity of the original work, there are sometimes problems with the original book or micro-film from which the books were digitized. This can result in minor errors in reproduction. Possible imperfections include missing and blurred pages, poor pictures, markings and other reproduction issues beyond our control. Because this work is culturally important, we have made it available as part of our commitment to protecting, preserving, and promoting the world's literature.

GUIDE TO FOLD-OUTS, MAPS and OVERSIZED IMAGES

In an online database, page images do not need to conform to the size restrictions found in a printed book. When converting these images back into a printed bound book, the page sizes are standardized in ways that maintain the detail of the original. For large images, such as fold-out maps, the original page image is split into two or more pages.

Guidelines used to determine the split of oversize pages:

• Some images are split vertically; large images require vertical and horizontal splits.
• For horizontal splits, the content is split left to right.
• For vertical splits, the content is split from top to bottom.
• For both vertical and horizontal splits, the image is processed from top left to bottom right.

10.68. p. 16

Ilchester Almshouse Deeds.

FROM THE TIME OF KING JOHN TO THE REIGN OF JAMES THE FIRST.
A.D. 1200—1625.

WITH APPENDIX:
CONTAINING SOME BRIEF TOPOGRAPHICAL NOTICES OF ANCIENT IVELCESTER.

BY THE
REV. W. BUCKLER, M.A.

QUID DIGNUM TANTO FERET HIC PROMISSOR HIATU?

HOR.

YEOVIL:
PRINTED AND PUBLISHED BY W. H. COATES.

MDCCCLXVI.

INTRODUCTION.

In the Autumn of 1858, several Packets of old Deeds, relating to the Property of the Almshouse at Ilchester, were restored by the Representative of the late Lord Huntingtower, (formerly Sir William Manners) to the custody of the newly constituted Board of Trustees of the Ilchester Almshouse Charity. *

These Manuscripts follow in regular succession, from the time of King John and Henry III., through the reigns of Edw. I, Edw. II, and Edw. III, Richard the Second, Henry IV, Henry V, and Henry VI, Edward IV, Hen. VII, Hen. VIII, Queen Elizabeth and James the First.

In some of them, the Regnal Date is wanting; and these undated Deeds are, most of them, anterior to the reign of Edward the First. One may probably be assigned to the time of King John, or to a period certainly not later than the commencement of Henry the Third's reign. The earliest recorded date is the seventh year of Edward I. Feb. 3rd, 1279.

They are written for the most part, in the usual contracted Latin; and some of the oldest of the manuscripts are very fine specimens of Calligraphy. A few, of the time of the Third Edward, are in Norman French; and two or three, belonging to the latter part of the 15th and the beginning of the 16th centuries, are in the quaint old English of the Period.

From the Reign of Henry VIII, the Deeds are few in number, of less comparative interest, and chiefly in the vernacular tongue.

* These Deeds are in the keeping of the Clerk to the Board.

The Documents thus unexpectedly brought to light, by their restoration to the right owners, refer to Lands and Tenements situate in the Parishes of Stocklinch Magdalen, Stocklinch Ottersay, Montacute, Chilthorne Domer, the Manor of Sock Dennis, Ilchester, Northover, Limington, Somerton Erleigh and the Parish of Somerton ; and a large proportion of the lands therein dealt with, including the Manor of Stocklinch, constitutes the Property of the Ilchester Almshouse Charity at the present time.

The most important of these Manuscripts, in relation to the Charity, are the two which bear date, respectively, on March 12, 1426, in the fourth year of Henry VI, and on Feb. 12, 1477, in the sixteenth year of Edward IV.

The former is the DEED OF FOUNDATION, executed by ROBERT VEEL; wherein he provides, that subsequently to the fulfilment of certain specified obligations, the Trustee-ship of the Almshouse, and of the Charity Lands, should be vested in the Bailiffs and Burgesses of Ilchester and their Successors, for ever. The other Deed, is the Indenture made by Swanne, a Canon of Wells, and others, to the Bailiffs and Burgesses; by which the intention and will of the Founder in this respect, were fully carried out.

These TRANSCRIPTS are arranged in Chronological oderr ; the contractions of the original text are for the most part omitted, and the abbreviated syllables are given *in extenso.* After each Transcript, is added an abstract of its contents, in English. The Appendix contains some brief notices of Mediæval Ilchester, arranged under separate heads, and elucidated by a Plan of the Town, on the basis of Dr. Stukeley's ISCHALIS.

W. BUCKLER.

THE RECTORY, ILCHESTER, 1865,

Ilchester Almshouse Deeds.

No. I. undated—Time of King John.

Sciant presentes et futuri quod ego Willielmus Dacus dedi et concessi et hac presenti carta confirmavi Herwardo pro homagio et servicio suo Mesuagium quod Paganus Hoperius tenuit cum duabus dimidiis acris quas predictus P (aganus) tenuit Et cum la Rig acra Et cum duobus sextariis prati que jacent juxta pratum H de Spegeton Quorum unum jacet versus Orientem et aliud versus Occidentem juxta predictum pratum H de Spegeton Et cum una perticata prati que jacet versus Occidentem juxta Kinges furlang Habendum et Tenendum sibi et heredibus suis de me et heredibus meis libere et quiete plenarie et integre Reddendo inde annuatim Undecim Solidos per quatuor anni Terminos Scilicet ad Festum Sancti Johannis tres et triginta denarios ad Festum S'c'i Michaelis xxxiii denar. Ad Natale Domini xxxiii den. Ad Pascham xxxiii den. pro omni servicio salvo servicio extrinseco Pro hac autem donacione mea et concessione dedit mihi predictus H (erward) dimidiam Marcam Argenti in recognicione Et ut hec donacio mea et concessio Rata et Stabilis permaneat Presentem Cartam Sigilli mei apposicione corroboravi Hiis Testibus Giliberto Daco Thoma de Cirencestre Roberto Triz Galfrido de Hospitale Willielmo Raffe Will de Geddi'g Henrico Caretio Ricardo clerico qui hanc Cartam fecit Et multis aliis.

William Dacus, (Dacres?) grants to Herward, for his homage and service, a Messuage held before by Hoper the Countryman; Also two half-acres held by the same countryman ; and the Ridge acre, and two sixth parts (of an acre) of Meadow adjoining land of H. de Spegeton ; and one quarter of an acre of meadow, eastward near Kinges furlang To Have and to Hold in consideration of a yearly rent of twelve shillings, to be paid quarterly, at the Feasts of St. John and St. Michael, at Christmas and Easter: in lieu of all service except special service. For this Grant Herward pays to Dacus as an acknowledgement or Fine half a mark of silver. Dacus ratifies the agreement by setting his Seal to the Deed—In the presence of Gilbert Dacus, Thomas of Cirencester, Robert Triz, Geoffry of the Hospital, Willm Raffe, William of Gedding, Henry Carter, Richard the Clerk, who drew up the Deed ; and many others.

Note.—The Charter of the Borough of Ilchester will assist in fixing the approximate age of this MS. In this Charter, granted by Philip and Mary, earlier Charters are cited ; and this extract from one of them is quoted— " King John gave to William Dacus a parcel of the Town."

No. 2, undated—Henry III.

Omnibus ad quos presens scriptum pervenerit Willielmus Cocul de Lumyntona Salutem in Domino Noverit universitas vestra me dedisse concessisse et hoc presenti scripto meo confirmasse Radulpho Herward de Ivelcestre in liberum Maritagium cum Matillida Filia mea unum mesuagium cum curtillagio et cum omnibus pertinenciis suis in villa de Lumyntona Illud scilicet quod jacet inter tenementum meum et tenementum Willielmi Busshup et quatuor acras terre arabilis in eodem manerio quarum una jacet in Suht broc furlange inter terram Willielmi le Vyngnur et terram Gyleberti clerici Et una jacet in Mydenhulle ex parte occidentali juxta terram que fuit Ricardi le Mey et terram Ade le Rns Et due jacent super la Dydehulle inter terram Roberti le Rat et terram Ade le Rus Et unam perticatam prati que jacet in la Mere inter pratum meum et pratum quod quondam fuit Domini Radulfi filii Herward Habendum et Tenendum dictum mesuagium cum curtillagiis et dictam terram cum prato predicto et cum omnibus aliis pertinenciis dictis Radulfo et Matillide et heredibus suis de predictis Radulfo et Matillida legitime procreatis De me et heredibus meis sive meis assignatis libere quiete bene et in pace jure hereditario imperpetuum Reddendo inde annuatim mihi et heredibus meis vel meis assignatis Unum Par Albarum Chirothecarum vel unum denarium ad Pascham pro omni servicio exactione et seculari demanda Et si contingat quod dicta Matillida sine herede de se et de predicto Radulfo legitime procreato obierit Volo et concedo pro me et heredibus meis sive meis assignatis quod predictus Radulfus sine aliqua contradiccione habeat et teneat dictum mesuagium cum curtillagio et dictam terram cum prato predicto et cum omnibus aliis pertinenciis per predictum servicium toto tempore vite sue Ita scilicet quod post terminum vite dicti Radulfi dictum mesuagium cum Curtillagio et dicta terra cum prato predicto et cum omnibus aliis pertinenciis mihi et heredibus meis sive meis assignatis sine aliqua contradiccione heredum suorum sive suorum assignatorum plenarie revertat Ego vero dictus Willielmus et heredes mei sive assignati dictum mesuagium et dictam terram cum prato predicto et cum omnibus predictis pertinenciis dictis Radulfo et Matillide et heredibus suis de predictis Radulfo et Matillida legitime procreatis Contra omnes mortales sicut predictum est Warantizabimus acquietabimus et per predictum servicium defendemus Et ut hec mea donacio concessio et presentis scripti confirmacio firmitatis robur obtineat Hoc presens Scriptum admodum chirographia confectum Sigilli mei impressione roboravi Hiis Testibus Johanne Albe Hugone de la Venele Willielmo Daubeny Roberto Tryz Stephano de Bromlyghe Will° Bbastard Willielmo Teissun clerico Et aliis.

———

William Cocul (otherwise le Keu) of Lumynton, gives to

Ralf Herward of Ivelcester, in free marriage with Matilda his daughter, a messuage with appurtenances in the village of Limington, situate between his own premises and those of Willm. Bishop. Also, four acres of arable land in the same Manor, one in South brook furlang, between land of William the Vintner and of Gilbert the Clerk, one in Middlehill westward, near land of Richard le Mey and Adam le Rus; the other two acres on Deadhill between land of Robert le Rat and Adam le Rus. Also, a quarter of an acre of meadow in the Mere, between a meadow of his own and one formerly belonging to Master Ralf the son of Herward. To Have and to Hold . . . By rendering thence every year one pair of white gloves or one penny, at Easter, in lieu of every service exaction and secular demand. Sealed in the presence of John Albe (White), Hugh de la Venele, William Daubeny, Robt. Tryz, Stephen de Bromlyghe, Willm Bastard, Willm. Teissun, clerk, and others.

Attached to this Deed is the Seal of Ralph Herward. The Device is, apparently, some ears of corn tied together with an ample fillet. The Motto, S (igillum) Radulfi Herward.

No. 3, undated—Henry III.

Omnibus ad quos presens scriptum pervenerit Johannes Albe de Ivelcestre Salutem in Domino Noverit universitas vestra me dedisse concessisse et presenti scripto meo confirmasse Radulpho Herward unam seldam in Chepstrete in villa Ivelcestre in liberum Maritagium cum Matillida filia Willielmi le Keu de Lymyntona nepte mea Que quidem Selda sita est inter seldam Hugonis le Rus et aream Rogeri Payvot exobposito tenementi dicti Hugonis juxta La Lane Habendum et Tenendum . . . Et ut hec mea donacio concessio et presentis scripti mei confirmacio firmitatis robur optineat Hoc presens scriptum admodum Cyrographya confectum Sigilli mei impressione roboravi Hiis Testibus—Will° Bastard, Hugone de la Venele, Stephano de Bromlyghe, Will° Daubeny, Roberto Tryz, Waltero Wytbryd, Will° Teissun clerico qui hoc scriptum composuit; Et aliis.

John Albe of Ivelcester to Ralph Herward—a shop in Chepstrete in the same Town, as a marriage portion with Matilda his grand-daughter, the daughter of William le Keu (Cocul No. 2) of Limington. The shop situate between the shop of Hugh le Rus and the yard of Roger Payvot near La Lane.

No. 4, undated—Henry III. or Edward I., early.

Sciant presentes et futuri quod ego Petrus de Draycote clericus dedi concessi et hac presenti carta mea confirmavi Willielmo le Keu de Lymyntone et Sarre uxori ejus unum mesuagium in Lymyntone quod quidem mesuagium situm est inter tenementum dicti Will¹ le Keu et tenementum tunc Will¹ Byssop Habendum et Tenendum totum dictum tenementum cum omnibus suis pertinenciis dictis Will° et Sarre uxori ejus et heredibus eorum de me et heredibus sive assignatis meis libere quiete integre bene et in pace jure hereditario imperpetuum Reddendo inde annuatim Deo et Beate Marie Ecclesie de Lymyntona duos solidos ad sustentationem quatuor cereorum in dicta Ecclesia per annum Videlicet ante Crucem duos cereos Et ante Altare Beate Marie Virginis unum cereum Et ante Altare Sancti Leonardi unum cereum Et mihi et heredibus meis vel meis assignatis dicti Willielmus et Sarra vel eorum heredes unam rosam ad Festum Nativitatis S'cti Johannis Baptiste pro omni servicio exactione et seculari demanda Et ut hec mea donacio concessio et presentis carte mee confirmatio Rata sit et stabilis imperpetuum Hanc presentem Cartam meam Sigilli mei impressione roboravi Hiis

Testibus—Dominis Mattheo de Ffurneus, Thoma de Hunteleghe, Militibus; Will° Fossard; Nicholao Cayllewey, Petro le
Rus; Johanne Colswayn, Will° Durre, Thoma Jakes, Waltero
de Wellesleghe clerico hujus carte notario Et multis aliis.

Peter of Draycote, clerk, to William le Keu (son of
Willm No. 3) of Lymntone and Sarah his wife, a messuage in
Limington, situate between the house of same Willm le Keu
and that of William Bishop. To Have . . . By render-
ing thereout every year, to God and the Church of the Blessed
Mary of Limington, Two Shillings, for the maintenance of four
wax tapers in the said church every year—Namely—Before
the Cross two Tapers, and before the Altar of the Blessed
Virgin Mary one Taper, and before the Altar of St. Leonard
one Taper . . . Witnesses, Sirs, Matthew de Furneus,
Thomas de Hunteleghe, Knights; Peter le Rus; Walter de
Wellesleghe, clerk, the notary of this Deed; and others.

No. 5, undated—Henry III. or Edward III., early.

Sciant presentes et futuri quod ego Willielmus Tessun de
Ivelcestre dedi concessi et hac presenti carta mea confirmavi
Ricardo filio Rogeri le Sepere et Alicie uxori sue et heredibus
et assignatis ejusdem Ricardi Unum Stabellum in Ivelcestre
Illud videlicet Stabellum quod situm est proximo juxta stabellum quod quondam fuit Thome Cabbel in Chepstret ville
predicte in parte australi et tenementum Luce Aurifabri in
parte boriali Tenend. et Habend. dictum Stabellum cum omnibus pertinenciis suis de me et heredibus meis vel meis assignatis dictis Ricardo et Alicie et heredibus vel assignatis ejusdem Ricardi libere quiete bene pacifice et integre jure hereditario inperpetuum Reddendo inde annuatim mihi et heredibus
meis vel meis assignatis dicti Ricardus et Alicia et heredes et
assignati dicti Ricardi sex denarios ad duos anni Terminos

Videlicet ad Pascha tres denarios et ad Festum S'cti Michaelis tres denarios et Firme ville predicte unum denarium ad Hocke- diem Et Willielmo Axstild unam rosam in Festo Nativitatis Beati Johannis Baptiste pro omni servicio ad me vel ad heredes meos pertinente   Pro hac autem mea donatione concessione et presentis carte mee confirmatione et Warantia habenda dederunt mihi predicti Ricardus et Alicia quatuor solidos stere- lingorum pre manibus Ego vero Willielmus et heredes mei et mei assignati dictum stabellum cum omnibus pertinenciis suis dictis Ric° et Alicie et heredibus et assignatis dicti Ric' War- antizabimus defendemus et ubique contra omnes homines et feminas aquietabimus inperpetuum Et ut hec mea donatio concessio et presentis carte mee confirmatio robur firmitatis inperpetuum optineat presentem cartam meam cum Sigilli mei impresione roboravi Hiis Testibus—Johanne de Koker, Thoma le Deghere, Waltero Frommie, Waltero Cole, Will° filio Stephani le Rus, Edwardo Cole, Ada Cole, Gilliberto de Tan- toune, Luca Aurifabro, Will° dicto Caretario Et aliis.

William Tessun of Ivelcester, to Richard the son of Roger le Sepere and Alice his wife, a stall in Ivelcestre, close to the stall once belonging to Thomas Cabbel in Chepstrete, on the south; and the house of Luke the Goldsmith on the north. To Have . . .   By a yearly payment of sixpence, one half at Easter, the other half at Michaelmas.   And to the Farm of the said Town one penny on Hockeday.   And to William Axstild one rose on the Feast of the Nativity of St. John the Baptist.   For this grant, Richard and Alice pay four shillings sterling, down, to Willm Tessun.

No. 6, undated—Edward I., early.

Sciant presentes et futuri quod Ego Cecilia Hereward de Ivelcestra in ligea viduetate mea dedi concessi et hac presenti

carta mea confirmavi Petro le Bere de Ivelcestra et Edithe
uxori sue unam acram terre arabilis jacentem in Campo de
Cilterne Dummere Videlicet apud Sewyesgore jacet una
dimidia acra proximo juxta terram Johannis Hagene in parte
occidentali Et alia dimidia acra jacet apud la Mere proximo
juxta terram predicti Johannis Hagene in parte occidentali
Tenend. et Habend. dictam unam acram terre arabilis de me
et heredibus meis vel assignatis Petro et Edithe et eorum
heredibus vel cuicumque eam dare assignare vendere vel legare
voluerint libere quiete bene et in pace in omnibus rebus et locis
jure hereditario inperpetuum Reddendo inde annuatim mihi et
heredibus meis unum par albarum cyrotecarum vel unum
obolum ad Pascha ad voluntatem tenentis pro omnimodis
serviciis sectis Curiarum scirarum hundredorum secularibus
exactionibus querelis et demandis ad quoscunque quocumque
modo spectantibus Pro hac autem mea donatione concessione
et presentis carte mee confirmatione dederunt mihi predicti
Petrus et Editha duas marcas esterelingorum pre manibus
Ego vero Cecilia et heredes mei et mei assignati predictam
acram terre cum omnibus pertinenciis suis dictis Petro et
Edithe et eorum heredibus vel cuicunque eam dare asignare
vendere vel legare voluerint ubique Warantizare et de omnimodis demandis secularibus exactionibus querelis sectis curiarum
scirarum hundredorum et omnimodis aliis ad quoscumque
quocumque modo pertinentibus adquitare et defendere tenemus
contra omnes homines et feminas Et ut hec mea donatio concessio et presentis carte mee confirmatio firma sit et stabilis
inperpetuum presentem cartam meam cum Sigilli mei impressione roboravi Hiis Testibus Waltero Cole, Will° de Aclere,
Thoma Cole, Johanne Pigaz, Thoma de Engelbi, Stephano de
Dummere, Johanne filio Radulphi, Johanne Hagene, Willielmo
dicto Caretario, hujus carte notario,   Et Aliis.

* Cecilia Hereward of Ivelcester, Widow, to Peter le

Bere of Ivelcester and Edith his wife; an acre of arable in Cilterne Dummere field.   By paying yearly one pair of white gloves, or one half-penny at Easter, at the option of the tenant; in lieu of all kinds of services, suits in County Courts and Courts of Hundreds . . . .   For which, Peter and Edith pay a Fine of two marks sterling in hand.   Among the Witnesses, William de Aclere (Oakley), and John son of Ralph (Herward).

No. 7, undated—Edw. I.

Sciant presentes et futuri quod Ego Matillis Hereward de Yvelcestre in pura viduitate mea dedi concessi et hac presenti carta mea confirmavi Will° le Keu de Lymintone fratri meo et Sarre uxori ejus duas acras terre arabilis et unam perticatam prati et unum denarium annui redditus cum pertinenciis in Manerio de Lymintone Illas scilicet duas acras que jacent super La Dedehylle inter terram que quondam fuit Roberti le Rat et terram Ade le Rus et illam perticatam prati que jacet in la Mere inter pratum quod quondam fuit Domini Radulphi Filii Hervardi et pratum Will¹ le Keu Et unum denarium annui redditus cum omni jure inde proveniente quem Rogerus de Crawecumbe mihi aliquando solebat solvere ad Pascha de uno tenemento quod situm est inter tenementum Will¹ Bissop et tenementum dicti Will¹ le Keu Hab. et Ten. dictas duas acras pratum et dictum denarium cum omnibus pertinenciis dicto Will° et Sarre uxori ejus et heredibus seu eorum assignatis de me et heredibus meis seu meis assignatis libere . . . . . Reddendo inde annuatim Capitalibus Dominis Feodi Unam Spicam Frumenti ad Festum S'cti Michaelis pro omni servicio . . . . Pro hac autem donatione concessione . . . . dederunt mihi dicti Willielmus et Sarra Viginti Solidos Argenti pre manibus Et Radulpho quondam viro meo viginti solidos et sex denarios Ego vero dicta Matillis Hereward et heredes mei . . . . . . contra omnes homines et feminas Waren-

tizabimus aquietabimus et ubique defendemus inperpetuum
Et ut hec mea . . . . hanc presentem Cartam Sigilli
mei proprii inpressione roboravi Hiis Testibus Will° de Romesyc,
Johanne Pigaz, Johanne Turke, Johanne de Estyntone, Will°
de Welesleghe, Et multis aliis.

Matilda Hereward of Yvelcester, Widow, to her brother
William le Keu (Nos. 2. 3.) of Limington, and Sarah his wife,
Two acres of arable, and a quarter of an acre of meadow, and
one penny of yearly rent, all in the Manor of Limington.
The two acres lie on the top of Deadhill; the quarter acre of
Meadow in La Mere, between land once the property of
Master Ralph son of Hervard, and land of Willm le Keu;
and one penny rent, formerly paid by Roger de Crawecumbe
at Easter, out of a tenement situate between the tenements of
Willm Bissop and William le Keu, By rendering yearly to
the Capital Lords of the Fee, one Ear of Corn at the Feast of
St. Michael. Fine paid by Willm and Sarah Twenty shillings
in Silver, in hand; "and to the Estate of Ralph my late
Husband, Twenty shillings and sixpence."

No. 8, undated—Edw. I.

Sciant presentes et futuri quod ego Thomas Capellanus
Dominus de Cilterne dedi et concessi et hac presenti carta mea
confirmavi Thome Cementario Nutricio meo pro humagio et
servicio suo unam acram terre Illam videlicet quam Christiana
mater Jordani Duket in puram et perpetuam Elimosynam
dedit Capelle mee de Cilterne Et jacet in Campo Australi
videlicet in Checfurlange versus Occidentem juxta Fossatam
de Thorne et incipit ab aquilone et protendit se versus
australem ad viam Regalem Hab. et Ten. de me et heredibus
meis vel meis assignatis sicut heredibus suis vel suis assignatis
Libere quiete pacifice integre et jure hereditario cum

omnibus libertatibus et liberis consuetudinibus Reddendo
inde annuatim Libere Capelle mee in Curia mea de Cilterne
erecte Tres denarios ad unum anni Terminum Scilicet ad
Vigiliam Assumcionis Beate Marie pro omni servicio
seculari exactione querela vel demandis ad me vel ad
heredes meos pertinentibus Ego vero Thomas et heredes
dictam acram terre cum omnibus pertinenciis suis prenominato
Thome et heredibus suis vel suis assignatis contra omnes
homines et feminas inperpetuum Warentizare tenemus et
defendere Et ut hec mea donacio et concessio firma et stabilis
perpetuis perseveret temporibus eam presenti scripto et Sigilli
mei impressione communivi Hiis Testibus Willo de Hewenebere, Johanne de Cinnoke, Rogero Pigaz, Ricardo Pingeho,
Galfrido de Hewenebere, Jordano Duket Et aliis.

Thomas the Chaplain, Lord of Cilterne, to Thomas the
Mason his Foster-father, an acre of land which Christiana, the
mother of Jordan Duket, gave in pure and perpetual Alms to
his Chapel of Cilterne. The acre situate in Checfurlange, in
South field, near Thorne Ditch. By paying thereout every
year to my Free Chapel, erected in my Parsonage House at
Cilterne, Three pence at one period of the year, namely on the
Eve of the Assumption of the Blessed Mary. Witnesses—
William de Hewenebere, Geoffry de Hewenebere, Jordan
Duket, and Others.

No. 9, undated—Edw. I.

Sciant pres. et fut. quod Ego Ricardus Pingeho de Chilterne
dedi concessi et hac presenti carta mea confirmavi pro me et
heredibus meis Stephano filio meo pro servicio suo unum
ferlingum terre in Chilterne Et domum et curtillagium quod
Magiota tenuit Partes vero terre sic jacent Super Montem
Liberorum hominum due acre In Hoka una acra In Lyvestede
una acra Ad caput de Livestede dimidia acra Ad a la Broke

dimidia acra In Bymera una acra In cultura de Coddecrofta una acra Super Smale hulle una acra In Holecumba una acra Juxta terram Radulfi Spihekat una acra ad parvam Manemede Et dimidia acra prati in Spmalemede Hab. et Ten. de me et heredibus meis sibi et heredibus suis vel assignatis libere et quiete pacifice et integre Reddendo inde annuatim unum par albarum cyrotecarum ad Pascha vel unum obolum et hoc ad libitum tenentis pro omni servicio et omni genere exactionis Salvo servicio Domini Regis quantum pertinet ad unum ferlingum terre in Manerio de Chilterne Et ego dictus Ricardus Pingeho dictum ferlingum terre cum omnibus pertinenciis suis contra omnes homines et feminas Warantizabimus imperpetuum et heredes mei Et ut hec mea donatio et concessio perpetuis temporibus perseveret presens scriptum Sigilli mei appositione roboravi Hiis Testibus Johanne de Eltone, Thoma Fageht, Jord. Duket, Thoma le Machum, Galfrido de Heuebere, Radulfo Faget, Thoma Grane de Bridiport, Radulfo le Machun de Bridiport, Et multis aliis.

Richard Pingeho of Chiltern, to Stephen his son, Ten acres of land in Chilterne, with a house and curtillage; On Free-mens' Hill two acres; In Hoka one acre; In Lyvestede one acre; At the head of Livestede half-an-acre; By the Brook half-an-acre; In Bymere one acre; In the ploughed ground of Coddecroft (now Cutcroft) one acre; On Smallhill one acre; In Holecumbe (Oakham) one acre; One acre at little Manemede (Manmead); and half-an-acre of Meadow in Smallmead. A pair of white gloves, or a half-penny, at the option of the tenant, to be rendered yearly at Easter, "in lieu of all kinds of service, save the service of our Lord the King as far as pertains to one ferlingus of land in the Manor of Chilterne."

No. 10, undated—Edw. I.

Notum sit omnibus presentes literas inspecturis quod Ego

Cristina filia Eustagii Carpentarii dedi et concessi et hac carta mea confirmavi Luce de la More et heredibus suis pro humagio et servicio suo totum jus meum quod habui in una virgata terre in Tintenelle quam predictus Eustagius pater meus et antecessores ejus et ego jure hereditario tenuimus Ten. et Hab. de me et heredibus meis Sibi et heredibus suis Libere et quiete cum omnibus liberis apendiciis suis ubicumque fuerint Reddendo mihi et heredibus meis annuatim Unum Par Cirotecarum de precio unius denarii pro omni servicio Salvo servicio Regali et Priori et Conventui Montis Acuti servicium quod antea solvebatur Pro hac autem donatione et concessione dedit mihi sepe dictus Lucas Unam Marcam argenti de garsume Ut igitur hec mea donatio et concessio firma permaneat in posterum Illam Sigillo meo roboravi Hiis Testibus Osberto de Stoke, Filippo Luvello Persona de Tintenelle, Amiano Persona de Crihg, Ricardo clerico de Tintenulle, Eustagio de Weleham, Rodulfo de la More, Et multis aliis.

. Cristina daughter of Eustace the Carpenter, to Luke de la More, all her right in one virgata (40 acres) of land in Tintenelle; " By rendering one pair of gloves of the price of one penny, in lieu of all service except the King's service, and the service which was heretofore customarily rendered to the Prior and Convent of Mont Acute." Luke pays to Cristina a fine (garsume) of one Mark in Silver. Witnesses—Osbert of Stoke, Philip Luvell Parson of Tintenelle; Amianus Parson of Crick; Richard, clerk, of Tintenulle; Eustace of Weleham,* Ralph de la More. *There is a Mill, about half way between Tintinhull and Stoke, which still goes by the name of Welham's Mill.

No. 11, undated—Edw. I.

Sci, pre. et fut. quod Ego Hugo de Valeze assensu et consensu Annie uxoris mee et heredum meorum dedi . . . . .

Matillidi que fuit filia Walteri Peck de Northovere quoddam
Mesuagium cum curt. in villa de Northovere quod situm est
juxta ten^m Henrici Bastard ex parte aust. Et undecim acras
terre arabilis in Campis de Northovere Quarum sex acre jacent
in Campo Boriali et quinque jacent in Campo Australi Quod
Mes. curt. et terram predictam dictus Walterus Peck
aliquando tenuit Ten. et Hab. dictum Mes. curt. et terram
predictam cum pert^s suis dicte Matillidi et hered, suis vel suis
assig. de me et hered. meis vel meis assig. libere quiete bene
et in pace jure hered^o inperp^m Reddendo inde annuatim mihi
et her. meis vel meis assig. dicta Matillis et her. sui et sui
assig. quinque Solidos et quatuor denarios obolum et quarterentem ad quatuor Anni terminos Videlicz Ad Fest. Nativit.
Beati Johannis Baptiste sexdecim denarios et quaderentem
Ad Fest. S'cti Mich'is sexdecim denarios et quarterentem Ad
Natale Domini sexdecim den. et quart. Et ad Fest. Pasche
sexdecim denarios pro omni servicio seculari exactione et
demanda Salvo servicio Regali quantum pertinet ad tantum
liberum tenementum in villa pred. Et salva Secta in Curia
mea ejusd. ville Et salvis amerciamentis Panis et Cervisie
Ego vero dictus Hugo et her. mei vel mei assig. dictum mes.
cum curt. et terra pred. et omnibus aliis perts. suis dicte
Matillidi et her^{us} suis et suis assig. contra omnes mortales
Warantizabimus inperp. Pro hac autem mea don. con. et hujus
carte mee confirm. dedit mihi dicta Matillis septem marcas
esterlingorum pre manibus Et ut hec mea don. con. et hujus
carte mee conf. rata et stabilis inperp. permaneat hanc cartam
Sigilli mei inpressione roboravi Hiis Testibus Domino Galfrido
de Northovere Capellano, Henrico Bastard, Will^o Fabro,
Filippo Bastard, Oseberto de Northovere Molendinario,
Turstano de Northovere Aurifabro, Ricardo Richeman de
Northovere, Et aliis.

Hugh de Valeze, with the assent and consent of Anna his

wife; to Matilda daughter of the late Walter Peck of North-over; a certain messuage in the village of Northover; and Eleven acres of Arable in Northover Fields; of which, six are in the North, and five in the South Field; which house and lands were some time in the occupation of the said Walter Peck. To render a yearly payment of five shillings and four-pence three farthings; thus—At Mid-summer, Michaelmas, and Christmas, one shilling and four-pence farthing; and at Easter one Shilling and four-pence—instead of all service . . . . . "saving suit in my Court of the same village, and saving the Assize of bread and beer." Matilda pays to Hugh a Fine of seven marks sterling in hand. Witnesses—Master Geoffry of Northover, chaplain; Willm Faber, Osbert of Northover, Miller; Turstan of Northover, Goldsmith; and others,

---

No. 12, undated,—probably Edw. III.

Sci pres. et fut. quod Ego Alicia quondam Uxor Johannis de Beauchampe de Somersete Militis Domini de Hatche dedi concessi et hac presenti Carta Indentata confirmavi Willielmo de Beauchampe Militi Fratri meo Will° de Burtone Militi Ricardo Craddoke Persone Ecclesie de Cury Malet et Henrico de Arderne Totum statum meum quem habeo in omnibus Maneriis terris tenementis redditibus serviciis et advocacionibus meis cum pert^s in Comitatibus Middelsex' Somersetee et Devonee Hab. et Ten. totum statum pred^m pred^is Will° Will° Ric° Henrico heredibus et assig^s eorum de Capitalibus Dominis Feodorum illorum per servicia inde debita et de jure consueta In cujus rei Testimonium presenti carte indentate Sigillum meum apposui Hiis Testibus Thoma de Bello Campo Comite Warr'; Hugone de Stafford Comite Stafford; Johanne de Seynlowe, Thoma Trenet', Nicholao Golafre, Militibus. Et aliis.

Alice, Widow of John de Beauchampe of Somerset,

Knight, Lord of Hatche, to William Beauchampe, Knight, her brother; William Burtone, Knight; Richard Craddoke Parson of the Church of Cury Malet; and Henry of Arderne; all her right and interest in all her Manors lands rents services and Advowsons in the Counties of Middlesex Somerset and Devon. To Have and to Hold of the Capital Lords of those Fees by the due and customary services. Witnesses—Thomas de Beauchampe Earl of Warwick, Hugh de Stafford Earl of Stafford; John de Seynlowe (St Lo)? Thomas Trenet', Nicholas Golafre, Knights; and others.

No. 13, A.D., 1279. Feb. 3.

Hec est Finalis Concordia facta in Curia Domini Regis apud Westmonasterium in Crastino Purificationis Beate Marie anno Regni Regis Edwardi Filii Regis Henrici Septimo Coram Thoma Welonde Waltero de Helym Johanne de Lovetot Rogero de Leyc Willielmo de Burntone Justiciariis et aliis Domini Regis fidelibus tunc ibi presentibus Inter Johannem de Bello Campo Querentem per Willielmum de Dakham positum loco suo ad lucrandum vel perdendum Et Adam de Lyscwys Impedientem De Manerio de Stoke-linche cum pertinenciis Unde Placitum fuit inter eos in eadem Curia Scilicet quod predictus Adam recognovit predictum Manerium cum pert⁵ esse jus ipsius Johannis ut illud quod idem Johannes habet de dono predicti Ade Et pro hac recognitione fine et concordia idem Johannes concessit predicto Ade et Johanne Uxori ejus predictum Manerium cum pert⁵ exceptis una acra terre et dimidia que jacent in Hethinge Advocacione Ecclesie ejusdem ville Et homagiis et omnibus serviciis libere tenure ejusdem Manerii que eidem Johanni et heredibus suis per finem istud* remanent imperpetuum Hab. et Ten. eisdem Ade et Johanne de predicto Johanne

* The occasional inaccuracies in Syntax occurring in the MSS. are retained, and marked in Italics, as above.

et heredibus suis tota vita utriusque ipsorum Ade et Johanne Reddendo inde per Annum unum denarium ad Pascha pro omni servicio consueto et exactione Et pred. Johannes et her. sui Warantio aquietabunt et defendent eisdem Ade et Johanne pred^m Maner^m cum pert^s quod eis per finem istum remaneat Integre revertetur ad pred. Johannem et her. suos quiete de her^us ipsorum Ade et Johanne Tenendum de Capitalibus Dominis Feodi illius per servicia que ad Illud Manerium pertinent imperpetuum Et preterea idem Johannes dedit predicto Ade Quadraginta Marcas argenti.   Somers.

This is a Final Agreement, made in the Court of our Lord the King at Westminster, on the Morrow of the Purification of the Blessed Mary, in the seventh year of the Reign of King Edward son of King Henry—Before Thomas Welonde, Walter de Helym, John de Lovetot, Roger de Leyc, William de Burntone, Justiciaries; Between John de Beauchampe, Plaintiff; and Adam de Lyscwys, Defendant—Concerning the Manor of Stocklinch   .   .   .   .

No. 14. A.D., 1304.   Sunday after Feby 2.

Omnibus Christi fidelibus ad quos presens Scriptum pervenerit Thomas de Speketone filius et heres Henrici de Speketone Salutem in Domino.   Noveritis me concessisse relaxasse et penitus quietum clamasse de me et heredibus meis vel assignatis inperpetuum Waltero Cole de Ivelcestra et her^us vel assig^is suis Totum jus et clamium quod habui vel quod aliquo modo habere potero vel mihi accidere poterit in toto illo Tenemento et curtil^o cum eorum pert^s in Ivelcestra quod situm est versus Portam Borialem ville In australi parte tenementi Albe Aule quod Thomas Axtil quondam tenuit Et quod datum fuit Willielmo dicto le Cartere in liberum Maritagium cum Matillide filia Willielmi de Speketone

et eorum heredibus inperpetuum Ita quod nec Ego
Thomas de Speketone nec heredes mei neque mei assignati nec aliquis nomine nostro aliquod jus vel clamium in
pred° tenem° cum curt° et eorum pert⁸ de cetero poterunt
exigere vel vendicare inperpet. Ego vero predictus Thomas
de Speketone . . . . . Pro hac autem mea re-
laxatione . . . . dedit mihi pred^us Walterus Viginti
solidos sterlingorum pre manibus In cujus rei testimonium
huic presenti Scripto meo Sigillum meum apposui Hiis Testibus Petro de Dray(cote), Will° Cocus de Lymyngtone, Roberto
de Scheptone, clerico. Thoma de Engelby, Magistro Roberto
de Nortone, Johanne Love, Thoma Tigel. Datum apud
Ivelcestram Die Dominica proxima post Festum Purificationis
Beate Marie Anno Regni Regis Edwardi tricesimo secundo.

———

Thomas of Speketone son and heir of Henry de Speketone
—to Walter Cole of Ivelcester—All that tenement, with
appurtenances, situate near the North Gate of the Town, to
the East of the edifice of White Hall; formerly in the
occupation of Thomas Axtil (No. 5), and given to William
called the Carter, in free Marriage with Matilda daughter of
William de Speketone. Walter Cole pays down to Tho⁸ de
Speketone a sum of twenty shillings sterling. Attested by—
Peter of Draycote, Willm Cocus of Limington, Robert of
Shepton, clerk, Thomas of Engelby, Master Robert of Norton,
and others. Given at Ivelcester on the Lord's Day next after
the Feast of the Purification of the Blessed Mary, in the thirty
second year of the Reign of King Edward.

———

No. 15. A D., 1308. Edw. II. Wednesday May I.
Omnibus Xti fidelibus ad quos presens scriptum pervenerit
Robertus Cole de Ivelcestra Salutem. Noveritis me con-
cessisse relaxasse et omnino de me et heredibus meis in-

perpetuum quietum clamasse Waltero Cole de Ivelcestra pro homagio et servicio suo totum jus et clamium quod habui vel aliquo modo habere potui in una acra et sextario prati in Manerio de Sock juxta Ivelcestram que sic jacent Una acra jacet in La Marysse inter pratum Domini exparte occidentali et pratum Persone ex parte orientali Et Sextarium jacet in La Lampull inter pratum Prioris de Bermundesie ex parte boriali et pratum Domini ex parte australi Hab. et Ten. pred^{am} acram et sextarium prati pred^{o} Waltero her^{bus} et assig^{s} suis de Capitalibus Dominis Feodi illius libere quiete bene integre et in pace jure hereditario inperp^{m}, Ita quod nec Ego pred^{s} Robertus et heredes mei nec aliquis nomine nostro aliquid juris vel clamii in pred^{is} acra et sexterio prati ratione hereditatis exigere poterimus vel vendicare nec alia quacumque ratione In cujus rei testimonium presenti Scripto Sigillum meum est appensum Hiis Testibus Johanne de Chitterne, Hugone de Draycote, Thoma Tigel, Thoma Cole, Adam Cole, Symone Bernard, Et multis aliis. Datum apud Ivelcestram die Mercurii in Festo Apostolorum Philippi et Jacobi anno regni Regis Edwardi Filii Regis Edwardi primo.

Robert Cole of Ivelcester to Walter Cole of Ivelcester, all his right and title in one acre, and one sixth part of an acre of meadow, in the Manor of Sock near Ivelcester, The one acre is in the Marsh, between the lord's land on the West, and the Parson's field on the East. The sixth part is in La Lampulle, between a Meadow of the Prior of * Bermondsey on the North, and a field of the lord (of Sock) on the South. Witnesses—John of Chitterne, Hugh of Draycote, and others. Given at Ivelcester on Wednesday in the Feast of the Apostles

* There was at this time, a Cluniac Priory "of our Holy Saviour of Bermondsey," at Preston near Yeovil. To this Priory, the field alluded to in the Deed no doubt belonged.

Philip and James, in the first year of the reign of King Edward son of King Edward.

No. 16, Edw., II, 1308. Wednesday, May I.

Omnib. Xti fidel. ad quos pres. Scrip. perven. Robertus Cole de Ivelcestra Salutem in Domino. Noveri. me remisisse concessisse relaxasse et penitus de me et her^bus meis quietum clamasse inperpet. Waltero Cole de Ivelcestra pro homagio et servicio suo totum jus et clamium quod habui vel aliquo modo habere potui vel mihi accedere poterit in una acra et uno sextario prati in Manerio de Soke Deneys juxta Ivelcestram Que acra jacet in La Merische inter pratum Domini de Socke ex parte occid. et Pratum Rectoris ejusdem ville ex parte orien. Et sexterium prati jacet in Sestermede in Forlango quod appellatur Laumphulle inter pratum Prioris de Bermundusye ex par. bori. et pratum Domini de Socke ex par. aust. Hab. et Ten. pred^am acram prati et pred^um sextarium prati cum suis pert^s pred^o Waltero her^bus et assig. suis de Capitalibus Dominis Feodi illius Libere quiete integre bene et in pace jure hereditario inperpet. Reddendo et facieneo predictis Dominis Capitalibus Redditus et Servicia inde debita et consueta Et ego vero dictus Robertus et hered. mei pred^am acram et Sextarium prati cum suis pert^s pred^o Walt^o et her^bus suis et suis as^tis contra omnes mortales Warantizare aquietare et defendere tenemus inperpet. Ita quod nec ego pred^s Robertus nec her. mei nec aliquis nomine nostro aliquid juris vel clamii causa cujuscumque rationis in pred^is acra et sexterio prati ratione hereditatis exigere vel vendicare poterimus inperpet. In cujus rei test. huic presenti quiete clamancie Sigillum meum apposui Hiis Test. Hugone de Draycote, Johanne de Chitterne, Thoma Tigel, Thoma Cole, Thoma le Dezare, Adam Cole, Simone

Bernard, Johanne Love seniore, Waltero Frommie, Rogero Page, Rogero de Trente, et multis aliis. Datum apud Ivelcestram die Mercurii in Festo Apostolorum Philippi et Jacobi Anno regni Regis Edwardi filii Regis Edwardi primo.

Robert Cole of Ivelcester to Walter Cole . . . . . one acre, and one sixth part of an acre, in the manor of Soke Deneys near Ivelcester. Which acre lies in the Marsh, between a field of the lord of Socke on the West, and a field of the Rector of the same town on the East. And the sixth part lies in Sestermede (Chestirmede), in the Forlang called Laumphylle, between the Meadow of the Prior of Bermondsey on the North, and that of the lord of Socke on the South. To Hold . . . . of the Head lords of that Fee . . . . (counterpart of preceding.)

No. 17. Edw. II. 1312. Saturday, Novr. 18.

Omnibus Christi Fidelibus ad quos pres. scrip. perven. Walterus dictus le Muleward de Suwerke Sal. in Dom. Noveritis me relaxasse et omnino quietum clamasse pro me her^bus et assig. meis Johanni de Middeltone hered. et assig. suis Totum jus et clamium quod habui vel aliquo modo habere potui in omnibus terris et tenementis que idem Johannes habuit de dono et feoffamento Johannis le Muleward patris mei in Ffaggeschilterne et Dummereschilterne in Comitatu Somersetie Ita quod nec ego dictus Walterus nec her. mei nec aliquis nomine nostro aliquid juris vel clamii in pred. ten^tis de cetero exigere vel clamare poterimus Se*t* ab omni actione sumus exclusi inperp^m. In cujus rei test. presentibus Sigillum meum apposui Datum apud Westmonasterium die Sabbati in Octavo Sancti Martini anno Regni Regis Edwardi Filii Regis Edwardi Sexto Hiis Test. Ricardo de Rodeny, Willielmo Malerbe, Waltero de Cumptone, Rogero le Gyldene, Johanne de Chiltone, Et aliis.

Walter called the Millward, of Southwark, to John of Middelton—All right and title in all lands . . . . . . which the same John held by the gift and feofment of John the Millward, father of the said Walter, in Faggeschilterne (Vagg) and Dummereschilterne, in the Co. of Somerset . . . . Given at Westminster, on Saturday in the Octave of St. Martin, in the sixth year of the reign of King Edward son of King Edward. Witnesses—Richard of Rodeny, William Malerbe, Walter de Cumptone, Roger le Gyldene, John de Chilton, and others.

No. 18. Edw. II. 1314. Sunday after Michaelmas Day.

Omn. Xti Fid. pres. scriptum visuris vel audituris Johannes Dummere, Miles, Sal. in Dom. sempiternam. Noveritis me tradidisse concess. et hoc pres^{ti} scripto confirmasse Waltero Isaac de Hulle sex acras terre arabilis cum suis pert^s in Chilterne Dommere Quarum due acre jacent super Smalemede inter terram tunc Henrici de Romesye, et Hulhamstrete Due acre jacent super Bymere inter terram tunc Nicholai Kayron et terram tunc Henrici de Pypelpenne una acra jacet Bymthecmermere inter terram tunc Henrici le Mone et terram tunc Johannis de Middeltone Una acra jacet super Riccherhulle inter terram tunc Henrici le Mone et terram tunc Will^i Suell Et quatuor solidatas annui redditus cum suis pert^s in Chilterne Dommere provenientes de tenemento et terra que Thomas de Remmysbury prius de me tenuit ad terminum vite sue in eadem villa Hab. et Ten. . . . . . In cujus rei testi. huic pres^i scr^o in modum cirographi confecto Sigilla nostra alternatim apposuimus Hiis Test. Domino Waltero de Romesye Milite, Johanne de Middeltone, Henrico de Pypelpenne, Johanne Ffagge, Roberto Pygaz, Et aliis. Datum apud Penne Die Dominica proxima post Festum S'cti Michaelis Anno Regni Regis Edwardi Filii Regis Edwardi octavo.

John de Dummere, Knight, to Walter Isaac of Hulle (Chilthorn Hill), six acres of arable land in Chilthorn Domere; two of which are above Smallmead, between land of Henry de Romesye, and Hulhamstrete; two acres above Bymere, between land of Nicholas Kayron and of Henry of Pypelpenne; one acre in Bymthecmermere, between land of Henry le Mone and of John de Middeltone; one acre on the top of Richerhill. Also a yearly Rent of Four shillings in Chilterne Dummere, accruing from the land and tenement which Thomas of Remmysbury held for his life. Witnesses—Sir Walter de Romesye, Knight; John de Middelton, Henry de Pypelpenne, John Fagge . . . . . Given at Penne on the Lord's Day next after the Feast of St. Michael, in the eighth year of the reign of King Edward son of King Edward.

No. 19. Edw. II. 1314. Wednesday before Octr. 18.

Omn. Xti Fidel. pres. scr. visuris vel audituris Johannes de Dommere, Miles, Sal. in Dom. sempit^m. Nov^{ls} me tradid. concess. et hoc pre^{ti} scpto confirmasse Waltero Isaac de Hulle sex acras terre arab. et unam dimidiam acram prati cum suis pert^s in Chilterne Dommere Quarum acrarum due jacent super Smalemede inter terram tunc Henrici de Romesye, et Hulhamstrete Due acre jacent super Bymere inter terram tunc Nicholai Kayron et terram tunc Henrici de Pupelpenne Due acre jacent super Irleghe inter terram tunc Roberti Pygaz et terram tunc Rectoris Ecclesie de Chilterne Dommere Una dimidia acra prati jacet in Chilterne Mere. juxta pratum tunc Johannis de Porta Quam dimidiam acram prati Thomas de Wayforde aliquando de me tenuit ibidem Et quatuor solidatas annui redditus cum suis pert^s in Chilterne Dommere provenientes de tenemento et terra que Thomas de Remmysbury prius de me tenuit ad terminum vite sue in eadem villa Hab. et Ten. . . . . . . In cujus rei testi.

huic pre^{ti} scpto in modum Cirographi confecto Sigilla nostra alternatim apposuimus Hiis Test. Domino Waltero de Romesye Milite, Johanne Ffagge, Johanne de Middeltone, Henrico de Pupelpenne, Roberto Pygaz, Et aliis. Datum apud Penne Die Mercurii proxima ante Festum Sancti Luce Evangeliste anno regni Regis Edwardi filii Regis Edwardi octavo.

John de Dommere, Knight, to Walter Isaac of Hylle, six acres of arable, and a half acre of meadow, in Chilterne Dommere. Two acres in Smallmead; two above Bymere; Two above Irleghe, between land of Robert Pygaz and of the Rector for the time being of the Church of Chilterne Dommere. The half acre is in Chilterne Mere, near the land of John de Porta . . . . . Given at Penne, on Wednesday next before the Feast of St. Luke the Evangelist, in the eighth year of the reign of King Edward son of King Edward.

No. 20. Edw. II. 1319. Saturday before 24th June.

Omn^s Xti Fid. pres. scr^m visuris vel aud^{is} Walterus de Romesye, Miles, Sal. in Dom. Nover^s me tradi. concess. et pre^{ti} scpto confirmasse Matillidi Isaac Waltero Isaac de Hulle et Will^o Isaac de eadem Pro quadam pecunie summa michi pre manibus soluta Totum Mesuagium Curt^m croftam gardinum Totam terram et pratum cum suis pert^s Que Isaac de Hulle de me aliquando tenuit in Hulle Juxta Chilterne Dommere in Com. Somers. Hab. et Ten. . . . . . In cujus rei testi. tam sigillum meum quam sigilla dictorum Matillidis Walteri et Willⁱ huic scripto bipartito in modum cirographi confecto alternatim sunt appensa Datum apud Romesye die Sabbati proxima ante Fest. Nativ. Sc^t Joh^{is} Baptiste Anno regni Regis Edwardi filii Regis Edwardi duodecimo Hiis Test. Domino Joh^e de Dommere, Milite; Joh^e de Middeltone, Joh^e de Dommere, Armigero; Henrico de Pupelpenne, Joh^e Ffagge, Johanne de Chitterne, Joh^e Pigaz, Et aliis.

Walter de Romesye, knight, to Matilda Isaac, Walter Isaac of Hylle, and William Isaac of the same, for a certain sum of money paid down to me—All that messuage, paddock, garden, arable land, and meadow, which Isaac of Hylle formerly held of me in Hylle near Chilterne Dommere in the Co. of Somers . . . . . Given at Romesye on Saturday next before the Feast of the Nativity of St John Baptist in the 12th year of the reign of King Edw. son of King Edward, Witnesses — Sir John de Dommere, Knight; John de Dommere, Esquire; and others.

No. 21. Edw. II. 1323. Sund. after Octr. 18.

Sci. pres. et fut. quod Ego Johannes Laueranz de Chilterne Vagge dedi con. et hac pre. car. mea confirmavi Johanni de Kayrhays perpetuo Vicario Ecclesie de Combe Kaygnes Unum Mesuagium cum curt° et curtil° et cum omnibus suis pert^s in Chilterne Vagge Et unum ferlingum terre in Campis de Chilterne Dommere Silicet unam acram in Stret forlange Unam acram juxta Langemer Unam acram super Erleyge Duas acras juxta Middilmer Unam acram juxta Oppemer Unam acram juxta Pratum Hominum versus occid. Unam acram et dimidiam juxta Seweyesgore Unam acram in Langelonde Unam acram juxta Greneweye Dimidiam acram in Mertforlange juxta Fossatum Unam acram super Smalhulle Dimidiam acram prati juxta pratum Galfridi de Heunebere Unam perticatam prati in Prato de Chilterne Vagge Dedi estiam dicto Johanni her. vel assig. suis Pasturam unius Affri trium Boum quatuor Vaccarum et quinqueaginta Bidentum in communa pastura in Campis de Chilterne Dommere Hab. et Ten. predicta Mesuag. Curt^m et Curtil^m terram pratum et pasturam cum libero ingressu . . . . . Et ut hec mea donacio con. et Warentizatio Rata et stabilis semper permaniat hanc pres. car. Sigilli mei inprescione roboravi Hiis Test. Joh^e Vagge, Joh^e de Dommere, Joh^e de Miltone, Luca

de Barri, Joh^e de Cruk' Joh^e Pynghou, Joh^e Torke, Et aliis
Data apu*t* Chilterne Vagge Die Domin. prox. post Fest S'cti
Luce Evangeliste Anno regni Regis Edwⁱ filii Regis Edwardi
Septimo decimo.

John Laueranz of Chiltern Vagge, to John de Kayrhays,
Perpetual Vicar of the Church of Combe Kaygnes—A
messuage in Chilterne Vagge, and one ferlingus (ten acres) of
land in Chilterne Dommere Fields. One acre in Stretforlang,
one near Longmere, one above Erleyge, Two by Middlemere,
Two near Upmere, One near the Mens' Field, westward, One
acre and a half near Sewersgore, one acre in Longland, one by
Greenway, Half-an-acre in Mertforlang near the Ditch, One
acre atop of Smallhill, Half-an-acre of Meadow near that of
Geoffry de Heunebere, One fourth part of an acre in the
Meadow of Chiltern Vagge. Also, pasturage for one heifer,
three oxen, four cows, and fifty two-year sheep in the common
pasture in Chiltern Dommere fields. Witnesses—John Vagge
John de Dommere, John de Milton, Luke de Barri, John of
Crewkerne, and others. Given at Chiltern Vagge on the
Lord's Day next after the Feast of St. Luke the Evangelist,
in the seventeenth year of the reign of King Edw. son of
King Edward.

No. 22. Edw. II. 1327. Monday after Feby 2.

Omn. Xti Fid. ad quos pres. scpt^m perven. Johannes
Herewarde de Ivvelchestre. Nover. me tradi. concess. et hoc
pres. scpto confirmasse Ricardo Herewarde Fratri meo Unum
Mesuagium cum curt° quatuor acras terre arab. quinque acras
prati cum una roda cum omn. aliis pert^s in Ivvelchestre
Quarum due acre jacent in Campo de Lymyngtone Un*um*
in Brokelonde et alter*um* in Midenille Due altere jacent in
Campo de Ivvelchestre Un*um* in Bridemere et alter*um* vocata

le Godacre Predicti vero prati due acre et dimidia jacent in
Botesmede et due altere et dimidia jacent in Chestirmede
Roda vero jacet desuper capu*d* pred. due acre Hab. et Ten.
. . . . . Salvo tamen secto Curie de Sakke . . . . . In
cujus rei testim . . . . . Hiis Test. Andree le Spicer,
Rob^to Blakebere sen. Petro Gonitz, Joh^e Quared, Joh^e Rypon-
ne, Ric^o Wolquir, Rob^to Bakebere Jun. Datum Ivvelchestre
die Lune prox. post Fest. Purificationis Beate Marie Virginis
Anno regni Regis Edw^1 filii Regis Edwardi vicesimo tertio
incipiente.

John Herewarde of Ivvelchester, to Richard Herewarde
his brother—One Messuage, four acres of arable, five of
meadow, and one rood. Two acres in Limington Field, one
in Brookland the other in Middlehill; two others in Ivvelchester Field, one in Bridemere the other called the Godacre.
Of the Meadow, Two acres and a half are in Botesmead, two
other acres and a half are in Chestirmead; and the rood is at
the top of the two acres aforesaid. To have . . . . . .
"save nevertheless suit in the Court of Exchequer." Witnesses
—Andrew the Spicer. Given at Ivvelchester on Monday
next after the Feast of the Purification of the Blessed Virgin
Mary in the beginning of the twenty *third year of the reign
of King Edward son of King Edward.

No. 23. Edw. II. 1327. Monday after Feby 2.
Omn. Xti Fid . . . . . Johannes Herward de Ivvel-

* Edward II. began to reign July 8. 1307; and his reign terminated
with his abdication, or more correctly, deposition. This event occurred on
the 20th of January, 1327; and his son, Edward III, was proclaimed King
on January 24th. So that at the time of his deposition, the King had only
reigned nineteen years and just over six months. In the same year, 1327,
on the 21st of September, Edward the Second was murdered in Berkeley
Castle. The regnal date given here, and repeated in the next Deed, must
consequently be an error There are likewise several grammatical inaccuracies
in both of these MSS. shewing the writer to have been ignorant or careless.

cestre . . . . . Noveritis me tradidisse . . . . .
Ricardo Hereward Fratri meo Unum Mesua. cum Curt°
Quatuor acras terre arabilis Quinque acras prati cum una roda
cum omnibus aliis pert⁸ in Ivvelsestre Quarum due acre jacent
in Campo de Lymyntone Unum in Brokelond et alterum in
Midenille Due altere jacent in Campo de Ivvelsestre Unum
in Bridemere et alterum vocata le Godacre Predicti vero prati
due acre et dimidia jacent in Votismede Et due altere et
dimidia jacent in Sestermede Roda vero jacet desuper caput
predict. due acre Hab. et Ten . . . . . . In cujus rei
testim. huic scripto indentato sigilla nostra alternatim apposuimus Hiis Test. Andree le Spycer, Rob^to Bakebere sen.
Petro Gonitz, Joh^e Quared, Joh^e Ryponn, Ric° Wolqir, Rob^to
Bakebere jun. Et multis aliis. Datum apud Ivvelcestre die
Lune prox. post Fest. Purific. Beate Marie Virginis Anno
regni Regis Edw^i filii Regis Edwardi vicesimo tercio incipienti.
(see No. 22.)

John Hereward of Ivvelcester, to Richard Hereward his
brother . . . . . with all appurt⁸ in Ivvelsester . . . .
Two acres of the meadow are in Votismede (Fotesmede)
Given at Ivvelcester on Monday . . . . in the beginning
of the 23rd year of the reign . . . . . . Counterpart
of foregoing.

No. 24. Edw. III. 1328. Sunday May 1.
Universis Xti Fidelibus pres. scr. visuris vel audituris
Walterus de Romesie Miles Sal. in Dom. Nover. quod ego
Walt⁸ pred⁸ Totum illud Tenementum Curtil^m gardinum
croftam totamque terr. arab^m et pratum cum pert⁸ apud Hulle
in Chilterne Dommere in Com. Somers. Que Isaac de Hulle
de me aliquando tenuit ibidem Matillidi Isaac de Hulle
Waltero Isaac de Hulle et Will° Isaac de Hulle die Sabbati

prox. ante Fest. Nativit' S'cti Joh'ᵉ Baptiste anno regni Regis
Edwardi duodecimo concessissem et tradidissem Habendum
et tenend. omnia predicta cum pertᵉ Eisdem Matillidi Waltero
Isaac et Willᵒ ad terminum vite eorundem vel cuilibet
eorundem diucius viventi de me et herᵇᵘˢ meis pro annuo
redditu quatuor solidorum quiete libere et in pace Ac prefati
Matillis quamdiu vixerat et Waltᵉ Isaac ac Willˢ omnia
predᵃ cum pertᵉ quousque iidem Waltˢ Isaac et Willˢ prout infra
scribitur ea mihi retradidissent juxta effectum concessionis et
tradicionis predictarum habuissent et possedissent pacifice et
quiete Tandem post mortem dicte Matillidis videlicet die Jovis
prox. post Fest. S'cti Marci Evangeliste Anno regni Regis
Edwardi Tercii post conquestum Secundo Iidem Walterus
Isaac et Willˢ Totum predᵐ tenᵐ curtilᵐ gardinum croftam
totamque terram arabᵐ et pratum cum pertˢ michi Waltero de
Romesie predᵒ. certis de causis retradiderunt et omni juri
quod eis compeciit in premissis simpliciter renunciarunt ac
omnia bona eorum et catalla infra dictum tenementum tunc
existencia certo precio in hac parte constituto et soluto michi
vendiderunt et eciam liberarunt Postea vero videlicet Die
Domin. in Fest. Apostolorum Philippi et Jacobi Anno reg.
Reg. Edwⁱ Tercii post Conqᵐ secundo Ego Waltˢ de Romesie
supradᵘˢ postquam plenariam seisinam et possᵐ omnium
premissorum habuissem juxta effectum retradicionis vendicionis
et liberacionis predictarum pro laudabili servicio quod Waltˢ
Isaac predˢ michi et meis impendit Totum predᵐ Ten'm curtil.
gardi. croft. totamque terram arabᵐ et pratum cum pertˢ predⁱˢ
Waltᵒ Isaac Willᵒ et Margarete Pigaz uxori ejusdem Willⁱ
concessi et tradidi Ac omnia bona et catalla mea in eodem tenᵒ
tunc existencia pro certa pecunie summa michi pre manibus
soluta vendidi et liberavi Hab. et Ten. . . . . In cujus
rei test. Ego Waltˢ de Romesie predˢ parti presentis Indenture
penes dictos Waltᵐ Isaac Willᵐ et Margaretam residenti

Sigillum meum apposui Et iidem Walt⁹ Isaac Will's et Margareta parti ejusdem Indenture penes me remanenti Sigilla sua apposuerunt. Datum Acle Die Domin. in Festo App. Philippi et Jacobi Anno regni Reg. Edwⁱ Tercii post Conqᵐ secundo Hiis Test. Domino Ricardo de Gyverney, Milite; Petro Colsweyn, Johᵉ Dommere, Willᵒ de Cantelo, Thoma de Pipelpenne, Johᵉ Ffagge, Johᵉ Pigaz, Et aliis.

Walter of Romesie, knight, (after citing a former Deed, No. 20, and premising, that on the death of Matilda Isaac named therein, her two co-tenants gave up possession to himself) declares—that in return for good service rendered by Walter to him and his; He (de Romesie) grants anew to Walter and Willᵐ Isaac (the late co-tenants with Matilda) and to Margaret Pigaz wife of the latter, the lands and tenements in question. Given at Acle (Oakley) on The Lord's Day, being the Feast of the Apostles Philip and James; in the second year of the reign of King Edward the Third after Conquest. Witnesses—Sir Richard de Gyverney * Knight; Peter Colsweyn, John Dommere, William de Cantelo, Thomas de Pipelpenne, John Fagge, John Pigaz, and others.

No. 25. Edw. III. 1329. Monday, April 24.

Sci. pre. et fut. quod ego Walterus de Multone filius et heres Johannis de Multone tradidi . . . . Johanni Stagon et Elene relicte Ade de Waltham sexdecim acras et unam rodam terre arrab et duas acras prati cum suis pertˢ

---

* The Family of the Gyverneys, Gournays, or Gurneys, was connected by property with Somersetshire. The relics of their Family Mansion, converted into a Farm House, are still to be seen at Stoke sub Hamdon. The recumbent effigy of a cross legged Knight on the Altar-tomb under the north window in the Transept of Limington Church, is thought to be that of a Gournay. A member of this Family was concerned in the murder of Edward the Second; and not long afterwards was summarily executed at sea for the alleged crime, during his passage to England for trial on a charge of high Treason.

in Campis de Chilterne Dummere Unde una acra jacet apud La Fflodghete Et una acra et dimidia jacent in Langgelonde Et una acra jacet in Ffilemede in parte boriali terre Turke Et una acra jacet in Schortehenedlonde Et una acra jacet in Holecombe Et dimidia acra jacet in Holecombe in le Marlyngputte Et due acre jacent in North Wonfelde Et dimidia acra jacet in Bynnch'hulle in parte occid. terre Walesleghe Et dimidia acra jacet inter Bymere et Saltereslake Et dimidia acra exstendit super Langgemere Et dimidia acra jacet desuper Hanggerlonde juxta terram Walesleghe Et dimidia acra super Overmere juxta terram quondam Domini Thome de Remmesbury ex parte orient. Et una acra jacet super Colderygge Et una acra jacet extra Torke's crofte Et dimidia acra jacet ex parte occid. Crofte Turke Et dimidia acra et una roda terre jacent extra le Mone'sheye Et una acra terre jacet apud Maydencresce in parte bori. terre Pyngho Et dimidia acra et una roda prati jacent in Langgemede in parte austr. prati quondam Welesleghe Et una roda prati jacet in Langgemede juxta pratum le Mone Et una acra prati jacet in Chilternemere in parte occid. prati Pygaz Hab. et Ten . . . . : In cujus rei testi. Huic Scripto bipartito alternatim sigilla nostra apposuimus Hiis test. Domino Johanne de Romesie, Milite; Johanne de Dummere, Joh⁰ Ffag' Joh⁰ Atteforde, Joh⁰ Torke, Joh⁰ Pigaz, Datum apud Chilterne Ffag' Die Lune in Crastino Sancti Georgii anno regni Regis Edwardi Tercii a conquestu Tercio.

Walter of Mylton, son and heir of John of Mylton, to John Stagon and Elena relict of Adam de Waltham; sixteen acres and one rood of arable, and two acres of Meadow in Chilterne Dummere fields; distributed in these localities— at the Floodgate, in Longland, in Ffile or Vilemead, in Shortenedland (now Shortlands) in Holecombe, and in Holccombe in the Marlpit, in North Wonfield, on Bynnchhill, between Bymere and Salterslake, above Longmere, beyond Hangerland, beyond Overmere, above Coldridge (now Chalridge), outside of Torke's Croft, and to the West of Turke's Croft, and to the West of Turke's Croft, beyond Le Mone'sheye, at Maiden Cross, in Longmead, and in Chilternemere. Witn. Sir John de Romesie, knight; Johnde Dummere, John Fagg . . . . Given at Chiltern Vagg, on Monday being the Morrow of St George, in the third year of the reign of King Edward the Third from the Conquest.

No. 26. Edw. III. 1336. Palm Sunday.

Le Jour de Palmes lan du Reigne le Roy Edward Tierz apres le conquest Disme Acouynt entre Monsieur Johan de Beauchampe de Somersete Chivaler et Seigneur de Hatche d une part Et Water Oseborn de Stokelynche Magdalen d autre part Issi c est a saver qe le dit Monsr Johan ad lesse baille et guarante au dit Water tutes celes teres et tenemenz en Stokelynche les queux il ad en fee d el donn l avandite Water Et auxi le dit Monsr Johan ad lesse Baille et guarante au dit Water un aqre de terre en mesmes la Vilé q est apele Churchstielaqre A aver et A tenir tutes les avantdites terres et tenemenz oue ses appertenaunces a tute la vie le dit Water fraunchement enterement bien et en pees Rendaunt de ceo dan en an a la Feste de Seynt Michel au dit Monsr Johan et a ses heirs un dener d argent pour tuz autres services et seculeres demaundes Et le dit Monsr Johan et ses heirs tutes les avantdites terres et tenemenz oue ses apportenaunces a tute la vie le dit Water countre tutes gentz garranteront et defenderont pour les services avant dites Et apres le deces le dit Water tutes les avant dites terres et tenemenz oue ses appurtenaunces au dit Monsr Johan et a ses heirs pleynement returgent Et ensus ceo veolt et garaunte le dit Monsr Johan

pur luy et ses heirs et en bone foi persmet qe apres
le deces le dit Water sera garaunte baille et lesse par
estre present pur luy ou pur ses heirs a Johane la Feme le
dit Watre et a Johan lour aynzne fitz le mies et le curtil
qe avaunt fust au dit Water et set aqres de terre arable
et un aqre de pree de les demeignes le dit Monsr Johan ou de
ses heirs en la dite Vile en leus covenables A tener fraunchement taunt come il vyveront ou un de eux qi plus longement
vivera Issi c est A saver qe si la dite Johane apres le deces le
dit Water vodra demaunder douwere des tenemenz qe son
Baron autre foith dona au dit Monsr Johan en fee quele soit
forclos des set aqres de terre et un aqre de pree susditz
tauntque ele eu fait un relees de son douwere en sa lige vesvete
au dit Monsr Johan ou a ses heirs En tesmoignaunce de queu
chose ataunt le dit Monsr Johan come le dit Water a cestz est
presentz Endentes entre chaungablement ount myis lour sealx
Est presentz a Hatche Beauchampe le jour et lan susdit
Par yces Tesmoignes—Roberd de Somertone, Roger de
Stokelynche, Johan Maloisel, Willame de Aisshlonde, Willame
Sarazyn, Et plusurs autres.

Palm Sunday, Tenth year of the reign of King Edward
the Third after Conquest. Undertaking between Sir John de
Beauchampe of Somerset, Knight and Lord of Hatche, on the
one part; and Walter Osborn of Stokelynche Magdalene on
the other part. Sir John lets to lease, and confirms to said
Walter for his life, and afterwards to his wife Johanna and their
eldest son John, certain lands and tenements in Stokelynche.
Also, an acre of land in the same village, called Churchstile
acre. By rendering at Michaelmas one silver penny, in lieu
of all other service and secular demands. But should Johanna
claim dower out of this property, after her husband's decease,
she was to be debarred from all benefit in the said property,

until she relinquished her claim. Given at Hatche Beauchampe, the day and year aforesaid.

No. 27. Edw. III. 1340. Sunday after March 25.

Noverint Universi me Walterum de Miltone filium et
heredem Johannis de Miltone tradidisse . . . . Johanni
Stagon et Elene Relicte Ade de Waltham sexdecim acras et
unam rodam terre arrabilis et duas acras prati cum suis pert⁸
in campis de Chilterne Dummere Unde una acra jacet apud
la Ffloudgate juxta Chilterneshassche Una acra et dimidia
jacet in Langelond inter terras Johannis Pigatz et Ricardi
Pouphorn Una acra jacet in Ffilemede juxta terram Johannis
Turke in parte bori. Una acra jacet Schorthenedlond juxta
terram meam in parte occid. Una acra in Holecombe juxta
terram meam in parte bori. Dimidia acra ibidem in La
Marlyngputte juxta terram Joh^is Turke in parte austr. Due
acre in North Wonfelde Quarum una juxta terram Stephani
le Monne in parte orient. Et una acra juxta terram Joh^is
Pigatz in par. occid. Una acra apud Sewyesgore jux. ter.
Joh^is Pigatz in par occid. Dimidia acra inter Chilterne mere et
Smalemede inter terram meam ex utraque parte Dimid. ac.
ibi Nicche hulle in par. occid. terre mee Dimid. ac. inter
Bymere et Saltereslake jux. ter. Joh^is Pigaz et Joh^is Beaushath
Dim. ac. extendit super Langemere jux. ter. quam Joh^es de
Rokebourne nunc tenet in par. bori. Dim. ac. desuper Hanger-
londe inter ter. meam ex utraq. parte Dim. ac. super Over-
mere jux. ter. Priorisse Albe Aule Ievelcestre in par. occid.
Una ac. super Chelderigge jux. ter. Joh^is Pigatz in par. occid.
Una ac. Bynuthe Turkes crofte jux. ter. Joh^is Pigatz in par.
occid. Dim. ac. in par. occid. dicte Crofte jux. ter. meam Dim.
ac. et una roda extra gardinum Joh^is Pigaz jux. ter. Prioris de
Brutone in par. bori. Una ac. apud Maydenecreyce jux. ter.
Joh^is de Rokebourne in par. bori. Dim. ac. et una roda prati

in Langemere jux. pratum meum in par. austr. Una roda prati ibid jux. pratum Joh[is] Dummere in par. austr. Et una ac. prati in Chilterne mere in par. occid. prati Joh[is] Pigatz Hab. et Ten. . . . . In cujus rei testi. Sigilla nostra presentibus alternatim sunt appensa Hiis Test. Joh[e] de Barrye, Joh[e] Atteffourde, Joh[e] Vag, Joh[e] Turke, Joh[e] Pigatz Joh[e] Englysshe, Joh[e] le Ffauconer Et aliis. Datum apud Chilterne Vagge Die Domin. prox. post Fest. Annunciacionis Beate Marie Virginis Anno regni Regis Edw[i] Tercii a con- questu quarto decimo Regni vero Ffrancie primo. (1340.)

Walter de Miltone, to John Stagon and Elena relict of Adam de Waltham. This MS. deals with the same lands specified before in No. 25. But in describing the boundaries, these names are mentioned, among others of conterminous owners, John de Rokebourne, The Prioress of White Hall, and the Prior of Bruton. Given at Chilterne Vagge on the Lord's Day next after the Annunciation of the Blessed Virgin Mary, in the fourteenth year of the reign of King Edward III, from the Conquest.

But in the first year of His Reign over France.*

No. 28. Edw. III. 1341. March 19.

Noverint universi me Walterum de Miltone filium et heredem Joh[is] de Miltone tradidisse et conc. Johanni Bokerel de Estlangbroke et Sibille uxori sue omnes terras et tenem[a] cum gardinis croftis curt[is] pratis pascuis et pasturis cum omnibus aliis suis pert[s] Que Joh[es] Stagon aliquando de me tenuit ad Firmam in Chilterne Vagge et Chilt. Domm. Concessi

* Although Edward III. assumed the style of King of France as early as the 7th of Octr. 1337, it was not until the 25th of January 1340, that in public documents he added the year of his nominal reign over that Country, to the year of his reign in England. (Nicolas, Chron. Hist.)

This addition does not appear in any other of the Almshouse Deeds.

eciam pred^ls Joh^l Bokerel et Sibille redditus et servicia Joh^is le Masson et Thome Pynghow tenentium in feodo in Chilt. Vagge pred^a Hab et Ten . . . . . In cujus rei testi. presenti Scr^o indentato Sigilla nostra alternatim apposuimus Hiis Test. Johanne Dommere, Joh^e Vagge, Joh^e Pygatz Joh^e Turke, Joh^e Baret, Henrico de Molyns, Will^o Cuaploke, Et aliis. Datum apud Chilterne Vagge nono decimo die Marcii Anno regni Regis Edwardi Tercii post conq^m quinto decimo.

Walter de Milton, son and heir of John de Milton; to John Bokerel of Eastlambrook, and Sibilla his Wife; all the lands and tenem^ts which John Stagon once held in Farm, in Chilt. Vagge and Chilt. Dom. Also to the same, the rents and services of John the Mason and Thomas Pinghow, tenants in fee in Chilt. Vagge aforesaid. Witn. John Baret, Henry de Molyns, and others. Given at Chilt. Vagge on the 19th day of March in the 15th year of the reign of King Edward III. after the Conquest.

No. 29. Edw. III. 1341. Wednesday after June 5.

Sachent tute gentz qe ore sont et qe sont avenirs qe jeo Johan Jurdan ai done et garaunte et par coste moie presente Chartre conferme a Muns^r Johan de Beauchampe de Somersete Chivaler deus acres de terre arable en Stokelinche Magdalene insauntz sur la Rydone, juxte la terre Roger de Stokelinche de une part et de aultre A avoir et a tenir les avantditz deus acres de terre oue lur apportenaunces a l avantdit Muns^r Johan de Beauchampe et a ses heirs et a ses assignes a tutz jours De chiefs Seignurs de mesmes le fee par les services de ceo duwes et custumables Et jeo l avantdit Johan Jurdan et mes heirs les avantditz deus acres de terre oue tutes lur appertenraunces a l avantdit Muns^r Johan de Beauchampe et a ses heirs et a ses assignes en cuntre tute gentz garanteronps acquiteronps et defenderonps as tutz jours En tesmoinaunce de quele chose ai ceste presente chartre ai mis meon Seal Par yces Tesmoignes Johan Sylveyn, Roger de Stokelinche, Richard de Dylyngtone, Thomas de Conndenham, Johan de Hilcumbe, Et autres. Done a Stokelinche Magdalene le Mekerdi proschien apres la Feste Seint Johan le Baptistre L an du regne le Roi Edward tierz apres le Conquest quinszime.

Know all men, present and to come, that I John Jurdan have given . . . . . to Sir John de Beauchampe of Somerset, Knight, Two acres of arable land in Stokelinche Magdalene, situate on the Rydone, bounded on both sides by land of Roger of Stokelynche . . . . . To have and to Hold . . . . Witnesses—John Sylveyn, Richard of Dylyngton, Thomas of Cortondenham, and others. Given at Stokelinche Magdalene, the Wednesday next after the Feast of St John Baptist, in the 15th year of the reign of king Edward III. after Conquest.

No. 30. Edw. III. 1345. Monday August 15.

Sci. pres. et fut. quod Ego Alicia quondam Uxor Hugonis Dodul Chalener in pura et ligia viduetate mea dedi conc. et hac pres. car. mea confirmavi Stephano filio meo Totum tenem^m meum in villa Ivelcestre quod Scitum est in la Chepstret exposito Ecclesie Marie Minoris inter ten. quondam Walteri de Northovere clerici filii Osmundi le Deghar' de Northovere ex parte una et tenem. Priorisse Albe Aule ex parte altera Hab. et Ten. totum pred^m ten^m cum om^{us} suis pert^s pred^o Stephano et her^{bus} suis et cuicunque dare vendere legare vel assingnare voluerit de Capitalibus Dominis Feodi illius libere quiete integre bene et in pace jure hereditario inperp. Reddendo inde annuatim Thome Cole et her^{bus} vel assig. suis Unam rosam ad Festum Nativitatis S'cti Johannis Baptiste Et ad Firmam ville Ivelcestre unam quadrentem ad Hockediem qui appellatur Worthingabull pro omni servicio exactione et demanda seculari Salvo servicio Regali et consuetudine ville predicte quantum pertinet ad tantum tenementum in eadem villa In cujus rei testi. huic pres^i carte mee Sigillum meum est appensum Hiis Test. Johanne Atte Broke, Joh^e Huldebrond, Ricardo de Chitterne, Ricardo de Sancto Johanne, Andrea Spicer, Joh^e Ive, Rogero Page, Will^o Romfray, Joh^e de Rypon, Roberto le Tannere, Roberto le Chalener, Walteroo Cole, Joh^e de Chitterne, Et aliis. Datum apud Ivelcestre die Lune in Festo Assumpcionis Beate Marie Virginis anno regni Regis Edwardi Tercii a Conq^u decimo nono.

————

Alice, formerly wife of Hugh Dodul, chalener, in her pure and true widowhood, to Stephen her son ; all her tenement in the town of Ivelcester, situate in la Chepstret, opposite the Church of Mary the Less ; between the tenement once belonging to Walter of Northover, clerk, son of Osmund the Deghar' of Northover, on one side, and that of the Prioress of Whitehall on the other. To have . . . . . By rendering yearly, to Thomas Cole and his heirs, one rose at the Feast of the Nativity of John Baptist ; and to the Farm of the town of Ivelcester, one farthing "on Hockeday, which is called Worthing a bull (a reference to Bull-baiting?), in lieu of all service save King's service ; and the custom of the aforesaid town, so far as pertains to certain tenements in the same. Witnesses—John at Brook, Rich^d of Chitterne, John Ive, Robert the Tanner, Robt the Chalener, Richard de St John. Given at Ivelcester, on Monday the Feast of the Assumption of the Blessed Virgin Mary, in the 19th year of the reign of King Edw III. from Conquest.

————

No. 31. Edw, III. 1346. Monday after May 26.

Noverint universi me Johannem de Dommere Filium Domini Johannis de Dommere Militis relaxasse ac pro me et heredibus meis quietum clamasse Magistro Waltero Ysaac de Hulle Archidiacono Bathoniensi ac ejus heredibus et assignatis Totum jus et clamium quod habui vel quoquo modo habere potui in omnibus terris pratis pascuis et pasturis et suis pertinentiis in Chilterne Dommere in Comitatu Somersetie Que predictus Walterus Ysaac et Isabella Ysaac Filia Willielmi Ysaac de Hulle de me tenent ad terminum vite eorum in eadem villa Ita quod nec Ego Johannes de Dommere . . . . . . In cujus rei testimonium Sigillum meum Presentibus apposui Hiis Testibus; Dominis Johanne de Clyvedone, Symone de Fforneaux, Militibus; Ricardo Barry, Joh⁰ Baret, David de Honteleghe, Will⁰ Welde, Rogero Page, Joh⁰ Turke, Joh⁰ Pigaz, Et Aliis. Datum apud Chilterne Dommere die Lune prox. post Festum Sancti Augustini Anglorum Apostoli Anno regni Regis Edwardi Tercii post Conquestum Vicesimo.

John de Dommere, Son of Sir John de Dommere, Knight, to Master Walter Ysaac of Hill, Archdeacon of Bath; all his right and title in all the arable and meadow lands in Chilterne Dommere, which the same Walter Ysaac and Isabella daughter of William Ysaac of Hill, held of me for the term of their lives. Witnesses; Sirs, John de Clyvedone; Simon de Fforneaux, Knights. David de Honteleghe, Willm Welde, ... Given at Chilterne Dommere, on Monday next after the Feast of St Augustine Apostle of the English, in the 20th year of the reign of King Edward III. after conquest.

No. 32. Edw. III. 1346. Saturday after Septr 8.

Omn. Xti Fid. Hoc pres. Scrp^m visuris vel audit uris Walterus de Miltone filius et heres Joh^is de Miltone de Com. Somers. Sal. in Dom⁰ sempiternam Cum nuper per quoddam Scriptum indentatum concesserim et dimiserim Joh^i Stagonn de Chilterne et Elene uxori ejus ad terminum vite eorundem sexdecim acras terre arabilis et duas acras prati cum pert' in Chilt. Fagge et Chilt Dmm. in Com. Somers. Reddendo inde annuatim michi et her^{bus} meis Unam Rosam ad Festum Nativi. S'cti Joh^{is} Baptiste Que quidem sexdecim acre . . . post decessum pre^{rum} Joh^{is} Stagonn et Elene ad me et heredes meos per formam dimissionis predicte reverti deberent Noveritis me pred^m Walt^m pro me et her^{bus} meis dictum annuum redditum unius rose Everardo Ffraunceys de Bristolle her^{bus} et assig. suis decetero concessisse et confirmasse Et ulterius concessisse quod predicte sexdecim acre . . . . que michi et her'bus meis post decessum dictor. Joh^{is} Stagonn et Elene reverti deberent ut predicitur statim post decessum eorundem Joh^{is} et Elene prefato Everardo libere integre et quiete remaneant Hab. et Ten. eidem Everardo . . . . . In cujus rei testi. huic pre'ti scrp° Sigillum meum apposui Hiis Test. Roberto de Schordiche, Thomas de Cantebrugia, Johanne atte Castel, Rogero de Woxebregge, Civibus London, Joh^e Turke, Joh^e Pygaz, Joh^e Fauconer, Ric° Barry, Will° de Warmwell, Joh^e Stagonn, Radulfo Mareschal de Chilterue, Et aliis. Datum London' die Sabbati prox. post Fest. Nativit. Beate Marie Virginis Anno regni Regis Edwardi III, post conq^m Vicesimo.

Walter de Milton: (a former Deed cited (27), wherein he granted to John Stagon and Elena his wife, certain lands in Chiltern Vagge and Dummere, for their lives; now grants in reversion to Everard Fraunceys of Bristol the rent of one rose, and also the said lands, after the death of John and and Elena. Witnesses; Robert of Shoreditch, Thomas of Cambridge, John atte Castel, Roger of Uxbridge, Citizens of London. Willm de Warmwelle, Ralph Mareschal of Chilterne . . . . Given at London, on Saturday next after the Feast of the Nativity of the Blessed Virgin Mary, in the 20th year of the reign of King Edward III. after Conquest.

No 33. Edw. III. 1346. Tuesday, in Holy Week.

Omnibus ad quos pres. sc'ptm perven. Johannes Bokerel de Estlangbroke et Sibilla uxor ejus Sal. in Dom. Quia Walt⁹ de Miltone nos pre^{tos} Joh^{em} et Sibillam per quoddam Scrip^m indentatum de omnibus terris et ten^{tis} que idem Walterus habuit in Chilterne Vagge et Chilterne Dommere Simul cum redditu et servicio Thome Pighow et Joh^{is} le Masson in eadem villa ad terminum vite nostre feoffavit Reddendo dicto Waltero per septem annos proximos post confectionem Scripti Indentati pre^{ti} Unum granum Piperis . . . . In cujus rei . . . . Hiis Test. Joh^e Turke, Joh^e Pygas, Joh^e de Rokeburne, Joh^e de Fauconer, Joh^e Stagon, Et aliis. Datum ap. Chilt. Vagge die Martis prox. post Fest. Dominice in Ramis Palmarum Ann. Reg. Reg. Edwⁱ III. a conq. Vicesimo.

John Bokerel of East Lambrook, and Sibilla his wife, cite a former Deed (28) wherein Walter de Milton grants to them, the Fee of certain lands; also the rent and service of Thomas Pighow and John the Mason; for their lives: By rendering to the said Walter, for seven years next following the execution of the said deed of Indenture, one Pepper corn. Witnesses; John de Rokeburne, John de Faukoner . . . Given at Chilterne Vagge on Tuesday next after the Feast of Palm Sunday, in the 20th year of the reign of King Edward III.

No. 34. Edw. III. 1346. Wednesday April 19.

Pateat universis per presentes quod Ego Walterus de Miltone coustituo et omnino dilectum michi in Xsto Dominum Johannem de Lodelawe Capellanum Ballivum meum ad disponendum et ordinandum in omnibus terris et tenementis

meis in Chilterne Vagge et Chilterne Dommere simul cum
redditibus et serviciis Thome Pynghow et Joh^is le Masson in
eadem villa Que quondam dimisi Joh^t Bokerel de Est lang-
broke et Sibille uxori ejus ad terminum vite eorum Et que
iidem Johannes et Sibilla per literas suas michi reddiderunt
Ratum et gratum habens et habiturus quicquid factum fuerit
per eundem Dominum Johannem Ballivum meum in premissis
In cujus rei testim. presentibus Sigillum meum apposui Et
quia Sigillum meum pluralibus est incognitum Sigillum Decanatus de Landaff hiis apponi procuravi Et Ego Decanus de
.Landaff ad rogatum ipsius Walteri presentibus Sigillum meum
apposui Datum apud Landaff die Mercurii in Festo Sancti
Alphegi Archiepiscopi et Martyris Anno regni Regis
Edwardi Tercii a conquestu Vicesimo.

Walter de Milton appoints Sir * John de Lodelawe,
chaplain, his Bailiff, to manage all his lands . . . in
Chilt. Vagge and Chilt. Dommere; which property he formerly
let to John Bokerel of Eastlambrook, and Sibilla his wife, for
their lives; and which, the same John and Sibilla by deed
(33) restored to him . . . . . "And because my Seal is
unknown to most persons, I have taken care, that the Seal of
the Deanery of Landaff should be affixed to these writings.
And I, the Dean of Landaff, at the request of Walter himself,
have affixed my Seal to these presents." Given at Landaff on
Wednesday in the Feast of St Alphege, Archbishop and
Martyr; in the 20th year of King Edward III.

No. 35. Edw. III. 1347. Wednesday after June 11.
Sci. pres. et fut. qnod ego Henricus de Romesye filius et
heres Henrici de Romesye dedi con. et hac pres. carta mea

* Sir (Dominus) was a title formerly applied to Clergymen; as we find
in Shakespeare, "Sir Nathaniel the Curate." When prefixed to the name of
an untitled layman, one below the grade of knight, Dominus appears to
correspond with Magister, Master, or by abbreviation Mr.

confirmavi Magistro Waltero Isaac de Hulle clerico Unam Croftam Inclusam Que jacet inter gardinum et croftas dicti Magistri Walteri et curtil^m mei Henrici in Hulle in Parochia de Chilterne Doumere Hab. et Ten. dictam Croftam Inclusam . . . . . In cujus . . . . . Sigillum . . . . apposui Datum apud Hulle die Mercurii prox. post Fest. S'cti Barnabe Apostoli Ann. reg. Reg Edw^l III. post conq^m vicesimo primo. Hiis Testib. Dominis, Johanne de Clyvedone, Simone de Fforneaux, et Nichola de Bolevyle, Militibus. Joh^e Baret, Ric^o de Warmwelle, Joh^e Turke, Joh^e Pigaz, Et aliis.

Henry de Romsey, son and heir of Henry de Romsey, to Master Walter Isaac of Hylle, clerk; an enclosed paddock, lying between the garden and crofts of the said Master Walter, and the Curtillage of the said Henry, in Hylle in the Parish of Chilterne Dommer . . . . . Given at Hylle, on Wednesday next after the Feast of St Barnabas the Apostle, in the 21st year of King Edward III. Witnesses; Sirs, John de Clyvedon, Simon de Forneaux, and Nicholas de Bolevyle, Knights.

No. 36. Edw. III. 1349. Monday after Octr 21.

Noverint universi me Walterum de Romesye filium et heredem Domini Johannis de Romesye Militis in plena etate mea relaxasse ac pro me et her'bus meis quietum clamasse Magistro Waltero Ysaac de Hulle Archidiacono Bathoniensi Will^o Ysaac de Hulle et Margarete Uxori ejusdem Will^l ac her'bus et assig. ejusdem Walteri Ysaac inperpet. Totum jus et clamium quod habui vel quoquo modo habere potui in omnibus mesua. terr. prat. pasc. et pasturis cum pert^s Que Ysaac de Hulle Pater ipsius Walteri Ysaac de Domino Waltero de Romesye Avo meo quondam tenuit in Hulle juxta Chilterne Dommere in Com. Somers. Et Que predicti Wal-

terus Ysaac Will⁵ et Margareta ante diem confectionis pre-
sencium de me tenuerunt ad terminum vite eorundem ex di-
missione D'ni Waltⁱ Avi mei supradicti Ita quod nec ego
Walterus de Romesye filius et heres . . . . . In cuj. rei
test. Sigil. me. pre'bus appos. Hiis Test. Dominis Johanne de
Clyvedone, Symone de Fforniaux, Militibus. Ricᵒ Barry, Johᵉ
Baret, Davyd de Honteleghe, Willᵒ Welde, Rogero Page,
Johᵉ Turke, Johᵉ Pygaz, Et aliis. Datum apud Acle die Lune
prox, post Fest. S'cti Dunstani Archiepiscopi Ann. reg. Reg.
Edwⁱ III. post conqᵐ vicesimo tercio,

Walter de Romsey, son and heir of Sir John de Romsey,
Knight, (on attaining his majority), to Master Walter Ysaac
of Hylle, Archdeacon of Bath, William Ysaac of Hylle, and
Margaret wife of the latter, for ever—all his right and title
in all the Messuages, lands, &c. which Ysaac of Hylle,
father of Walter Ysaac, formerly held in Hylle near Chilterne Domer in Co. of Somerset, of Sir Walter de Romsey
the Grandfather . . . . . Witnesses; Sirs, John de
Clyvedon, Symon de Forniaux, Knights . . . . Given
at Oakley (Acle), on Monday next after the Feast of St.
Dunstan Archbishop; in the 23rd year of King Edward III.

No. 37. Edw. III. 1349. Sunday before Octʳ 28.

Sci. pres. et fut. quod Nos Thomas de Moltone dictus
Baker et Agnes uxor mea unanimi assensu et consensu dedimus concess. et hac pres. car. nost. confirmavimus Johanni
Josep de Ivelcestra et Alicie uxori sue et her'bus dicte Alicie
Illud tenementum cum pertˢ quod situm est in Chepstrete
ejusdem ville inter tenem. Domini Nicholai de Bolevylle Militis juxta Viam que se extendit versus Novam Molendinam
et tenem. pertinens ad Albam Aulam Hab. et Ten . . . .
cuj. rei testi. Sigil. nost. huic pres. carte apposuimus Hiis
Test. Thoma de Broke, Andrea Spicer, Ricᵒ Ffolquy, Waltero

Belfamite, Joh⁰ atter Wille, Joh⁰ de Ryponn, Et aliis Datum apud Ivelcestram Die Domin, prox. ante Fest Apostolorum Simonis et Jude Ann. reg. Reg. Edwardi III. Vicesimo tercio· Endorsement on this Deed—Johannes Hubarde Webbe de Yevele filius Is (abelle) Hubardes sororis Alicie infra nominate dat &c., R' Veel.

Thomas de Moltone, called Baker, and Agnes his wife, with one assent and consent—to John Josep of Ivelcester; That tenement situate in Chepstrete, between the tenement of Sir Nicholas de Bolevylle, Knight, near the Road which leads towards the New Mill, and a tenement belonging to Whitehall . . . . Witn. Thomas de Broke, and others Given at Ivelcester on the Lord's Day next before the Feast of the App. Simon and Jude, in the 23rd year of King Edwd. III.

Endorsed John Hubarde Webbe of Yeovil, son of Isabella Hubardes, sister of Alicia within named, grants, &c., to Robert Veel.

No. 38, Edw. III. 1351, Thursday after Ascension Day.

Universis ad quorum noticiam presentes litere pervenerint Ricardus Michel et Elizabet uxor ejus filia et heres Domini Johannis Wake Sal. in D'no Noveritis nos unanimi assensu et concensu remisisse relaxasse et omnino de nobis et her'bus nostris quietum clamasse Thome Sperman her'bus suis et assig. suis Totum jus Nostrum et clamium quod habuimus habemus vel aliquo modo habere poterimus in Toto illo Tenemento et Columbario cum singulis eorum pert⁸ in Ivelcestra Et quod quidem tum Dominus Johannes Wake pater meus habuit ex concessione Johannis de Chilterne prout in quodam Scripto D'ni Joh^is quiete clemancie penes D'num Joh^em Wake remanentis plenius continetur In cujus

rei test. Sigil. nost. pre'bus sunt apposita Hiis Test. Nich°
de Bolevylle, Milite, Thoma de Broke, Will° de Bolevylle,
Thoma de Honteley, Ric° Folquy, Joh° de Ryponne, Et aliis.
Datum apud Ivelcestram die Jovis prox. post Fest. Adcensionis
Domini Ann. reg. Reg. Edwardi Tercii a conquestu vicesimo
quinto.

Richard Michel and Elizabeth his wife, daughter and heir
of Dr. John Wake—to Thomas Sperman—all their right
in that Tenement and Dovecot in Ivelcester, which Master
John Wake, the father of Elizabeth, held of John de Chilterne
. . . Witn. Nicholas de Bolevylle, knight; Thomas de
Broke, Willm de Bolevylle, Thos de Honteley . . . .
Given at Ivelcester on Thursday next after the Feast of our
Lord's Ascension; in the 25th year of Edward III.

No. 39. Edw. III. 1355. Saturday before March 25.

Omn. Xti Fid. ad quos pres. sc'ptm perven. Thomas
Machon de Chilterne Fagge Sal. in D'no. Noveritis me tradi.
. . . . . Johanni Bule de Chilterne Dummere Unam
dimidiam acram terre arrabilis in Campo de Chilt. Dum.
apud le to Creyce jacentem in cultura que vocatur Mert-
furghlang inter terram Roggeri Torel ex una par. et Cam-
pum de Thourne ex altera Hab. et Ten . . . . Hiis Test.
Mermeduce Ffagge, Thoma Pighou, Rob^to Pygaz, Thoma
Warmwelle, Will° Isaac, Et aliis. Datum apud Chilt.
Fagge die Sabbati prox. ante Fest. Annunciacionis Beate
Marie Ann. reg. Reg, Edw^i Tercii post conq^m Vicesimo nono.

Thomas Machon of Chilterne Fagge, to John Bule of
Chilterne Dummer; half-an-acre of arable land in Chilt. Dum.
field, at the Cross, lying in the ploughed ground called Mert-
furghlang, between the land of Roger Torel on one side, and

Thourne field on the other . . . . . Witn. Marma-
duke Fagge, . . . Given at Chilt. Fagge, on Saturday
next before the Feast of the Annunciation of the Blessed
Mary. In 29th year of Edward.

No. 40. Edw. III. 1358. Sunday, Septr 30.

Sci. pres. et fut. quod ego Wills Isaake de Hulle dedi
. . . . Domino Stephano Pygacz Vicario Ecclesie de
Chilterne Dummere Omnia et singula terras et tenementa
mea cum perts Que habui de confectione presentum in Hulle
et Chilt. Dummere predictis Hab. et Ten . . . . .
Datum apud Hulle predictam die Domin. in Crastino Festi
S'cti Mich'is Archangeli Ann. reg. Reg. Edwi III. a conqu
Tricesimo secundo Hiis Test. Johe Fauconer, Willo Brok,
Robto Pygacz, Johe Huchyn, Daniele Broke, Et aliis.

William Isaake of Hylle—to Sir Stephen Pygacz, Vicar
of the Church of Chiltern Dummer—All and singular the
lands and tenements belonging to him, in Hylle and Chilt.
Dum. . . . Given at Hylle, on the Lord's Day, being the
Morrow of the Feast of St Michael the Archangel; in the
32d year of Edwd III. Witn. John Fauconer, Willm Brok,
John Huchin, Daniel Broke.

No. 41. Edw. III. 1360. Saturday after April 23.

Noverint universi me Thomam Machon de Chylterne
Vagge dedisse . . . . Willielmo de Byngham Unum
annuum redditum centum solidorum percipiendum de omnibus
terris et ten'tis meis in Chylterne Vag et Hardyngtone
Maundevylle in Com. Somers. Hab. et percipiendum predm
redditum . . . . Hiis Test. Robto Forde, Robto Basset
Willo Wither, Thoma Brytone, Johe Stagone, Thoma Monne,
Rico de Penne, Johe Waspray, Johe Sprot, Et aliis Datum

apud Hardyngtone predictam Die Sabbati prox. post Fest
S'cti Georgi Ann. reg. Reg. Edw^t Tercii post conq^m Tricesimo
quarto.

Thomas Machon of Chylterne Vag, to William de
Byngham, a yearly rent of one hundred shillings; to be
levied upon all his lands and tenements in Chylterne Vag and
Hardyngton Maundevylle, in the Co. of Somerset . . . .
Richard of Penne . . . . Given at Hardyngtone, on
Saturday next after the Feast of St. George. In the 34th
year of Edward III.

No. 42. Edw. III. 1361. Tuesday Novr 30.

Pateat universis per presentes quod ego Walterus de
Miltone de North Peret attornavi et in loco meo apposui
dilectos michi in X'sto Nicholaum Dynygtone et Willm Mercere
de North peret conjunctim et divisim ad ponendum Robertum
James in plenam et pacificam seisinam in omnibus terris et
tenementis pratis et pasturis Que Johannes Stagonn de me
tenuit in Chilt. Vagge et Chilt. Dom. Sibi et her'bus suis
inperpet. Sicu*d* in quadam carta inde confecta plenius continetur Ratum et gratum habiturus quicquid iidem Nic^{us} et
Will^s fecerit vel fecerint nomine meo in premissis In cujus
rei testi. pres'bus Sigil. meum apposui Datum apud North
Peret die Martis in Festo S'cti Andree Apostoli Ann. reg.
Reg. Edwardi Tercii a conquestu tricesimo quinto.

Endorsed. Lett' of Attornay by Wat' of Myltone.

Walter de Milton of North Peret, appoints Nicholas
Dynygton and Willm Mercer of North peret, his Attorneys to
put Robert James in full and peaceable possession of all the
lands and tenements which John Stagonn held of him, in
Chilt. Vagge and Chilt Dom. Given at North Peret on
Tuesday, the Feast of St. Andrew the Apostle. In the 35 year
of Edward III.

No. 43. Edw. III. 1361. November 30.

Sci. pres. et fut. quod ego Walterus de Miltone de North Peret dedi . . . . . Roberto James omnes terras et tenementa Que Joh^{es} Stagon de me tenuit in Chilterne . . . . . Hab. et Ten . . . . . Hiis Test. Nich° Dynygton, Will° Mercere, Will° Welde, Rogero Warmwelle, Rob^{to} Pigas, Et aliis. Dat. ap. North peret die Martis in Festo S'ci Andree Apostoli Ann. reg. Reg. Edw^l III. a conquestu tricesmo quinto.

Walter de Milton of North Peret to Robert James (No 42.)

No. 44. Edw. III. 1361. Septr 21.

Sci. pres. et fut. quod nos Walterus Cary et Willielmus Craddoke dedimus . . . . . Roberto Lange et Johanne Gyot tenementum nostrum in Bischepistone cum curt° et septem acras terre Que vocatur Gyotesplace cum suis pert' Hab. et Ten . . . . . In cujus rei test. Sigil. nost. apposuimus Hiis Test. Domino Ricardo Grigory Capellano, Will° Hayward, Will° Eatone, Waltero Seymour, Joh^e Salisbury, Will° Warman, Joh^e Janot, Et aliis. Datum apud Bischepistone pred^m die Martis in Festo S'ci Mathei Apostoli et Ewangeliste Ann. reg. Reg. Edwardi Tercii a conq^u tricesimo quinto.

Walter Cary and William Craddoke, to Robert Lang and Johanna Gyot; Their Tenement in Bishopstone, with Curtillage, and seven acres of land, called Gyot's place . . . . . Witn. Sir Richard Grigory, chaplain . . . . . Given at * Bishopstone aforesaid, on Tuesday, the Feast of St Matthew the Apostle and Evangelist. In the 35th year of Edward III.

* Bishopstone—called Montacute after the Conquest. The street and Tithing of Bishopstone, remain distinguishable in the Parish of Montacute at the present day.

No. 45, Edw. III. 1362. Thursday after Feby 12.

Pateat universis per presentes quod ego Walterus Isaac de Hulle Fateor et reco*n*gnosco me esse Ballivum Stephani Fratris mei et Will^i de Modeforde consanguinei mei Tenere terras prata et pasturas cum pert^s eorundem apud Hulle et Chylterne Et de omnibus bonis et catallis provenientibus eorum me esse coram quocunque judice illis et utrique eorundem computabilem. In cujus rei test. Sigil. meum apposui. Data apud Hulle in Parochia de Chylterne Dommere die Jovis prox. post Fest. Purificationis Beate Marie Ann. reg. Reg. Edw^i Tercii post conq^m tricesimo sexto intrante.

Walter Isaac of Hylle acknowledges, that he is steward for his brother Stephen, and Willm of Modeford his cousin, to hold possession of their lands at Hylle and Chyltern, and to render an account before any judge, to both and each of them, of all the goods and chattels accruing from the property. Given at Hylle, in the Parish of Chyltern Dommere, on Thursday next after the Feast of the Purification of the Blessed Mary, in the beginning of the 36th year of King Edward III.

No. 46. Edw. III. 1361. Thursday Novr 25.

Sci pres. et fut. quod Ego Stephanus Pygacz Perpetuus Vicarius de Chilterne Dommere dedi . . . . Waltero Isaac de Hulle filio Will^i Isaac de Hulle defuncti et Stephano Isaac Fratri suo omnia et singula terras et tenementa crofta cum pert^s Que habui die confectionis presentum in Hulle et Chilterne Dummere ex dono et feffiamento predicti Willi Isaac de Hulle dum vixit Hab. et Ten . . . . In cujus rei test. huic pre^{tt} car. mee Sigil. meum apposui Et de omnibus supradictis predictis Waltero et Stephano seisinam personaliter liberavi Datum apud Hulle die Jovis in Festo Sancte Katerine

Virginis Ann. reg. regis Edw¹ Tercii a conqᵘ tricesimo quinto. Hiis Test. Domino Waltero de Romesye, Domino Edmundo Dummere, Militibus. Rogero Warmwille, Robᵗᵒ Pigacz, Thoma Mone, Willᵒ Cayrene, Et aliis.

Stephen Pygacz, Perpetual Vicar of Chilterne Dommere, to Walter Isaac of Hylle, son of Willᵐ Isaac of Hylle, deceased, and to Stephen his brother—All and singular the lands and tenements which he (Stephen Pygacz) then had in Hylle and Chilterne Dummere, by gift from the aforesaid Willᵐ Isaac of Hylle during his life time . . . . And he puts the said Walter and Stephen into full and corporal possession of the same property. Given at Hylle, on Thursday in the Feast of St Catherine the Virgin. In the 35th year of King Edward III. Witnesses. Sir Walter de Romesye, Sir Edmund Dummer, Knights. Roger Warmwille, &c.

No. 47. Edw. III. 1362. Friday after March 25.

Omn. Xti Fid. ad quos pres. sc'ptm perven. Robertus James et Walterus de Miltone Sal. in D'no. Noveritis nos tradidisse . . . . Stephano Godewyne et Edithe uxori ejus Quatuor acras terre cum suis pertˢ in Campo de Chilterne Dummere Quarum una acra jacet super Cheldrygge inter terram Roberti Pygas ex parte una et terram Stephani Swan ex altera Et tres dimidie acre terre jacent in le Estlangelonde inter terram Robᵗⁱ Pygas ex parte una et Ricⁱ Pouphorn ex altera Et una acra jacet in Vilemede juxta terram Rogeri Torel Et tres virgate terre jacent Bytwynetone juxta terram Prioris de Brutone ex parte una et unam virg' terre de Ecclesie ex altera Hab. et Ten. . . . . Hiis Test. Willᵒ Welde, Rogero Warmwelle, Robᵗᵒ Wrenche, Willᵒ Cayron, Et aliis Datum apud Chilterne Dommere die Veneris prox. post Fest. Annunciacionis Beate Marie Virginis Ann. reg. Reg. Edwardi Tercii a conqᵘ tricesimo sexto.

Robert James and Walter de Milton, to Stephen Godewyne and Edith his wife; Four acres in Chiltern Dummer field. One acre lies above Chalridge; three half-acres are in East longland; one acre is in Vilemead, near land of Roger Torel; three roods at Bytwyneton, near lands of the Prior of Bruton on one side, and a rood belonging to the Church on the other side. Given at Chilt. Dom. on Friday next after the Feast of the Annunciation of the Blessed Virgin Mary. In the 36th year of King Edward III.

No. 48. Edw. III. 1362. Whit Monday.

Sci. pre. et fut. quod ego Willielmus de Peyto tradidi . . . . . Roberto James her'bus et assig. suis omnes terras ac ten^{ta} prata pascuas et pasturas communes (cum) viis semitis et omnibus aliis suis pert^s Que quondam fuerunt Walteri de Miltone in Chilterne Vagge et Chilterne in Com. Somers. Hab. et Ten. . . . . Hiis Test. Will^o Bynghame, Will^o Welde, Joh^e le Doo, Rogero de Warmwelle, Rob^{to} Pygas de Com. Somers. Et aliis. Datum apud Westone juxta Brayles in Comitatu Warr' Die Lune in Crastino Pentecoste Ann. reg. Reg. Edw^i Tercii a conq^u tricesimo sexto.

William de Peyto to Robert James—All lands and tenements which formerly belonged to Walter de Milton in Chiltern Vagge and Chiltern. Witnesses, William Byngham, Willm Welde, ... Given at Weston near Brayles, in the County of Warwick, on Monday the Morrow of Pentecost (Whit Monday) in the 36th year of King Edward III.

No. 49. Edw. III. 1362. Sunday after Augt 24.

Omn. Xti Fid. ad quos pres. sc'pm perven. Walterus de Miltone Sal. in Dno. Noveritis me tradidisse . . . . . Roberto Yonge Vicario Ecclesie de Bradepole et Hugoni

Couffe de Brideporte Omnia terras ten^{ta} prata pascuas pasturas bostra mor' alvet ward' maritag' relevia escaet' redditus reversiones et servicia cum omn. suis pert^s Que habui in Chilterne Vagge et in Chilterne Dommere Concessi eciam predictis Roberto et Hugoni quatuor denarratus annui redditus cum pert^s que Stephanus Godewyne et Agnes uxor ejus michi reddere consueverunt Simul cum reversione quatuor acrarum terre cum pert^s que acciderit post mortem predictorum Stephani et Agnetis Hab. et Ten . . . . Reddendo mihi et her'bus meis unam rosam rubeam . . . . Hiis Test. Will^o Welde, Rogero Warmewelle, Joh^e Botere, Rob^{to} Pygaz, Rob^{to} Bertone, Et aliis. Datum apud Brideporte Die Domin. prox. post Fest. S'ci Bartholomei Apostoli Ann. reg. Reg. Edwⁱ Tercii a conq^u tricesimo sexto.

Walter de Milton to Robert Yonge, Vicar of the church of Bradepole, and Hugh Couffe of Bridport—All lands, &c., which he held in Chilt. Vagge and Chilt. Dom. Also, a yearly rent of four-pence, which Stephen Godewyne and Agnes his wife (Edith No. 47) used to pay to me; together with the reversion of four acres of land, to fall in at the death of the said Stephen and Agnes . . . . By rendering to me and my heirs one red rose . . . Witnesses; Willm Welde and others. Given at Bridport on the Lord's Day next after the Feast of St. Bartholomew the Apostle. In the 36th year of Edward III.

No. 50, Edw. III. 1363. Tuesday before Augt 24.

Noverint Universi me Edmundum Dommere Militem remisisse relax: ac pro me et her'bus meis quietum clamasse Waltero Isaac et Stephano Isaac fratri ejusdem Walteri ac eorum her'bus vel assig. Totum jus meum et clameum quod habui vel quoquo modo habere potui in omn. terris pratis

pasc. et pastu, cum suis pert⁸ in Chilt. Dom. in Com. Somers.
Que quondam Walterus Isaac et Isabella Isaac filia Willⁱ
Isaac de Hulle aliquando tenuerunt de Johanne Dommere
patre meo ad terminum vite eorum in eadem villa Ita quod
nec ego dictus Edmundus Dommere nec heredes mei nec
aliquis alius nomine nostro aliqui*t* juris vel clamei in pred.
terris . . . exigere vel vendicare poterimus in futurum
Se*t* inde ab omni accione juris inperp. sumus exclusi per presentes Et ego vero dictus Edmundus Dommere Miles et her⁹
mei omnia pred. terras, &c., predictis Waltero et Stephano
her'bus et assig. eorum contra omnes mortales Warantizabimus
aquietabimus et defendemus inperp. In cujus rei test. pre'bus
Sigil. meum apposui Hiis Test. Will° de Bynghame, Will°
Welde, Joh° Atte Forde, Will° Broke, Rob⁹ Pygas, Et aliis
Datum apud Chilt. Dom. die Martis prox. ante Fest. S'ci
Bartho'i Apostoli Ann. reg. Reg. Edwardi Tercii a conq⁹
tricesimo septimo.

Endorsed. Relaxatio Edmundi Dommere Militis concessa
Waltero Isaac et Stephano, &c.,

Edmund Dommer, Knight, to Walter Isaac and Stephen
Isaac, brother of Walter; all his right and claim in all lands,
of every description, in Chiltern Dommer; which property,
Walter Isaac and Isabella Isaac, daughter of William Isaac of
Hylle, at one time held of John Dommer, father of Sir
Edmund, for the term of their lives . . . . Given at
Chilt. Dom. on Tuesday next before the Feast of St. Bar-
tholomew the Apostle. In the 37th year of Edward III.

No. 51. Edw. III. 1364. Monday after April 4.
Omn. Xti Fid. ad quos pres. sc'pm perven. Robertus
Yonge Vicarius Ecclesie de Bradepol et Hugo Couffe de
Brudeport Sal. in Dno Noveritis nos concessisse . . . .

Waltero de Cloptone Omnia terras et ten^{ta} cum pratis pasc. pastu. boscis moris alvetis Wardis Maritagiis releviis escaetis redditibus serviciis reversionibus quando acciderint et cum omn. suis pert^s Que nos predicti Robertus et Hugo prius habuimus ad totam vitam nostram ex dimissione Walteri de Myltone in Chilt. Vagge et in Chilt. Dom. Concessimus eciam predicto Waltero de Cloptone quatuor denarratus annuⁱ redditus cum perts. quas Stephanus Godewyne et Agnes uxor ejus nobis annuatim reddere consueverunt Simul cum quatuor acris terre quas de nobis tenet ad totam vitam eorum ibidem cum reversione dictarum quatuor acrarum terre post mortem pre'orum Stephani et Agnetis quando acciderit Hab. et Ten . . . . Hiis Test. Will^o de Bynghame, Will^o Welde, Joh^e Leddrede, Joh^e Longhe, Rogero Warmwelle, Rob^{to} Pigatz, Rob^{to} Alfford, et multis aliis. Datum · apud Crukerne die Lune prox. post Fest. Sci Ambrosii Ann. reg. Reg. Edwardi Tercii post conq^m tricesimo octavo.

Robert Yonge, Vicar of the Church of Bradepol, and Hugh Couffe of Bridport—to Walter de Cloptone—all lands and tenements whatsoever, with appurtenances of every kind. Which property they formerly held for the whole term of their lives, by the quittance of Walter de Mylton; in Chilt. Vagg and Chilt. Dommer. Also, to the same Walter de Cloptone, a yearly rent of four-pence . . . . (No. 49) Given at Crukerne, on Monday next after the Feast of St. Ambrose. In the 38th year of Edward III.

No. 52. Edw. III. 1364. Monday after Augt 4.

Omn. Xti Fid. ad quos pres. scrip. perven. Walterus de Cloptone Sal. in Dno. Noveritis me tradidisse . . . . . Stephano Godewyne et Edithe uxori ejus quatuor acras terre arabilis cum perts in Campis de Chilterne Dummere Quarum una acra jacet super Cheldrigge inter terram Rob^ti Pygaz ex parte una et terram Stephani Swan ex altera Et una acra et dimidia jacent in Estelangelond inter terram Rob^ti Pygas ex par. una et terram Ric^i Pouphorn ex altera Et una acra jacet in Vilemede juxta terram nuper Rogeri Torel Et tres rode terre jacent Bytwynetone inter terram Prioris de Brutone ex parte una et unam rodam terre pertinentem Ecclesie ex altera Hab. et Ten . . . Datum apud Chilt. Vagge die Lune prox. post Fest. S'ci Ambrosii Ann. reg. Reg. Edw^i Tercii post conq^m tricesimo octavo Hiis. Test. Will° Welde, Rogero Warmewille, Robt° Pigaz, Robt° Wrenche Will° Cayron, et multis aliis.

Walter de Cloptone to Stephen Godewyne and Edith his wife—lands, &c. (No. 47.)

No. 53. Edw. III. 1364. Wednesday after May 1.

Omn. Xti Fid. ad quos pres. scrip. perven. Walterus de Cloptone Sal. in Dno. Noveritis me tradidisse . . . . Johanni Couke et Stephano Tribulacz tres acras terre arabilis in Campis de Chilt. Dum. cum toto prato meo de Manymede Una acra jacet in cultura de Hirleighe inter terram nuper Joh^is Turke et terram Rob^ti Pigaz Una acra jacet in cultura de Lonstede inter terram nuper Joh^is Turke et terram Sarre Rokkebourn Dimidia acra jacet apud Manymede Croise inter terram Johanne Smythes et terram nuper Joh^is Stagon Et dimidia acra jacet ad occidentalem finem bosci de Ocle inter terram Thome Pynghow et terram nuper Domini Johannis de Beauchampe Hab. et Ten . . . . salva secta curie mee de Chilterne Vagge semel per annum . . . . Hiis Test. Will° Bynghame, Robt° Boure, Rog° Warmewelle, Robt° Pigaz, Robt° Wrenche Et aliis Datum ap. Chilterne die Mercurii prox. post Fest, Apostolorum Philippi et Jacobi ann. reg. Reg. Edw^i Tercii a conq^u tricesimo octavo.

Walter de Cloptone to John Couke and Stephen Tribulacz, three acres of arable in Chilt. Dum. fields, together with all his meadow of Manymead; one acre in the ploughed ground of Hirleigh; one acre in the ploughed ground of Lonstede; half-an-acre at Manymead Cross; and half-an-acre at the Western extremity of Oakley wood, between land of Tho⁸ Pynghow, and land which belonged lately to Sir John de Beauchampe. To Have . . . . saving suit in my court of Chilterne Vagge once a year . . . . . Given at Chilterne, on Wednesday next after the Feast of the Apostles, Philip and James. In the 38th year of Edward III.

No. 54. Edw. III. 1365. The second Sunday after Easter.

Omn. Xti Fid. ad quos pres. scr. perven. Walterus de Cloptone filius et heres Joh^{is} de Cloptone Sal. in Dno. Noveritis me dimisisse . . . . Willielmo Phelpys et Margarete uxori ejusdem Unum mesuagium cum curtill° et clauso adjacenti et decem acris terre arabilis et tribus acris prati et suis pert, quibus cunque Que michi jure hereditario inperp. descendebant post mortem Johannis de Cloptone Fratris mei senioris in Tyntenhulle Quod quidem mesuagium situm est ibidem inter mesuagium Nicholai Phelpys ex parte una et mesuagium Johanne Dorsetes ex parte altera Concessi insuper eisdem Will° et Margarete omnia terras et ten^{ta} mea redditus et servicia cum omnibus et singulis suis pert³ quibuscumque que adquisivi mihi her'bus et assig. meis de Edmundo Dummere Milite in Tyntenhulle predicta tota vita Isabelle Mascalys Hab. et Ten . . . . cum curtill° clauso adjacenti . . . In cujus rei testi. tam ego pred. Walterus quam pred. Willielmus et Margareta sigil. nost. alternatim apposuimus Hiis Test. Joh° Bondman, Nich° Trut, Will° Broke, Rob^{to} Atte Yerde, Rob^{to} le Bour, et Multis aliis. Datum apud

Tyntenhulle Die Domin. prox. post Fest. Clausi Pascha ann. reg. Reg. Edwardi Tercii post conq^m tricesimo nono.

Endorsed. Tynternhelle.

Walter de Clopton son and heir of John de Clopton, to William Phelpys (Phelyps) and Margaret his wife; a messuage, with Curtillage and a close of ground adjoining, and ten acres of arable land, and three acres of meadow, and all appurtenances—which descended to me by hereditary right, for ever, after the death of John de Clopton my elder brother; in Tyntenhull. The messuage is situate in that village between property of Nicholas Phelpys (Phelyps) on one side, and of Johanna Dorsetes on the other. Moreover, I have given up to the same William and Margaret, all my lands and tenements, rents, services, &c., acquired by me from Edmund Dummer, knight, in Tyntenhull aforesaid, for the natural life of Isabella Mascalys . . . . Witn. Robert Atte Yard, and others. Given at Tyntenhull, on the Lord's Day next after the Feast of the Close of Easter (i. e. on the second Sunday after Easter); in the 39th year of Edw. III.

No. 55. Edw. III. 1365. Tuesday after Octr 21.

Omn. Xti Fid. ad quos pres. litere perven. Johannes Martyn de Stokelynche Sal. in Dno. Noveritis me tradidisse . . . . . Waltero de Cloptone omnia terras et ten^ta mea redditus et servicia cum omn. suis pert^s Que habeo in Stokelynche Ostriser Hab. et Ten . . . . . In cujus rei testi. presentibus literis indentatis presentes pred^ti alternatim sigilla sua apposuerunt Hiis test. Joh^e de Moltone, Joh^e Beauchampe de Lillesdone, Militibus; Rogero Sylveyn, Joh^e de Dylyngtone, Joh^e Cropp Et aliis. Datum apud Stokelynche die Martis prox. post Fest. S'ci Dunstani ann. reg. Regis Edw'i Tercii a conq^u tricesimo nono.

John Martyn of Stokelynche to Walter de Clopton, all the lands and tenements, rents and services belonging to me in Stokelynche Ostriser . . . . Witnesses—John de Molton, John Beauchampe de Lillesdone, knights. John of Dylyngtone, &c. Given at Stokelynche, on Tuesday next after the Feast of St. Dunstan. In the 39th year of Edward III.

No. 56. Edw. III. 1365. Counterpart of No. 54, supra.

Omn. Xti Fid . . . . Walterus de Cloptone filius et heres Joh^ls de Cloptone Sal. in. Dno. Noveritis me dimisisse . . . . Willielmo Phelypes et Margarete uxori ejusdem unum Mesuagium cum curtill^o clauso adjacente . . . . . Quod quidem Mesuagium situm est ibidem inter mes^m Nicholai Phelypes, &c.

Walter de Cloptone son and heir of John de Cloptone, to Willm Phelypes and Margaret his wife. No. 54.

No. 57. Edw. III. 1366. Sunday after Michaelmas Day.

Sciant pres. et fut. quod nos Walterus Cary et Willielmus Cradduke dedimus . . . . Rob^to le Langebakere et Johanne uxori ejusdem, filie et heredi Johannis Gyot, Omnia illa terras et ten^ta cum omn. suis pert^s quibus cumque Que habuimus ex dono feofamento predicte Johanne nobis et her'bus nostris inperp. Et que quidem terre et ten^ta scita sunt in la Hyde in Byschepestone juxta Burgum Montis Acuti Hab. et Ten. Hiis test. Joh^e le Doo, Rob^to Yerde, Joh^e Peny, Rob^to Peystour, Waltero Saymour, Will^o Dollynge seniore, Will^o Warman, et Multis aliis Datum apud Montagu Die Domin. prox. post. Fest. S'ci Michaelis Archangeli ann. reg. Reg. Edwardi Tercii post conq^m Quadragesimo. Et seisinam eisdem Rob^to et Johanne et her'bus ipsius Johanne in forma prenotata personaliter liberavimus.

Walter Cary and Willm Cradduke, to Robert le Langebakere and Johanna his wife, daughter and heir of John Gyot; certain lands and tenements (44) in La Hyde in Bishopstone, near the Castle of Montacute . . . . Given at Montacute on the Lord's Day next after the Feast of St. Michael the Archangel; in the 40th year of Edward III. " And we, in person, have delivered possession to the same Robert and Johanna, in manner before described.

No. 58, Edw. III. 1366. Monday after Christmas Day.

Sci. pres. et fut. quod ego Thomas Hullard de Stoforde dedi . . . . Johanni Mallynge de Stoforde Unum burgagium situatum in la Southstrete ville de Stoforde ex parte austr. inter tenementa Joh^{is} Cole ex utraque parte Hab. et Ten. Totum pred. burga. &c. Hiis Test. Joh^e Martyn tunc Preposito Ville de Stoforde, Will^o Payn junr., Johe Galyet, Will^o Mone, Joh^e Blew, Joh^e Trunket, Will^o Fateman, Et multis aliis. Datum apud Stoforde die Lune prox. post Fest, Natalis Domini Ann. reg, Reg. Edw^i Tercii post conq^m quadragesimo.

Thomas Hullard of Stoford, to John Mallynge of Stoford; a burgage situate in la Southstrete of the village of Stoford . . . . Witn. John Martyn, Provost (or Mayor) of the village of Stoford, and others. Given at Stoford on Monday next after the Feast of our Lord's Nativity; in the 40th year of Edward III.

No. 59. Edw. III. 1368. Sunday after June 29.

Universis pateat per presentes me Walterum Moritz concessisse remis. relax. et omnino de me et her'bus meis imperp, quietum clamasse Ricardo Brice et her'bus suis omne jus meum et clamium quod habeo habui vel aliquo modo habere potero quacunque ratione vel titulo in toto illo tenemento et curtillagio cum Columbario et singulis eorum pert^s

Quod quidem tenementum quondam fuit Rogeri Hardarey et quod situm est in Chepstrete ville Ivelcestre Hab. et Ten. Hiis test. Domino Will° Power Capellano, Rob¹° Pervyes, Waltero Fflatchere, Will° Bouchere, Joh° Ffyssche, Joh° Atte Wille, et aliis. Datum apud Ivelcestram Die Domin. prox. post Fest. Apostolorum Petri et Pauli ann. reg. Reg. Edwardi Tercii post conq™ quadragesimo secundo.

Walter Moritz to Richard Brice—All his right and title in that tenement and curtillage together with a Dovecot, which formerly belonged to Roger Hardarey, situate in Chepstrete in the town of Ivelcester . . . . Witn. Sir William Power, Chaplain, and others. Given at Ivelcester on the Lord's Day next after the Feast of the Apostles, Peter and Paul; in the 42d year of Edward III.

No. 60, Edw. III. 1368. Sunday after July 7.

Omn. Xti Fid. ad quos pres. hoc scrip. perven. Ricardus Brice Sal. in Dno. Noveritis me concessisse . . . Waltero Moritz Totum illud tenem. meum et curtill™ cum Columbario et eorum pert⁹ quod fuit Rogeri Hardarey et quod situm est in West strete ville Ivelcestre. Hab. et Ten. Hiis Test. (No 59) Datum apud Ivelcestre die Domin. prox. post Fest. Translacionis S'ci Thome Martyris ann. reg. Regis Edw¹ Tercii post conq™ quadragesimo secundo.

Richard Brice to Walter Moritz—all that my tenement and curtillage with Dovecot, formerly the property of Roger Hardarey; situate in West Strete (Chepstrete, 59,) Given at Ivelcester, on Sunday next after the Feast of the Translation of St. Thomas, Martyr. In the 42d year of Edw. III.

No. 61. Edw. III. 1369. Monday after June 24.

Omn. Xti Fid. ad quos pres. scr. perven. Reginaldus Atte Watre de West Cammele Sal. in Dno. Noveritis me tradidisse . . . . . Thome Hore Burgensi Wellie et Johanne uxori ejus Unum tenementum apud Northovere ex opposito Pontem de Ievelcestre inter aquam decurrentem ibidem ex parte austr. et tenem. Johannis Merman ex parte bori. Hab. et Ten. totum pred. tenem. cum terris pasturis clausturis et omn. aliis suis pert⁹ adeo plene et integre sicut Mabilla Atte Watre ea dum vixit similiter tenuit. Hiis test. Ric° Bryce, Joh° Hamond, Joh° Rypon, Waltero Fletchere, Joh° Breuere, Adam Bat, Thoma Noreys, Waltero Blankpayn, Et aliis. Datum apud Ievelcestre die Lune prox. post Fest. Nativitatis S'ci Johannis Baptiste—Ann. reg. Reg. Edwⁱ III. post conqᵐ quadragesimo tercio.

Reginald atte Water of West Camel, to Thomas Hore a Burgess of Wells, and Johanna his wife; a tenement at Northovere, opposite to the Bridge of Ievelcester, bounded by the River on the South, and John Merman's house on the North . . . . To have, &c. with the lands, pastures, brushwood, &c., on the same full and complete tenure as that by which Mabel atte Watre held them for her life . . . . Given at Ievelcester, on Monday next after the Feast of the Nativity of St John Baptist. In the 43rd year of Edw. III.

No. 62. Edw. III. 1369. Sunday after Octr. 18.

Omn. Xti Fid . . . . Johannes de Erleghe Sal. in Dno. Noveritis me remisisse relaxasse et omnino de me et her'bus meis quietum clamasse Ric° Brysz de Somertone et her'bus suis inperpet. Totum jus meum et clamium que habeo habui seu quoquo modo habere potero in una separali pecia

prati vocata Leverham prout includitur et limitatur in Somertone Erleghe jacente inter le Voreham de Carybrigge et
Kyngesleverham Remisi insuper et relaxavi eidem Ricardo et
her'bus suis inperp. Totum jus meum et clamium que habeo
seu quovis modo habere potero in decem acris prati cum
pert⁸ in Somerton Erleghe jacentibus in quodam prato vocato
Southmor juxta Ivelcestre in diversis locis Videlicet In la
More sex acre In la Gore tres acre Et una acra vocata le
Averokacra jacet in eodem prato ex opposito la Wyche Que
omnia pred⁸ Ricardus prius de me tenuit Hab. et Ten. Hiis
Test. Joh⁶ de Ledrede, Ric⁰ de Ledrede, Joh⁶ Kynge, Waltero
Leveriche, Rob⁶ᵒ Bakwylle, Hugone Ffokle, Joh⁶ Isaak, Et
aliis. Datum apud Somertone Erleghe Die Domin. prox. post
Fest. S'ci Luce Evangeliste Ann. reg. Reg. Edwardi Tercii
post conq^m Quadragesimo tercio.

John de Erleghe, to Richard Brysz of Somertone; all
his right and claim to one particular piece of Meadow called
Leverham: so far as the boundaries thereof extend within
Somerton Erleghe; lying between the Voreham of Carybridge
and Kings leverham. Also, ten acres of Meadow in Somerton Erleghe. lying in a certain meadow called Southmore,
near Ivelcester, in different parts; viz. In the Moor six acres;
in the Gore three acres; and one acre, called the Averokacre,
is in the same field, opposite la Wyche. All which lands and
tenements, the aforesaid Richard held of me before. Given
at Somerton Erleghe, on Sunday next after the Feast of
St. Luke the Evangelist; In the 43rd year of Edward III.

No. 63. Edw. III. 1370. Friday in Whitsunweek.
Omn. Xti Fid. . . . Johannes Cole de Bruggewatere
Sal. in Dno. Noveritis me tradidisse . . . . Waltero
Blannk payn et Juliane uxori sue Sorori mee Unum bur-

gagium cum parvo curtill° Que scita sunt in Regio Vico de Yevelcestre ex opposito Ecclesie Beate Marie inter burgagium quod fuit Joh^is Draycote et burg. Marie Priorisse de Nywehalle. Hab. et Ten, Hiis Test. Rob^to Pryvyere, Joh^e Rypon, Waltero Fletchere, Joh^e atte wille, Joh^e Vysshere, Willo Wynsam, et multis aliis. Datum apud Yevelchestre die Veneris prox. post Fest. Pentecoste ann reg. Reg. Edwardi Tercii post conq^m Quadragesimo quarto.

Endorsed. Carta Walteri Blanpayn de ten. in Yevelchestre.

John Cole of Bridgwater, to Walter Blannkpayn and Juliana his wife, sister of John Cole—a burgage with small curtillage, in the public street of Yevelchester, opposite the Church of the blessed Mary; between a tenement formerly belonging to John Draycote, and another belonging to Mary Prioress of the New Hall . . . . Given at Yevelchester, on Friday next after the Feast of Whitsunday. In the 44th year of Edw. III.

No. 64, Edw. III. 1370. Sunday July 7.

Sciant pres. et fut. quod ego Johannes de Erleghe dedi . . . . Johanni de Chorletone decem acras prati pertinentis ad manerium meum de Somertone Erleghe Que vocantur le Rygge in prato vocato le Sothmore Hab. et Ten. Hiis Test. Johanne Ledrede, Ric° Ledrede, Waltero Leveriche, Rob^to Bakwille, Joh^e Kaillewey, Hugone Fokle, Joh^e Isaak, et Aliis. Datum apud Somertone Erleghe Die Domin. in Festo Translacionis S'ci Thome Martyris Ann. reg. Reg. Edwardi Tercii post Conquestum Quadragesimo quarto.

John of Erleghe to John Charlton, ten acres of Meadow belonging to my Manor of Somerton Erleghe; which are known by the name of the Ridge; in the mead called Southmore. . . . . Given at Somerton Erleghe. on Sunday, being the Feast of the Translation of St. Thomas, the Martyr. In the 44th year of Edward III.

Written on the same parchment as the preceding, 22 years subsequently.

Richard II. 1392. Monday in the Third week in Lent.

Sciant pres. et fut. quod ego Willielmus de Chorletone filius et heres Joh^ls de Chorletone dedi . . . Willielmo Ekerdone Capellano et Roberto Veel Decem acras prati cum pert^s in Sothmor que vocantur le Rygge Que predictus Johannes pater meus nuper adquisivit de Johanne de Erleghe Videlicet de parcella Manerii de Somertone Erleghe Hab. et Ten. Hiis Test. Philippo Spore, Joh^e Burcy, Joh^e Isaak, Will^o Whittok, Joh^e atte Yerd, Rogero Arundelle, Will^o Dole, Et aliis. Datum apud Yevelchestre die Lune in tercia Septimana Quadragesime Ann. reg. Reg. Ricardi Secundi Quinto decimo.

Endorsed. Copia Joh^ls de Erleghe de Somertone Erleghe.

Willm of Charlton son and heir of John de Charlton, to Willm Ekerdone, Chaplain, and Robert Veel—Ten acres of Meadow in Sothmor, called the Ridge; which the aforesaid, John, my father, lately bought of John de Erleghe; out of a portion, that is to say, of the Manor of Somerton Erleghe . . . Given at Yevelchester on Monday, in the third week in Lent; in the 15th year of Richard the Second.

No. 66. Edw. III. 1370. July 7.

Sci. pres. et fut. quod ego Joh^es de Erleghe dedi . . . Joh^i de Chorletone Decem acras prati pertinentis ad Manerium meum de Somertone Erleghe Que vocantur le Rygge in prato vocato le Sothmore Hab. et Ten. [Counterpart of No. 64]

Endorsed. M'dum quod Johannes de Chorletone infra
fuit seisitus de prato infra et illud dimisit Ric° Bris ad terminum vite sue Et idem Joh⁰ˢ obiit Et Ric⁰ˢ Bris obiit Post
cujusque mortem Will⁵ Chorletone filius predicti Johannis et
Johanne filie et heredis ejusdem Ricardi intravit, &c., et
inde feoffavit Willielmum Ekerdone Capellanum et Robertum
Veel.

John of Erleghe to John of Charlton—Ten acres of
Meadow belonging to my manor of Somerton Erleghe; called
the Ridge; in Southmore. (counterpart of No 64) Endorsed.
Mem^dum that the within John of Charlton was seised of the
meadow herein described; and made it over to Richard Bris
for the remainder of his own life. And the same John died;
and Richard Bris died. And after the death of both, William
Charlton, son of the aforesaid John and of Johanna daughter
and heir of the same Richard, entered on possession; and afterwards granted in fee to William Ekerdone Chaplain, and
Robert Veel.

No. 67. Edw. III. 1372.

Ceste Endente faite par entre Dame Alice Beauchampe
de Somersete dune parte Et Wauter Cloptone dautre parte
Tesmoigne ge la dite dame Alice ad lesse et par y cestes conferme a dit Wauter tout son Manoir de Stokelynche oue les
appurtenances a tute de la vie Dame Alice Rendant a la Dame
Alice diz Marz par an a deux termes Cest assavvoir cynk
marz a la Feste de Seint Michel Et cynk marz a la Feste de
Pasqz annuelment pour la vie la dite Dame Alice Et le dit
Wauter garante qen cas qe la dite rente soit aderere en partie
ou en tout apres quinsze jours apres ascun terme avandite qa
donqz bien lise a la dite Dame Alice et a ses ministres a

destreindre en le Manoir avandit et la destreste' retelner
tanqz gree soit fait de la rente et les arrerages Et le dit
Wauter sustendra le Manoir avandit sanz Wast ou destrucion
faire En temoignance des qeux choses les parties avanditz as
y cestes entrechaungeablement onnt mys los Sealx. Done a
Stoke Southe Hamedone l an de regne le Roi Edwarde Tierce
puis la Conqueste quaraunte quinte.

Endorsed. Irrotulatio in Memorand' Scaccarii inter Re-
corda de Termino Pasche Anno octavo Regis Ricardi S'c'di
ex parte Rem. . . . . , Thes. . . . . .

This Indenture, made between Dame Alice Beauchampe
of Somerset, on the one part, and Walter Cloptone on the
other, Witnesseth—That the said Dame Alice leases, and by
these presents doth confirm to said Walter, all her manor of
Stokelynche with pertinents, during Dame Alice's life time ;
He paying to Dame Alice ten marks a year, five at Michaelmas and five at Easter. Whenever the rent should be wholly
or partially in arrear, the agents of Dame Alice to be at liberty
to distrain on the Manor; and to keep possession until full
satisfaction should have been made for the rent due, and
arrears. The said Walter to keep up the Manor without
committing waste or wilful havoc. Given at Stoke South
Hamedone ; in the 45th year of Edward III.

Endorsed. Enrolment, as Memorandum, among the
Records of the Exchequer, of Easter Term ; in the 8th year
of King Richard the Second. . . . .

No. 68, Edw. III. 1373. Friday next after Dec' 13.

A tous ceux qe cestes lettres verronnt ou oyrent Roberd
Langebakere de Mountagu Salutacion en Dieu Sachetz moy
avoir ordeine et assigne William Balryche Chatellain a
deliverer plein seisine a Wautere de Cloptone de tous lez

teres. . . . qeux je ai en Mountagu Bisshopestene et
Hyde. . . . Done a Mountagu le Venderdi proschein
apres la Feste de seinte Lucie la Virgine Lan du Regne le
Roy Edwarde Tierce apres le conqueste Quarante Septisme.

To all who shall see or hear these letters, Robert Langebaker of Montacute wishes health in the Lord. Know, that
I have commissioned and appointed William Balryche,
steward, to deliver full possession to Walter de Cloptone of
all the lands. . . . Which I possess in Montacute,
Bishopstone and Hyde. . . . Given at Montacute, the
Friday next after the Feast of St. Lucy the Virgin; in the
47th year of Edward III.

No. 69. Edw. III. 1373. Friday next after Decr 13.

Omn. Xti Fid. ad quos pres. scr. perven. Robertus Lange-
bakere de Mountagu Sal. in Dno. Noveritis me dedisse
. . . . . Waltero de Cloptone Totum statum meum quod
habeo habui seu quovis modo habere potero in omnibus terris
et ten^{tis} . . . . in Mountagu Bisshopestone et Hyde
Que omnia habui ex dono et concessione Walteri Cary et
Will^t Craddok Hab. et Ten. In Cujus rei test. presentibus
Sigil. meum apposui. Data apud Mountagu die Veneris
prox. post Fest. Sancte Lucie Virginis ann. reg. Reg. Edwardi
Tercii post conq^m Quadragesimo Septimo. Hiis Test. Roberto
Peyghtour, Ric^o Loverynge, Joh^e Doget, Philippo Bat, Will^o
Dollynge, Et aliis.

Robert Langebaker of Montacute, to Walter de Cloptone;
All my rights whatsoever, in all the lands &c., in Montacute
Bishopstone and Hyde, which I held by grant of Walter
Cary and William Craddok (57) Given at Montacute, &c.

No. 70. Edw. III. 1373.   Monday next before July 7.

A touz y ceaux q'ceste lettre verronnt ou oyronnt Cecile Turburvyle Salutz en Dieu Sachez moi avoir relesse a Wauter Cloptone tut le droit que le j ay en touz lez terrez et tenementz queux il tient en Stokelynche Issint qe moy l avauntdite Cecile mes heirs ne autres en nostre nom en lez dit'z terrez et tent'z ou les aportynaunz desore rein ne pursommez chalenger mes de tut droit se . . .' forclos a touz jours par cestez mes presentes lettres en sealles de meme Seal Done le Lundy proschein devant le Feste de Seint Thomas Translacion L an du regne le Roy Edwarde Tierce puis le Conqueste qaraunte septisme.

Endorsed. Un reles fait par Dame Cecile Turberville a Wauter Cloptone de Stokelynche.

Cecilia Turburvylle wishes health in the Lord, &c., know, that I have made over to Walter Cloptone, all my right in all the lands and tenements occupied by him in Stokelynche . . . . . Given on Monday next before the Feast of the Translation of St. Thomas; in the 47th year of Edw. III.

No. 71. Richard. II. 1380.   Thursday after March 25.

Sciant pres. et fut. quod ego Thomas Machon filius et heres Johannis Machon dedi . . . Domino Nicholao Rectori Ecclesie de Stokegyffard Domino Will⁰ Welde Capellano et Johanni Chilterne, clerico, duos solidos annui redditus quos Willᵘˢ Wrode michi reddere consuevit pro duabus acris prati que de me tenet in Hardyngtone Hab. et Ten. . . . Hiis Test. Will⁰ Carent, Will⁰ Rycheman, Johe Hurdcote, Johᵉ Fauconer, Rogero Warmwille, Will⁰ Cloke, Robᵗ⁰ Boule, Et aliis. Data apud Chilterne Dummere die Jovis prox. post Fest. Annunciacionis Beate Marie Ann. reg. Reg. Ricardi Secundi post conquestum tercio.

Thomas Machon, son and heir of John Machon, to Master Nicholas, Rector of the Church of Stokegyffard; Master Willm Welde, chaplain; and John Chilterne, clerk; a rent of two shillings a year, which Willm Wrode is accustomed to pay to me for two acres of meadow, which he holds of me in Hardyngton. Given at Chilterne Dummere, on Thursday next after the Feast of the Annunciation of the Blessed Mary; in the 3rd year of King Richard the Second.

No. 72. Richard II. 1383. Thursday, January 1.

Omnibus Xti Fidelibus ad quos presens scriptum pervenerit Nicholaus Stylard capellanus nuper Rector Ecclesie Parochialis de Stokegyffard Sal. in Dno. Noveritis me remisisse relax. et omnino de me et her'bus meis quietum clamasse D'no Will° Welde Capellano Vicario in Ecclesia Cathedrali Wellensi her'bus et assig. suis Totum jus meum et clameum quod habui habeo seu in futurum habere potero in omnibus illis terris ten^tis pra. pasc. et past. Que quondam fuerunt Thome Machon filii et heredis Joh^is Machon defuncti in Chilt. Vagge et Chilt. Dommere Ac eciam in duobus solidis annui redditus exeuntis de duabus acris prati que Will^us Wrode et Editha uxor ejus nunc tenent per redditum predictum ad terminum vite eorundem una cum reversione predictarum duarum acrarum prati post mortem dictorum Will^t Wrode et Edithe uxoris ejus quando acciderit Ita quod ego prefatus Nicholaus . . . . Hiis test; Will° Carente, Joh^e Hurdecote, Joh^e Fauconer, Will° Cloke, Will° Rycheman, Et aliis. Datum apud Chilterne Domer die Jovis in Festo Circumcisionis Domini Ann. reg. Reg. Ricardi Secundi post conquestum sexto.

Nicholas Stylard, Chaplain, lately Rector of the Parish Church of Stokegifford, to Master Willm Welde, chaplain, vicar in the Cathedral Church of Wells; all my right and title in all those lands . . . . which formerly belonged to Thomas Machon, son and heir of John Machon, deceased, in Chilt. Vagge and Chilt. Dom. and also, in a rent of two shillings a year, accruing from two acres of meadow which Willm Wrode and Edith his wife now hold by such payment, for the term of their lives; together with the reversion of the said two acres, after the death of Willm Wrode and his wife Edith . . . . Given at Chilterne Domer, on Thursday in the Feast of the Circumcision of our Lord ; in the 6th year of Richard II.

No. 73, Richard II. 1386. October 28.

Pateat universis per presentes quod nos Johannes Aysshwyke Magister Domus Hospitalis Sancti Johannis Baptiste de Bathonia Et ejusdem Domus Confratres unanimi assensu Attornavimus et in loco nostro posuimus dilectos nobis in Christo Johannem Churcheman et Robertum Veel conjunctim et divisim ad deliberandum pro nobis et nomine nostro Willielmo Whyttoke plenariam seisinam in uno Mesuagio cum Curtillagio in Yevelchestre et una pecia prati continente unam cestram in Chestremede in Manerio de Soke Denys cum suis pert^s Que ei concessimus ad terminum centum annorum juxta Formam Indenture inde inter nos facte Ratum et gratum habituri quicquid predicti Johannes Churcheman et Robertus fecerint vel alter eorum fecerit in premissis juxta Formam Scripti predicti In cujus rei testimonium presentibus Sigillum nostrum Commune apposuimus Datum Vicesimo octavo die Mensis Octobris Ann. reg. Reg Ricardi Secundi Decimo.

Be it known to all by these presents, that we, John Aysshwyke, Master of the Hospital House of St. John Baptist of Bath, and the Co-Brethren of the same House, have with one consent, attorneyed and substituted for ourselves,

our beloved in Christ, John Churcheman and Robert Veel *
conjointly and severally, for us and in our name, to deliver
to William Whyttoke full possession in one Messuage with
Curtillage in Yevelchester; and one plot of Meadow containing
one sixth part of an acre, in Chestermead in the manor of
Sock Denis. with their pert⁸. Which we have granted to him
for the term of one hundred years, according to the form of
Indenture then executed between us; confirming and approve-
ing all that the aforesaid John Churchman and Robert, or the
one of them, shall have done in the premisses in accordance
with the terms of the before-named writing. In witness
whereof, we have put our Common Seal to these Presents.
Given on the 28th day of the Month of October, in the tenth
year of the Reign of King Richard the Second.

No. 74. Richard II. 1387. Tuesday after July 25.
Sciant pres. et fut. quod Ego Johannes Herwarde dedi
. . . . . Roberto Veele Unum Mesuagium cum Curtillᵒ
adjacente situatum extra Portam Occidentalem Ville de
Yevelchestre Et duas acras terre arrabilis Duas acras dimidias
prati Duas Sextarias et unam peciam prati cum. pert⁸ in la
West felde ejusdem ville de tenura de Sooke Denys Hab. et
Ten. omnia predicta mesuagia terram et pratum cum suis
pert⁸ Prefato Roberto her'bus et assig. suis inperp. de Capitalibus Dominis Feodi illius per redditus et servicia inde debita
et de jure consueta Et ego vero pred⁸ Johannes et heredes mei
omn. predᵃ mesⁱᵃ terram et pratum cum omn. suis pert⁸ prefato
Roberto her'bus et assig. suis contra omnes gentes Warantizabimus aquietabimus et inperpetuum defendemus In cujus
rei testim. Huic carte mee Sigil. me. apposui Hiis Test. Willₒ
Carent, Willᵒ Whittoke, Willᵒ Wilby, Johᵉ Warmwelle, Johᵉ
Bondeman, Ricᵒ Brice, Johᵉ Lidiarde, Et aliis. Data apud

* This is the earliest date, 1386, under which the name of ROBERT
VEEL occurs in these Deeds.

Yevelchestre die Martis prox. post Fest. S'cti Jacobi Apostoli
Ann. reg. Reg. Ricardi Secundi Undecimo.

John Herwarde to Robert Veel—A messuage with Curt.
adjacent, situate outside the West Gate of the Town of
Yevelchester; and two acres of arable land, two half-acres of
meadow, two sixth parts and one parcel of Meadow in the
West field of the same town, of the tenure of Sock Denys,
At Yevelchester on Tuesday next after the Feast of. St, James
James the Apostle; in the 11th year of Richard II.

No. 75. Richard. II. 1389. November 2.

Sci. pres. et fut. quod ego Johanna filia et heres Ricardi
Brice de Ivelchestre dedi. . . . . Domino Petro de
Courtenay Militi Jacobo Fitzjamys Johanni Mannyngford
Thome Knoel Will° Whyttoke de Ivelchestre predicta et Will°
Charletone omnia terras et ten^a mea Molendina Columbaria
prata boscos, &c. . . . . in Ivelchestre et Northovere
Et que omnia michi hereditarie descendebant per mortem
predicti Ric^i patris mei Hab. et Ten. . . , . Hiis test.
Joh^e Trenet; Joh^e Cary de Blundyshey Milite; Joh^e Bevyn,
Nicholao Poulet, Philippo Spore, Joh^e Burcy, Et alils. Datum
apud Northovere Secundo die Novembris Ann. reg. Reg.
Ricardi Secundi post conq^m tercio decimo.

Johanna, daughter and heir of Richard Brice of Ivelches-
ter, to Sir Peter de Courtenay, knight, James Fitz James,
John Mannyngford, Thomas Knoel, William Whyttoke of
Ivelchester, and Willm Charlton—All my land and tenements,
Mills, Dovecots, Woods, &c., in Ivelchester and Northover.
. . . . John Cary of Blundyshey, knight; Nicholas
Poulet, and others. At Northover, Novr 2, in 13th year of
Richard II.

No. 76. Richard II. 1390. Monday after Nov. 1.

Sci. pres. et fut. quod Ego Johannes Ffysshe de Ievelchestre dedi . . . . Willo Whittoke Burgagium meum apud
Ievelchestre in Alto Vico situatum inter burg. Nicholai Trot
ex par. bori. et burg. Walteri Morys ex par. austr. Hab. et Ten.
Hiis Test. Joh⁰ Brice, Thoma Brice, Joh⁰ Churcheman, Nicho.
Trot, Et multis aliis. Data apud Ievelchestre die Lune prox.
post Fest. Omnium Sanctorum Ann. reg. Reg. Ricardi S'c'di
post conq^m Quarto Decimo.

John Fysshe of Ievelchester to Willm Whittoke My
burgage in the High-street of Ievelchester , ... At
Ievelchester, on Monday next after the Feast of All Saints;
in the 14th year of Richard II.

No. 77. Richard II. 1390. Friday after Novr 12.

Omn. Xti Fid . . . . Willielmus Whittoke Salutem
in Dno. Noveritis me tradidisse et dimis. Johanni Fysshe
Totam aulam et caudam ab ostio aule in par. bori. illius
burgagii quod habeo ex dono et conces. dicti Joh^is Fysshe in
Villa de Icvclchestre situati inter burg. Nich^i Trot ex par.
bori. et burg. Walteri Morys ex par. austr. Hab. et Ten.
predictam aulam cum cauda ab ostio aule predicte modo
supradicto cum libero introitu et exitu sibi et assig. suis ad
terminum vite sue Reddendo inde annuatim michi et her'bus
vel assig. meis unam rosam rubiam ad Festum Nativit. S'ci
Joh^is Baptiste pro omnibus serviciis Ita tamen quod ego dictus
Will⁵ aulam et caudam predictam heredes et assig. mei sis-
tentabimus et manutenebimus sumptibus nostris propriis termino supradicto Et predictum Joh^m Fysshe erga Dominum
Regem et alios quoscunque de om'bus oneribus dicto burg⁰
pertinentibus termino suprad⁰ aquietabimus et defendemus
In cujus rei testim. hiis Indenturis sigil. nost. alternatim sunt
appensa Hiis test. Joh⁰ Brice de Yerde, Nich⁰ Trot, Thoma

Brice, Et aliis. Datum apud Ievelchestre die Veneris prox. post Fest. S'ci Martini Episcopi et Confessoris Ann. reg. Reg. Ricardi S'c'di post conq^m Quarto decimo.

———————

Willm Whittoke to John Fysshe—All the court, and the strip of ground from the entry of the court, at the North end of that tenement which I hold by grant of the said John Fysshe, in the town of Ievelchester. At Ievelchester, on Friday next after the Feast of St. Martin, Bishop and Confessor; in the 14th year of Richard II.

———————

No. 78, Richard II. 1391. Friday after June 11.

Omn. Xti Fid. ad quos . . . . Johannes Cole de Briggewater Sal. in Dno. Noveritis me tradidisse conces. &c., Willielmo Whittok et Agneti uxori ejus Unam acram prati cum pert^s in prato vocato Southmoreys mede in Somertone Hab. et Ten. pred^am acram prati cum pert^s prefatis Will^o et Agneti ad terminum vite eorum et unius eorum diucius viventis de me her'bus et assig meis Reddendo inde annuatim michi prefato Johanni et her'bus meis unam rosam ad Fest. S'ci Joh'is Bap'te pro omn. serviciis Salvo servicio Regali Et ego vero pred^s Joh^es et heredes mei predictam acram . . . . . Warentizabimus aquietabimus et defendemus In cujus rei testim. huic pre^ti scr^o indentato Sigil. nost. alternatim apposuimus Hiis test. Thoma Carssbroke, Nich^o Poulet, Joh^e Caylewey, Edmundo Lyte, Joh^e Bryce, Philippo Spore, Will^o Scherpe, Et aliis. Datum apud Yevelchestre die Veneris prox. post Fest. S'ci Barnabe Apostoli Ann. reg. Reg. Ricardi S'c'di Quarto decimo.

Endorsed. 1 acra prati in Somertone.

———————

John Cole of Bridgwater, to Willm Whittok and Agnes his wife—one acre in the Meadow called Southmore Mead, in Somerton . . . . Edmund Lyte . . . . At Yevelchester on Friday next after the Feast of St. Barnabas the Apostle; in the 14th year of Richard II.

No. 79. Richard II. 1392. Monday of the Third week in Lent.

Sciant pre. et fut. quod ego Willielmus de Chorletone filius et heres Joh^is de Chorletone dedi . . . . . Will^o Ekerdone Capellano et Roberto Veel decem acras prati cum pert^s in Sothmor Que vocantur le Rygge Que pred^s Johannes pater meus nuper adquisivit de Johanne de Erleghe Videlicet de parcella Manerii de Somertone Erleghe Hab. et Ten. Hiis Test. Phillipo Spore Joh^e Burcy. Joh^e Isaake, Will^o Whyttoke, Joh^e Atte Yerde, Rogero Arundelle, Will^o Dole, Et aliis, Data apud Yevelchestre die Lune in Tercia Septimana Quadragesime Ann. reg. Reg. Ricardi Secundi Quinto decimo.

Willm of Charlton, son and heir of John of Charlton, to Willm Ekerdone, chaplain, and Robert Veel—ten acres in Southmore. No. 65, is a "Copy" of this Deed.

No. 80. Richard II. 1392. July 26.

Omn. Xti Fid. ad quos . . . . . Willielmus Ekerdone Capellanus Sal in Dno. Noveritis me remisisse relax. et omnino pro me et her'bus meis inperp. quietum clamasse Roberto Veel Totum jus meum et clameum que habui habeo seu quovismodo in futurum habere potero in decem acris prati cum pert^s in Somertone Erleglie que vocantur le Rygge in prato vocato le Sothmor Que predictus Robertus et ego antedictus Will^us nuper adquisivimus de Will^o de Chorletone filio et herede Joh^is de Chorletone Ita quod nec ego prefatus Will^s Ekerdone heredes aut assignati mei aliquid juris seu clamei in predictis decem acris prati aut aliqua parcella earumdem versus predictum Robertum heredes vel assig. suos decetero exigere habero seu vendicare potero aut poterimus Set ab accione juris vel clamei inde petendi simus exclusi per presentes inperpet. In cujus rei testi. Sigil. meum pres'bus apposui Hiis test. Elia Fitz Payn, Joh⁸ Atte Yerde, Joh⁸ Burcy, Will° Whittoke, Joh⁸ Isaake, et aliis. Datum apud Yevelchestre vicesimo sexto die Julii ann. reg. Reg. Ricardi secundi sexto decimo.

———

Willm Ekerdone, chaplain, to Robert Veel; all my right and claim whatsoever in ten acres of meadow in Somerton Erleghe, called the Ridge, in Southmore; which the said Robert and I bought of William of Charlton, &c. Elias Fitz Payn . . . . at Yevelchester, July 26th, in the 16th year of Richard II.

———

No. 81. Richard. II. 1396. Monday after March 25.

Sciant pres. et fut. quod ego Ricardus Mulborne filius et heres Will¹ Mulborne dedi . . . . Roberto Veel et Alicie uxori ejus her'bus et assig ipsius Roberti unum mesuagium cum curtill° adjacente in Yevelchestre scituatum ex opposito Curie vocate Torellys court Hab. et Ten. Hiis Test. Will° Wyttok, Henrico Leddred, Joh⁸ Corteys, Rogero Bochel, Ric° Bryan Data apud Yevelchestre die Lune prox. post Fest. Annunciationis Beate Marie Virginis Ann. reg. Reg. Ricardi S'cdi Decimo nono.

Endorsed. Postea Robertus Veel illud dedit Thome Cole pro alio, &c.

———

Richard Mulborne, son and heir of Willm Mulborne, to Robert Veel and Alice his wife; a messuage with curtillage adjacent in Yevelchester; situate opposite to the Mansion called Torellys court . . . . At Yevelchester, on Monday next after the Feast of the Annunciation of the Blessed Virgin Mary; in the 19th year of Richard II.

No. 82. Richard II. 1398. Sunday before August 10.

Omnibus Xti Fid. ad quos . . . . Johannes Cole de Briggewater Sal. in Dno. Noveritis me remisisse . . . . Willielmo Whyttoke Totum jus meum et clameum . . . . in una acra prati cum pert⁸ in prato vocato Southmoreysmede in Somertone Quam quidem acram nuper tradidi et conc. prefato Will⁰ et Agneti uxori ejus jam defuncte ad terminum vite eorum . . . . Hiis test. Edmundo Lyte, Nich⁰ Polet, Joh⁰ Brice, Roberto Veel qui hoc scripsit, Joh⁰ Mascalle, Et aliis Datum apud Yevelchestre Die Domin. prox. ante Fest. S'ci Laurentii Martiris ann reg. Reg. Ricardi Secundi Vicesimo Secundo.

John Cole of Bridgwater, to Willm Whyttoke; all my right and title in one acre in South-more-mead in Somertone; which acre I lately granted to the said Willm and to Agnes his wife now deceased, for the term of their lives. Witn. Edmund Lyte, Nicholas Polet, " Robert Veel, who wrote this," and others. At Yevelchester, on Sunday next before the Feast of St. Laurence, Martyr; in the 22d year of Richard II.

No. 83. Henry IV. 1400. Sunday before August 10.

Omn. Xti Fid . . . . Nicholaus Yonge clericus et Petrus Blount Sal. in Dno. Noveritis nos remis. relax. et omnino pro nobis . . . quietum clamasse Ricardo Cloptone Will⁰ Ekerdone clerico Will⁰ Coventre et Roberto Veel Totum jus nostrum . . . . in Manerio de Stokelynche cum suis pert⁸ Ac in omnibus aliis terris tenem. pratis, &c., ... in eadem villa. Ita quod, &c., Hiis Testibus Humfredo Stafforde Milite, Ric⁰ Warre, Joh⁰ Deneband, Joh⁰

Asshelonde, Joh^e Rollour, Et aliis. Datum die Domin. prox. ante Fest. S'ci Laurentii Ann. reg. Reg. Henrici Quarti post conq^m primo.

Nicholas Yonge, clerk, and Peter Blount—to Richard Cloptone, Willm Ekerdone clerk, Willm Coventre, and Robert Veel; all our right and title in the manor of Stokelynche, and in all other lands and tenements in the same village. Witnesses. Humfrey Stafford, knight, Richard Warre. John Asshelonde . . . . Given on Sunday next before the Feast of St. Laurence, in the first year of the reign of King Henry the Fourth after Conquest.

No. 84. Henry IV. 1401. Saturday, March 12.

Noverint universi per presentes me Joh^{em} Chilterne clericum dedisse . . . . Johⁱ Drapere de Ievelchestre duos solidos annui redditus quos Will^s Brode michi reddere consuevit pro duabus acris prati in Hardyngtone Hab. et Ten. pre^{os} duos solidos annui redditus simul cum reversione pred, duarum acrarum prati cum acciderint post mortem pred^t Willⁱ predicto Johⁱ Drapere . . . . . Hiis Test. Will^o Carent. Joh^e Holme, Henrico Morgan, Joh^e Passewir, Joh^e Cloke Datum ap. Chilterne Dommere die Sabbati in Festo Sancti Gregorii Primi, Pape, Ann. reg. Reg. Henrici Quarti post conq^m secundo.

John Chilterne, clerk, to John Draper of Ievelchester; a rent of two shillings a year . . . . (No. 71.) at Chilt. Dom. on Saturday, being the Feast of Pope St. Gregory the First. In the second year of Henry IV.

No. 85. Henry IV. 1401. Tuesday after Oct. 18.

Omn. Xti Fid . . . . Ricardus Cloptone Will^s

Ekerdone clericus Nich's Yonge cl'icus Will$ Coventre Petrus
Blount et Robertus Veel Sal. in Dno. Noveritis nos attornasse
et loco nostro posuisse dilectos nobis in Christo Willm Roucetre
et Willm Kyngestone conjunctim et divisim ad ponendum
Johannem Wadham Militem, Willm Haukeforde Militem,
Henricum Fulleforde Robertum Hulle filium Joh^is Hulle,
Joh^em Faunteleroy Juniorem, Edmundum Elyot cl'cum Joh^em
Lopenford et Joh^em Lovelle in plenam et pacificam seisinam in
Manerio de Stokelynche Maudeleyne cum suis pert$ Necnon
omnibus terris, &c, cum suis ubique pert$ in eadem villa que
eis her'bus et assig. suis dedimus et per quandam cartam nos-
tram confirmavimus Secundum vim formam et effectum
ejusdem carte nostre sibi inde confecte Ratum et gratum
habentes et habituri quicquid predicti Will$ Roucetre et Will$
Kyngestone fecerint aut alter eorum fecerit nomine nostro in
Premissis In cujus rei testim Sigil nost. pres'bus apposuimus.
Datum die Martis prox. post Fest. S'ci Luce Evangeliste
Ann. reg. Reg. Henrici Quarti tercio.

Richd Clopton, Willm Ekerdon, clk. Nich$ Yonge clk.
Willm Coventre, Peter Blount, and Robert Veel—appoint as
their attorneys, Willm Roucetre and Willm Kyngeston, to put
John Wadham kn^t., Willm Haukeforde, kn^t., Henry Fulleford,
Robert Hulle son of John Hulle, John Faunteleroy, jun^r
Edmund Elyot clk. John Lopenford and John Lovelle, in full
and peaccable possession of the manor of Stokelynche Maudeleyne, and of all the lands and other property in the same
village, conveyed to them by a deed previously executed
. . . . Given on Tuesday next after the Feast of St. Luke
the Evangelist. In the 3rd year of Henry IV.

No. 86, Henry IV. 1402. April 12.
Omn. Xti Fid . . . . , . Johannes Herewarde de
Yeveltone filius et heres Ricardi Herewarde de Lymyngtone

fratris Johannis Herewarde de Yevelchestre Sal. in Dno.
Noveritis me remisisse . . . . . Roberto Veel her'bus et
assig. suis Totum jus meum . . . . . in omnibus terris et
ten^{tis} . . . . que idem Robertus Veel habet et tenet in
Yevelchestre Sooke Denys et Lymyngtone Ita quod ego
pred^s Joh^{es} Herewarde de Yeveltone nec heredes . . . .
Sed ab omni accione juris seu clamei inde petendi aut habendi
simul exclusi per pres'tes inperp. Et ego vero pred^s Joh^{es}
Herewarde de Yeveltone et heredes mei omnia predicta terras,
&c., prefato Roberto Veel her'bus et assig. suis contra omnes
gentes Warantizabimus aquietabimus et defendemus per presentes imperp. In cujus rei test. Sigil. meum pres'bus
apposui Et quia Sigillum meum pluribus est incognitum
sigillum Willielmi Whittoke de Yevelchestre hiis apponi
procuravi Et ego pred's Will^s Whittoke ad specialem
rogatum ejusdem Joh^{is} Herewarde de Yeveltone Sigillum
meum in testimonium premissorum apponi feci Hiis Test.
Joh^e Wike de Nyenhude Thoma Niter Will^o Roucetre Joh^e
Comelonde Will^o Kyngestone Joh^e Mascalle et aliis Datum
duodecimo die Mensis Aprilis ann. reg. Reg. Henrici Quarti
tercio.

John Herewarde of Yeovilton, son and heir of Richard
Herewarde of Limington, brother of John Hereward of
Yevelchester—to Robert Veel. All my right and title in all
the lands ten^{ts} and other property which Robert Veel has and
holds in Yevelchester, Sock Denys, and Limington . . . .
and because my seal is unknown to most persons, I have taken
care that the Seal of Willm Whittoke, of Yevelchester, should
be set to these presents. And I the aforenamed Willm
Whyttoke, at the special request of the same John Herewarde
of Yeovilton, have caused my Seal to be affixed, in witness
of the premisses . . . . John Wike of Nynehead, John
Comelonde, &c., April 12, 3rd Hen. IV.

No. 87. Henry IV. 1402. Friday before Whitsunday **Eve.**

Omn. Xti Fid . . . . . Ricardus Dierre Sal. in Dno. Noveritis me dimisisse, &c., Wyll° Chepman totum jus meum et clameum que vel quod habui habeo aut quovismodo in futurum habere potero in omnibus illis tenementis redditibus terris in villa Yevilchestre cum suis pert° Que nuper Nicholao Hoper constat' *jacens inter tenementum Beate Sancte Marie Majoris exuna par. borriali Altera vero juxta viam regiam apparte hawstrali predictum et que prefata predictus ejusdem Willielmo nuper habuerunt ex dono et concessione mea in loco supradicto prout in quadam carta mea de terris et ten^{tis} predictis Will^i deinde facta cum libera seisina eisdem liberata plenius continetur Hab. et Ten . . . . Hiis testibis Wyllielmum Wyttok Johannem Brice Joh^e Schephurde Et multis aliis Datum apud Yevilchestre die Veneris prox. ante Fest. in Vigilia Penticoste ann. reg. Reg. Henrici Quarti post conq^m Anglorum tercio.

Richard Dierre to Willm Chepman—all my right in all those tenements, &c., in Yevilchester, which were lately in the occupation of Nicholas Hoper, lying between the *tenement* of Blessed St. Mary Major to the North and the high road on the South . . . . . at Yevilchestre, on the day before Whitsun Eve. In 3rd year of Hen. IV. after conq^t of the English.

No. 88, Hen IV. 1403. Tuesday before May 6.

Sci. pres. et fut. quod ego Johanna Fateman quondam uxor Will^i Cole mercer de Ievelchestre in pura viduetate dedi • . . . . Johanni Drapere de Ievelchestre Johanne uxori sue her'bus et assig. suis Totum burgagium meum in Ievelchestre cum omn. perts. Quiquidem jacent juxta regiam viam

* Some scribe of very thirsty propensities must have thrown this odd jumble of words together, in defiance of all grammatical propriety.

ex austr. parte ex par. una Et Ecclesiam Beate Marie Majoris ex. par, bori. ex par altera Hab. et Ten . . . . Hiis Test. Will° Wyttoke Joh'i Bryce. Joh'i Maschal Joh'i Schephurde et Thome Ffolkey Et aliis Data apud Ievelchestre die Martis prox. ante Fest. S'ci Johannis ante Portam Latinam Ann. reg. Reg, Henrici Quarti post conqᵐ Anglie quarto.

Endorsed, long subsequently. Carta Joh'e Fatman pro terr' in Ievelchestre juxta Ecclesiam Marie Majoris.

Johanna Fateman widow of William Cole, mercer, of Ievelchester, in her pure widowhood; grants to John Drapere, Johanna his wife, and their heirs—all her burgage in Ievelchester, being next the road on the South, and towards the church of the Blessed Mary Major on the North. At Ievelchester, on Tuesday next before the Feast of St John " before the Latin Gate." In the 4th year of Henry IV. after conquest of England.

No. 89. Henry IV. 1404. Tuesday before Whitsunday.

Sciant pres. et fut. quod ego Reginaldus atte Watre de West Cammel dedi, &c., . . . Ricardo filio meo Will° Whyttoke Will° Gosse et Roberto Veel her. et assig. suis Omnia terras et tenᵗᵃ mea cum suis pertˢ in Northovere juxta Yevelchestre Hab. et Ten. Hiis Test. Ricᵒ Otery Johᵉ Brice Johe Mascalle Andrea Tour Ricᵒ Dole Johᵉ Smythe de Northovere Thoma Mulleward de eadem Et aliis. Data apud Northovere die Martis prox. ante Fest. Pentecostes ann. reg. Reg. Henrici Quarti post conqᵐ Quinto.

Reginald atte Water of West Cammel, to Richard his son, Willᵐ Whyttoke, Willᵐ Gosse, and Robert Veel—all my lands and tenᵗˢ in Northover near Yevelchester . . . . .

John Smythe of Northovere, Thomas the Millward of the same place . . . Given at Northover. on Tuesday next before Whitsunday. 5th year of Hen. IV.

No. 90 Henry IV. 1404. Friday before Whitsunday.

Noverint universi per presentes me Ricardum filium Reginaldi atte Watere de West Cammel remisisse, &c . . . Will° Whyttoke Will° Gosse et Roberto Veel her'bus et assig, suis Totum jus meum, &c., . . . in omnibus terris et ten^tis que nuper habui simul cum predictis Will° Will° et Roberto ex dono et concessione pred^i Reginaldi patris mei in Northovere juxta Yevelchestre prout in carta ejusdem patris mei nobis inde confecta plenius poterit apparere Ita quod ego, &c., · . . Hiis test. Ric° Otery Andrea Tour Joh^e Brice Joh^e Mascalle Ric° Dole Joh^e Smythe de Northovere Will° Lovecoke Et aliis. Data die Veneris prox. ante Fest. Pentecostes ann. reg. Reg. Henrici Quarti post conq^m Quinto.

Richard, son of Reginald atte Water of West Camel, to Willm Whyttoke, Willm Gosse, and Robert Veel—All my right in all the lands and ten^ts in Northover, near Ilchester, which I lately had in conjunction with them, by gift of said Reginald my father . . . . . Given on Friday next before Whitsunday, in the 5th year of Henry IV.

No 91. Henry IV. 1404. Whitsunday.

Noverint universi per pres. me Reginaldum atte Watre de West Cammel remisisse . . : . Will° Whyttoke Will° Gosse et Roberto Veel her. et assig. suis Totum jus meum . . . . in omnibus terris et ten^tis que ipsi simul cum Ricardo filio meo nuper habuerunt exdono et concess. mea in Northovere juxta Yevelchestre . . . . Hiis test, Ric°

Otery Andrea Tour Joh⁰ Brice Joh⁰ Mascalle Ric⁰ Dole Joh⁰ Smythe Will⁰ Lovecoke Et aliis. Data in Festo Pentecostes ann. reg. Reg. Henrici Quarti post conqᵐ Quinto.

Reginald atte Water of West Camel, to Willᵐ Whyttoke, Willᵐ Gosse, and Robert Veel—all my right in all the lands and tenᵗˢ in Northover, near Yevelchester, which they, with Richard my son, lately held by my grant . . . . Given on Whitsunday. In 5th year of Henry IV.

No. 92. Henry IV. 1405. Sunday after July 7.

Hec indentura testatur quod Johannes Drapere de Yevelchestre concessit et ad Firmam dimisit Johanni Hawth et Matilde uxori ejus aut uni eorum diucius viventi Unam acram terre arabilis jacentem in Campo de Chilterne Vagge qui vocatur Chatforlange inter terram Prioris de Charterhowse ex par. orient. et Thorne Coffyne ex par. occid. Hab. et Ten . . . . Reddendo inde annuatim Domino Feodi illius her. et assig. suis iiiiᵈ ad Fest. S'ci Mich'is Archangeli Et si predicti quatuor denarii a retro fuerint per quadraginta dies post Fest. predᵐ quod extunc bene licebit prefato Johⁱ Drapere et her'bus suis in prefatam acram terre reintrare et retinere sicut ante concessum istum fecerint . . . . In cujus rei testim. partes predic. sigil. sua hiis indent'is alternatim apposuerunt Hiis Test. Edmundo Dommere Will⁰ Stauntone Joh⁰ Wynforde Et aliis. Data apud Yevylchestre Die Domin. prox. post Fest. S'ci Thome Martiris ann. reg. Reg. Henrici Quarti post conqᵐ Sexto.

John Draper of Yevelchester, grants and lets to Farm, to John Hawth and Matilda his wife, or the survivor of them, one acre of arable in a field at Chilterne Vagge, called Chatforlang, between land of the Prior of Charterhouse on the

East, and Thorne Coffyn on the West. To have . . . .
by rendering thence every year to the Lord of that Fee, four-
pence at Michaelmas . . . . Edmund Dommer . . .
Given at Yevylchester on Sunday next after the Feast of
St. Thomas, Martyr. In the 6th year of Henry IV.

No. 93. Henry IV. 1405. February 9.

Pateat universis per pres. me Thomam Stanshade
Custodem Ffeodi Mag'ne Cur' Bristolle honor' Glouc' re-
cepisse tres solidos et quatuor sterlingorum de Will° Whittocke
Will° Gosse et Roberto Veel pro t'nsgr' pardonand' de eo
quod adquis' [iverunt] unum toftum et undecim acre terre in
Northovere juxta Yevelchestre sibi et her'bus suis de Reginaldo
de la Watere Et quibus iiis iiiid fateor me esse solut' Et dictos
Willm Willm et Robertum inde fore quietos per pres. In cujus
rei test. Sigil. meum apposui. Data Bristollie nono die Febr'i
ann. reg. Reg. Henrici Quarti post conq^m Sexto.

Thomas Stanshade, keeper, [or * Treasurer of the Fee, of
the . . . . Court at Bristol, in the Lordship of Gloucester?]
acknowledges to have received of Willm Whittoke, Willm
Gosse, and Robert Veel, 3s. and 4d. sterling, for * condoning
of trespass? Consequent on their purchase of messuage, and
eleven acres of land in Northover near Yevelchester, of
Reginald de la Water. Given at Bristol, Feby 9. In 6th
year of Hen. IV.

No. 94. Henry IV. 1405. Friday after Ascension Day.

Sciant pres. et fut. quod ego Cristiana Spensere filia et
heres Andree Spensere et Johanne uxoris ejus dedi . . . . .
Joh^t Drapere de Yevelchestre et Johanne uxori ejus et heredes

* This document is written in a lawyer's cursive hand, and is very
difficult to decipher; the passages marked are merely rendered at hazard.

ipsius Unam placeam in Chepstrete ville de Yevilchestre
quondam fuit edificatam *(sic)* juxta Crucem S'ci Petri, et continet in se octodecim pedes in longitudine et sexdecim in
latitudine Infra Muros. Hab. et Ten. predictam placeam
predicto Johanni Drapere et Johanne uxori ejus . . . . .
Reddendo inde annuatim Burgencibus de Yevilchestre unam
quadrantem ad Festum Natalis Domini pro omni servicio . . .
Hiis test. Will⁰ Wyttok Joh⁰ Brise Waltero Bowchere
Hugone Westone Will⁰ Bakere Joh⁰ Schepert. Datum apud
Yevilchestre die Veneris prox. post Fest. Assencionis Domini
ann. reg. Reg. Henrici Quarti post conqᵐ Anglie Sexto.

———

Christiana Spensere, daughter and heir of Andrew
Spensere and Johanna his wife—to John Draper of Yevelchester and Johanna his wife—One plot of ground in Chepstrete
in Yevilchester, formerly built on, near the Cross of St. Peter;
being 18 feet in length, and 16 feet wide, underneath the Walls
. . . . . By paying thence yearly to the Burgesses of
Yevilchester, one farthing at the Feast of the Nativity of our
Lord. Given at Yevilchester, on Friday next after the Feast
of our Lord's Ascension. In the 6th year of Henry IV. after
the conquest of England.

———

No. 95, Henry IV. 1406. Monday after Septʳ 14.

Noverint univ. per pres. me Ricardum Cloptone Fratrem
et heredem Walteri Cloptone Militis defuncti Remisisse, &c.,
Willielmo Haukeforde Militi Johⁱ Fauntleroy juniori Johⁱ
Lopenforde Roberto Veel et Alianore que fuit uxor Walteri
Cloptone Militis defuncti . . . . Totum jus meum, &c.,
in Manerio de Stokelynche Maudeleyne ac omnibus terris et
tenᵗⁱˢ cum pertˢ que nuper fuerunt predicti Walteri in eadem
villa . . . . Et ego vero predictus Ricardus . . . .
contra omnes gentes Warantizabimus . , . . . Ita quod

Warantia ista non se extendat aut vim habeat ad reddend' in valorem eorum licet per aliquem alium vocati erimus ad Warantizand' Set warantia ista locum et vim habeat ad barrand' et excludend' inde me et heredes meos imperp. In cujus rei testim. Sigil. meum pres'bus apposui. Hiis test. Roberto Grey Joh⁰ Crukerne Will⁰ Coventre Joh⁰ Hunte clerico Et aliis Datum die Lune prox. post Fest. Exaltacionis S'cte Crucis ann. reg. Reg. Henrici Quarti post conq^m Septimo.

Richard Clopton brother and heir of Walter Clopton, knight, deceased; to Willm Haukeford, kn^t . . . Robert Veel, and Alianor widow of Walter Clopton, kn^t, deceased— All his right in the manor of Stokelynche Maudeleyne, and in all lands and tenements in that Village, which formerly belonged to the said Walter . . . . Robert Grey, John Crukerne . . . Given on Monday next after the Feast of the Elevation of Holy Cross. In the 7th year of Henry IV.

No. 96. Henry IV. 1408. September 1.

Noveritis Univ. per pres. Nos Thomam Knoel et Willm Charletone remisisse . . . Will⁰ Whittoke de Ivelchestre Totum jus nostrum . . . . in uno Cotagio cum curtill⁰ in Northovere situato inter tenementum Willi Dole in par. orient. et ten. Cecilie Deigberes in par. austr. Nec non in duabus acris terre arrabilis jacentibus in Northovere in diversis culturis et campis Que Cotagium curtill^m et terram Nos pred^i Thomas et Will^s Charletone simul cum eodem Will⁰ Whittocke nuper habuimus cum aliis personis ex dono et feoffamento Johanne filie et heredis Ricardi Brice de Ivelchestre Ita quod . . . . Hiis Test. Will⁰ Stauntone Will⁰ Carente Will⁰ Neutone Roberto Veel Ric⁰ Dole Joh⁰ Mascalle. Data primo die Mensis Septembris ann. reg. Reg Henrici Quarti post conq^m nono.

Thomas Knoel and Willm Charletone, to Willm Whittoke of Ivelchester—All our right to a cottage with curtillage in Northover; also in two acres of arable in Northover, lying in several ploughed grounds and fields. Which cottage and land, we and the same Willm Whittocke lately held conjointly with others, by the grant and feoffment of Johanna, daughter and heir of Richard Brice of Ivelchester . . . . September 1. 9th year of Henry IV.

No. 97. Henry IV. 1409. September 12.

Sciant pres. et fut. quod ego Johannes Hubarde de Yevele Webbe filius et heres Isabelle Hubardes sororis Alicie que fuit uxor Joh^is Josep dedi . . . . Roberto Veel unum burg^m cum suis pert^s in Ivelchestre situatum in le Chepstrete ejusdem ville inter tenem. quod Thomas Ffolqui tenet de herede Will^i Bonevyle et tenem. Priorisse Albe Aule ex opposito ten^ti Johannis Courteys Hab. et Ten . . . . Hiis test, Will^o Whittoke Will^o Nywetone Joh^e Brys Joh^e Drapere Joh^e Mascalle et aliis Data apud Yvelchestram pred^am duodecimo die Mensis Septembris ann. reg. Reg. Hen. IV. post conq^m decimo. Endorsed—De burgagio quod Thomas Folky tenet.

John Hubarde of Yeovil Webbe, son and Heir of Isabella Hubardes, sister of Alice, widow of John Josep—to Robert Veel; a burgage in Ivelchester, in Chepstrete; between a tenement held by Thomas Folqui of the heir of Willm Bonevyle, and one belonging to the Prioress of White Hall. At Yevelchester, Septr 12. 10th year of Henry IV.

No. 98, Henry IV. 1409. September 13.

Noverint Univ. per pres. me Johannem Hubarde de Yevele Webbe filium et heredem Isabelle Hubardes sororis Alicie que fuit uxor Joh^is Josep ordinasse et loco meo constituisse Willm Whittoke de Ivelchestre et Walterum Bochere de eadem veros Attornatos meos conjunctim et divisim ad deliberandum nomine meo Roberto Veel plenam et pacificam seisinam de uno burgagio cum pert^s in Yevelchestre Quod quidem bnrgagium pred^s Robertus habet ex conces. mea prout in quadam carta mea inde prefato Roberto confecta plenius continetur Ratum et gratum habens et habiturus quicquid iidem Will^s et Walterus fecerint aut unus eorum fecerit circa premissa imperpetuum In cuj. rei test. pres'bus sigil. meum apposui Datum apud Yvelchestram pred'am Tercio decimo die Mensis Septembris ann. reg. Reg. Henrici Quarti post conq^m decimo.

Endorsed, long subsequently—Burgagium in Chepstrete in Ivelchestre.

———

John Hubarde of Yeovil Webbe, empowers Willm Whittoke and Walter Bocher of Ivelchester, to deliver possession of the burgage before named to Robert Veel. Septr 13. 10th of Hen. IV.

———

No. 99. Henry IV. 1409. Monday after Novr 11.

Sciant pres. et fut. quod ego Will^us Whyttoke dedi . . . Joh^i Strecche Will^o Gosse Roberto Veel et Will^o Kyngestone Omnia burgagia terras tenem'ta mea stabellas prata pasturas redditus servicia et reversiones cum omn. suis pert^s in Mountagu Somertone Yevelchestre Northovere et in omn. aliis villis et locis in Com. Somers. Hab. et Ten; . . . . Hiis Test. Will^o Neutone Joh^e Drapere Thoma Cole Joh^e Curteys Waltero Bouchere Will^o Bakere de Yevelchestre Will^o Trot Et aliis. Datum die Lune prox. post Fest. S'ci Martini ann. reg. Reg. Henrici Quarti undecimo.

———

William Whyttoke—to Robert Veel, and others named, all his burgages, lands, &c., in Montacute, Somerton, Yevelchester, Northover, and all other places in the Co, of Somerset;

To have . . . . Given on Monday next after the Feast
of St. Martin. 11th year of Henry IV.

No. 100. Henry IV. 1409. Monday before November 30.

Om'bus Xti Fid. ad quos . . . . . Willielmus
Whyttoke Sal. in Dno. Noveritis me remisisse . . . . .
Johi Strecche Willo Gosse Roberto Veel et Will° Kyngestone
her'bus et assig. suis Totum jus meum . . . . . in
omnibus burgagiis terris tenementis, &c., ... Que eis
her'bus et assig. suis nuper per cartam meam dedi et conc.
imperp. in Mountagu Somertone Yevelchestre Northovere et
in omn. aliis villis et locis in Com. Somers. De quibus omnibus
eis seisinam liberavi personaliter Ac ipsi inde seisiti ad presens
existunt Ita quod . . . . . Hiis Test. Will° Neutone
Thoma Cole Joh° Drapere Joh° Curteys Will° Bakere Waltero
Bouchere Joh° Mascalle Et aliis. Data die Lune prox. ante
Fest. S'ci Andree Apostoli ann. reg. Reg. Henrici Quarti
undecimo.

William Whyttoke, to Robert Veel and others (99).
Given on Monday next before the Feast of St. Andrew the
Apostle. In the 11th year of Henry IV.

No. 101. Henry IV. 1410. Friday before January 6.

Omn. Xti Fid. ad quos . . . . Thomas Machon
filius et heres Joh^{is} Machon Sal. in Dno. Noveritis me prefatum Thomam remisisse . . . . Johanni Drapere de
Ivelchestre Totum jus meum . . . , in om'bus terris et
ten'tis cum eorum pert^s Que fuerunt Joh^{is} Machon patris mei
in Chilterne Vagge Chilt. Dum. et Hardyngtone Ita quod nec
ego . . . . Hiis test. Will° Whittoke Joh° Brice Joh°
Curteys Thoma Ffolky Ric° Dole Et aliis. Data apud Ievel-

chestram pred'am die Veneris prox. ante Fest. Epiphanie
Domini ann. reg. Reg. Henrici Quarti post conq^m undecimo.

Thomas Machon son and heir of John Machon, to John
Draper of Ivelchester—all his right, in all the lands and
tenements which once belonged to his father John Machon, in
Chiltern Vagge and Chiltern Dummer, and in Hardington.
At Ievelchester, on Friday next before the Feast of the
Epiphany of our Lord, 11th of Henry IV.

No. 102. Henry IV. 1410. April I.

Johannes Tyssebury clericus, Reverendi in Christo Patris et
Domini Domini Nicholai Dei gratia Bathoniensis et Wellensis
Episcopi Commissarius Generalis, Discretis Viris Will° Gosse
Roberto Vele Willo Newtone et Will° Kingestone Bathoniensis
et Wellensis Diocesis Salutem in Auctore Salutis. Cum Com-
missio administracionis omnium et singulorum bonorum et
catallorum quorumcumque infra Diocesim Bathoniensem et
Wellensem ab intestato decedentium ad dictum Reverendum
Patrem et Nos de jure et antiqua consuetudine in Diocesi
predicta observata pertineat Ad administrandum igitur colli-
gendum adimandum et recipiendum omnia et singula bona et
catalla cujusdam Willielmi Whittok de Ivelchester ab intestato
jam nuper decedentis in quorumcumque manibus existant
Vobis primitus juratis de fideli inventario bonorum et catallorum hujusmodi conficiendo et ratiocinio integro et legali
cum super hoc debite fueritis requisiti inde reddendo plenariam
committimus potestatem Vosque administratores bonorum et
catallorum hujusmodi perfecimus per presentes In cujus rei
(testim.) Sigillum Officii nostri presentibus est appensum. Data
Wellie primo die Mensis Aprilis Anno Domini Millesimo
Quadringentesimo decimo.

John Tyssebury, clerk, Commissary General of the Reverend Father and Lord in Christ, Lord Nicholas, By the Grace of God Bishop of Bath and Wells, to William Gosse, Robert Vele, Willm Newton and Willm Kingeston, discreet (or select) men of the diocese of Bath and Wells, Health in the Author of Health. Whereas Commission of Administration, of all and singular the goods and chattels of such persons as die intestate within the Diocese of Bath and Wells, pertains of right and by ancient custom observed in the aforesaid Diocese, to the said Reverend Father and to us: Therefore we commit full power to you, to administer, to collect, take away and take possession of all and singular the goods and chattels of one William Whittok of Ivelchester, now lately deceased intestate, in whose hands soever they may be. Ye being first sworn, to make a faithful Inventory of such goods and chattels; and to render a true and lawful account, whenever ye shall be duly called upon about this matter. And by these presents. we have fully appointed you the Administrators of such goods and chattels. In witness whereof, our Seal of Office is affixed to these presents. Given at Wells, on the first day of the Month of April, in the year of our Lord one thousand four hundred and ten.

No. 103. Henry IV. 1412. August 6.

Sciant pres. et fut. quod nos David Persona Ecclesie de South Cadebury Joh^{es} Venables Will^{us} Pontone et Thomas Meere dedimus . . . Will^o Haukeforde Militi Roberto Veel Johⁱ Fauntleroy juniori Hugoni Deverelle Will^o Kyngstone Roberto Walsham Thome Ffrome et Ric^o Wrynge Omnia terras et ten^{ta} nostra . . . que nuper habuimus exdono et concess. Willⁱ Martyn filii et heredis Joh^{is} Martyn de South-cadebury in Stokelynche Ostryzer et Stokelynche Maudeleyne Hab. et Ten: . . . . Hiis Test. Joh^e Mountagu Roberto Saymour Joh^e Rollour Will^o Roucetre Will^o Meredene Data sexto die Mensis Augusti ann. reg. Reg. Henrici Quarti post conq^m tercio decimo.

David, Parson of the Church of South Cadbury, (and others)—to Willm Haukeforde, knight, Robert Veel, and others—All our lands, tenements, &c., which we lately held by grant from Willm Martyn, son and heir of John Martyn of South Cadbury, in Stokelynche Ostryzer and Stokelynche Maudeleyne . . . . John Montacute . . . Augt 6. 13th year Hen. IV.

No. 104. Henry IV. 1412. August 7.

Nov'nt univ. per pres. Nos David Personam Ecclesie de Southcadebury Johe^m Venables Willm Pontone et Thomam Meere Attornasse et loco nostro posuisse dilectos nobis Willm Roucetre et Joh^{em} Havegod conj. et div. ad liber^m pro nobis et nom. nost. Willielmo Haukeforde Militi Roberto Veel Johⁱ Ffauntleroy jun. Hugⁱ Deverelle Will^o Kyngestone Roberto Walsham Thome Frome et Ric^o Wrynge plenam et pacif. seis. in et de om'bus terris ten'tis . . . nostris que nuper habuimus ex dono et concess. Willⁱ Martyn filii et heredis Johis Martyn de Southcadebury in Stokelynche Ostryzer et Stokelynche Maudeleyne Ratum et gratum habentes, &c. Data septimo die Mensis Augusti ann. reg. Reg. Henrici Quarti post conq^m tercio decimo.

A Power of Attorney from David, Parson of the Church of South Cadbury, and others; to Willm Roucetre and John Havegod, to deliver full possession to Willm Haukeforde, kn^t Robert Veel and others, of all the lands in Stokelynche lately granted to said David and others by Willm Martyn. Aug. 7. 13th year of Henry IV.

No. 105. Henry IV. 1412. November 20.

Omn. Xti Fid. ad quos hoc scr'pt'm indent. perven Will

Haukeforde Miles Robertus Veel Joh^{es} Fauntleroy jun. Hugo Deverelle Wills Kyngstone Robertus Walsham Thomas Frome et Ric^{us} Wrynge Sal. in Dno. Noveritis nos dedisse . . . . Nicholao Yonge clerico quendam annualem redditum viginti et sex solidorum et octo denariorum Hab. percipiend' et levand' in et de oi'bus terris ten'tis, &c., nostris Que nuper habuimus ex dono 'et concess. Davidis Persone Ecclesie de South-cadebury Joh^{is} Venables Willⁱ Pontone et Thome Meere in Stokelynche Ostryzer in Stokelynche Maudeleyne eidem Nicholao durante vita sua ad quatuor anni terminos principales equis porcionibus Et volumus et concedimus pro nobis . , . Proviso semper quod pred^s Nicholaus non implacitabit nos . . . . in aliqua Curia Domini Regis per Breve de an-nuetate ratione doni seu concessionis annui redditus predicti nec personas nostras pro premissis aliquo modo onerabit nec gravabit in futurum Et nos pre'ti . . . . posuimus pred'm Nich'm in plenam et pacificam seisinam . . . in forma pred'a per solucionem unius denarii impressi in quolibet sigillo nostro hujus scripti . . . . Data vicesimo die Novembris ann. reg. Reg. Henrici Quarti post conq^m quarto decimo.

Endorsed (temp. Eliz. or Ja^s 1.) Carta Willⁱ Haukeforde Militis Roberti Veel et aliorum cuidam Nich^o Younge clerico de annuitate xxvi^s viii^d in Southcadbury, Stocklinche, et alibi.

Willm Haukeforde, kn^t, Robert Veel and others—to Nicholas Yonge, clerk, for his life—A yearly rent of 26 shillings and 8 pence—to be raised out of all the lands . . . which we lately became possessed of by grant from David, the Parson of South Cadbury, and others; in Stokelynche. Novr 20. 14th Hen IV.

No. 106. Henry IV. 1413, Monday after Jany 6.
Omn. Xti Fid . . . . Will^{us} Haukeforde Miles

Robertus Veel Joh^{es} Fauntleroy jun^r Hugo Deverelle Will[•] Kyngstone Robertus Walsham Thomas Frome et Ricardus Wrynge Sal. in Dno. Noveritis nos tradidisse . . . . . Will^o Ffysshemere et Sonote uxori ejus unum mesuagium unum cotagium tria curtillagia Quadraginta acras et dimidiam terre Quatuor acras et dimidiam prati cum suis pert^s Que nuper habuimus ex dono et feoffamento Davidis Persone Ecclesie de Southcadebury Joh^{is} Venables Willⁱ Pontone et Thome Meere Et Que ipsi prius habuerunt ex dono et concess. Willi Martyn filii et heredis Joh^{is} Martyn de Southcadebury in Stokelynche Ostrizer et Stokelynche Maudeleyne Que eciam idem Johes Martyn quondam tradidit et concessit Waltero Cloptone et Edithe uxori ejus ad terminum vite eorum Hab. et Ten . . . . Reddendo inde annuatim nobis her'bus sive assig. nostris quadraginta et sex solidos et octo denarios ad quatuor anni terminos principales . . . . Et. ego prefatus Robertus Veel et her'es mei omnia pred'a mes'a cum suis pert^s pref'^{is} Will^o Fysshemere et Sonote ad terminum vite eorum et alterius eorum diucius viventis modo forma et condicione pred'is Contra omnes gentes Warantizabimus aquietabimus et defendemus per presentes In cujus rei testim. tam nos quam predicti Will^s Fysshemere et Sonota sigilla nostra hiis indenturis alternatim apposuimus Hiis Test. Roberto Seymour Will^o Roucetre Joh^e Roller Johe Welwetone sen. Joh^e Wottone Et aliis. Data apud Stokelynche die Lune prox. post Fest. Epiphanie Domini ann. reg. Reg. Henrici Quarti post conquestum Quarto decimo.

Willm Haukeforde, kn^t, Robert Veel, and others—to William Fysshemere and Sonota his wife—one messuage, one cottage, 3 curtillages, forty acres and a half of arable, four acres and a half of meadow, in Stokelynche—which we lately acquired possession of by grant of David, Parson of Southcadbury and others; and which they had previously acquired

by the gift of Willm Martyn son of John Martyn of Southcadbury; and which property the said John Martyn formerly
made over to Walter Clopton and Edith his wife, during their
lives. To have . . . by paying thereout yearly to us 46
shillings and 8 pence, in quarterly instalments. At Stokelynche,
on Monday next after the Feast of our Lord's Epiphany.

No. 107. Henry Fifth. 1416. March 5.

Hec Indentura Facta apud Stokelynche Maudeleyne in
Comitatu Somersetie Quinto die Marcii Anno regni Regis
Henrici Quinti post conquestum Tercio Inter Alianoram Que
fuit uxor Walteri Cloptone Militis ex parte una Et Nicholaum
Yonge clericum, Robertum Veel seniorem, et Willielmum
Kyngstone ex altera parte Testatur Quod eadem Alianora
tradidit concessit et presenti Indentura confirmavit prefatis
Nicholao Roberto et Will° omnia terras et tenem. sua redditus
et servicia cum suis pert^s Que eidem Alianore nuper liberata
et assignata fuerunt in dotem ex dotacione predicti Walteri
nuper viri sui in Stokelynche predicta Hab. et Ten . . . . ,
Reddendo inde annuatim eidem Alianore durante vita sua
Quadraginta et quatuor solidos et quatuor denarios legalis
monete apud Silveyns juxta Stokelynche predictam. . . . .
Hiis test. Nicho Reede Johe Keynes Will° Stauntone Will°
Roucetre Ric° Huwet Joh^e Roller Roberto Geffrey Et aliis
Data loco die et anno supradictis.

Endorsed. Mem. quod parcelle subscripte diu ante confectionem hujus Indenture assignate et liberate fuerunt
Alianore infranominate de dote sibi contingente de terris et
ten'tis que fuerunt Walteri Cloptone Militis quondam viri sui
in Stokelynche Maudeleyne. xvi^s quos Nich^us Wattes pro
1 ten' continente Vacras terre 1 roda prati de antiquo astro et
xi acras terre et 1 acr' prati de dominicis (dmcis) xxi^s quos
Johannes Nicol reddit pro 1 ten^to continente vii acr' terre
1 acr' prati de antiquo astro Et xi acr' et 1 acr' prati de

dominicis. V⁴ viii⁴ quos Will⁴ˢ Reede reddit pro 1 ten. continente Vacr' terre 1 roda prati de antiquo astro et uno clauso vocato Whyffynes. xviii⁴ quos Nich⁴ˢ Yonge Rector loci reddit pro 1 acr' dimid. terre dominicalis. 1⁴ quem Alicia Sylveyns reddit pro via vocata Mullewey. 1⁴ quem Sonota nuper uxor Walteri Peyntour reddit in feodo pro ii acr' terre S'ma per Ann. XLiiiiˢ iiii⁴.

By indenture made at Stokelynche, on the 5th day of March, in the 3rd year of the reign of King Henry the Fifth; Alianor, widow of Walter Cloptone, knight, grants to Nicholas Yonge, clerk, Robert Veel senior, and William Kyngestone—All her lands and tenements in Stokelynche, those viz. which were delivered and assigned to her in Dowry, by the Endowment of the said Walter her late husband: on condition of the grantees paying yearly to Alianor, during her life, 44 shillings and 4 pence of legal money, at Sylveyns (her residence) near Stokelynche.

No. 108. Henry V. 1416. March 6.

Noverint univ. per pres. me Alianoram que fui uxor Walteri Cloptone Militis Attornasse et loco meo posuisse dilectos michi Joh⁵ᵐ Havegod et Joh⁵ᵐ Webbe de Stokelynche Maudeleyne conj. et div. ad lib'dum pro me et nom. meo Nich° Yonge cl'ico Roberto Veel seniori et Will° Kyngstone plen'am sei'am in et de om'bus terris et ten'tis redd'bus et serviciis cum pert⁵ Que eis tradidi et concessi ad term. vite mee in Stokelynche Maudeleyne Hab. et ten. secundum vim formam et effectum quarundam Indenturarum inter Nos inde confectarum Ratum et gratum habens et habitura id quod iidem Joh⁵ˢ et Joh⁵ˢ fecerint aut alter eorum fecerit nomine meo in premissis In cujus rei testim. Sigil. meum pres'bus apposui Data sexto die Marcii ann. reg. Reg. Henrici Quinti post conquestum Tercio.

Alianor, widow of Sir Walter Clopton, appoints John Havegod and John Webbe of Stokelynche, her Attorneys; to to put Nicholas Yonge, clerk, Robert Veel senior, and Willm Kyngston, into full possession of her lands in Stokelynche. March 6. In 3rd year of Henry Fifth.

No. 109. Henry V. 1416. July 1,

Omn. Xti Fid . . . . Marcus Whittoke Sal. in Dno. Noveritis me tradidisse . . . . Will° Newtone unum Burgagium cum curtill° adjacente in Yevelchestre situa. in Vico Occidentali ejusdem ville inter burga. nuper Ricⁱ Bryce ex par. austr. et burga. nuper Willⁱ Trutte ex par. boria. Hab. et Ten . . . . . Hiis Test. Joh^e Gerarde Joh^e Gyldene Joh^e Bryce Will° Balsham Joh^e Drapere et multis aliis Datum apud Yevelchestre primo die Julii ann. reg. Reg. Henrici Quinti post conq^m quarto.

Marcus Whittoke to Willm Newton—a tenement in West-street, Yevelchester. July 1. 4th year of Henry, V,

---

No. 110, Henry V, 1416. Sunday August 30.

Sciant pres. et fut. quod nos Johannes Strecche Will^s Gosse Robertus Veel et Wills Kyngestone concessimus . . . Marco Whittok filio et heredi Willⁱ Whittok de Yevelchestre omnia burgagia terras et ten'ta nostra Stabellas prata past. redd. serv. et revers. cum om'bus suis pert^s Que nuper habuimus ex dona et feoff. pred'i Willⁱ Whittok in Somertone Yevelchestre et Northovere in Comit. Somers. Hab. et Ten. omnia pre'ta burg'a, &c., prefato Marco et her'bus de corpore suo legitime procreatis imperp. De Capitalibus Dominis Feodorum illorum per servicia inde debita et jure consueta . . . . Hiis Test. Will° Baker Et aliis, Datum apud Yevelchestram pred'am Die Domin. in Crastino Decollacionis

S'ci Joh'is Baptiste ann. reg. Reg. Henrici Quinti post conqᵐ Quarto.

John Strecche (Strachey?) Robᵗ Veel, and others—to Marcus Whittok, son and heir of Willᵐ Whittok of Yevelchester—All the lands and tenem. which they acquired by grant of said Willᵐ Whittok; in Somertone, Yevelchester, and Northover. At Yevelchester, on the Lord's Day, being the Morrow of the Beheading of St John Baptist. 4th of Henry V.

No. 111. Henry V. 1418. October 20.

Omn. Xti Fid . . . . . Robertus Veel Sal. in Dno. Noveritis me tradidisse . . . . Johanni Dountone aliter dicto Couke et Edithe uxori ejus Omnia terras et ten'ta mea prata pasc. et past. Que nuper habui ex concess. Johannis Croukerne in Chedyngtone Hab. et Ten. . . . . Hiis test. Thoma Bolour Willᵒ Leyghe Ricᵒ More Et aliis Datum apud Chedyngtone vicesimo die Octobris ann. reg. Reg. Henrici Quinti post conqᵐ sexto.

Robert Veel to John Dountone, otherwise named Couke (Cook), and Edith his wife—All the lands and tenements which I acquired by grant of John Crewkerne in Chedyngton. Given at Chedyngton, Octʳ 20. in 6th year of Henry V.

No. 112. Henry V. 1421. Tuesday after Octʳ 18.

Omn. Xti Fid. presens scriptum visuris vel audituris Willˢ Gosse Sal. in Dno. Noveritis me remisisse . . . . Roberto Veel , . . . Totum jus meum . . . . . in om'bus terris et ten'tis Que quondam Willⁿˢ Whittok dum vixit habuit tenuit seu occupavit in Yevelchestre Northovere Somertone et Mountagu in Com. Somers. Et etiam in et de omnibus terris et ten'tis que idem Robertus et ego conjunctim

habemus seu tenemus in villis pred'is . . . . Hiis Test.
Will⁰ Gascoigne Will⁰ Neutone Joh⁰ Bryce Joh⁰ Mascalle
Joh⁰ Glainville Et aliis Datum die Martis prox. post Fest.
S'ci Luce Evangeliste ann. reg. Reg. Henrici Quinti post
conqᵐ nono.

William Gosse to Robert Veel—All his right in all lands,
&c., which belonged to Willᵐ Whittok, in Yevelchester,
Northover, Somerton, and Montacute. Also, all lands which
Robert Veel then held conjointly with him in those places.
Given on Tuesday after the Feast of St. Luke the Evangelist;
in 9th year of Henry V.

No. 113. Henry Sixth. 1423. Tuesday after Michaelmas Day.

Noverint universi per presentes Nos Cristinam Priorissam
Albe Aule de Yevelchestre et Johannam Whyttokes Monialem
et Consororem ejusdem Priorisse Johannem Peny Thomam
Drapere Gilbertum Bouche et David Hawes Attornasse et
loco nostro posuisse dilectum nobis Johᵉᵐ Smythe de Northovere ad liberandum pro nobis et nomine nostro Roberto Veel
Ric⁰ Serle et Johⁱ Glainville plenam et pacificam seisinam in
et de om'bus terris et ten'tis Que nuper fuerunt Marci Whyttok
in Northovere et Somertone . . . . Data die Martis
prox. post Fest. S'ci Michaelis Archangeli ann. reg. Regis
Henrici Sexti post conquestum Secundo.

Cristina, Prioress of White Hall in Yevelchester, and
Johanna Whyttokes, Nun and Sister associate of the same
Prioress, and others—Appoint as their Attorney, John Smythe
of Northover; to put Robert Veel, and others, into full
possession of all the lands and tenements which lately belonged
to Marcus Whyttok, in Northover and Somerton. Tuesday
after Michaelmas Day: 2d year of Henry Sixth.

No. 114. Henry VI. 1423. Tuesday after Michaelmas Day.

Sciant pres. et fut. quod nos Cristina Priorissa Albe Aule de Yevelchestre et Johanna Whyttokes Monialis et Consoror ejusdem Priorisse Joh^{es} Peny Thos Drapere Gilbertum Bouche et David Hawes dimisimus conces. et pre'ti sc'to confirmavimus Roberto Veel Ric° Serle et Johⁱ Glainville omnia terras et ten'ta cum pert^s Que nuper fuerunt Marci Whittok in North-overe et Somertone Hab. et Ten . . . . Hiis Test. Nich° Moleyns Joh^e Welwetone jun. Joh^e Smythe de Northovere Ric° Dole Et aliis Data die Martis prox. post Fest S'ci Michaelis Archangeli ann. reg. Reg. Henrici Sexti post conq^m Secundo.

Cristina Prioress of White Hall, and Johanna Whyttokes, Nun and Sister associate of the same Prioress, with others —to Robert Veel and others; All the lands once the property of Marcus Whyttok in Northover and Somerton . . . . Nicholas Moleyns . . . . Tuesday after Feast of St. Michael Archangel, in the 2d year of Henry VI.

No. 115. Henry VI. 1424. May 9.

Sci. pres. et fut. quod ego Johannes Abbot consanguineus et heres Thome Cole de Yevelchestre dedi . . . Alexandro de la Lynde Will° Walkdene Ric° Cerle Henrico Havegod Johⁱ Glainville David Hawys Thome Drapere Thome Saymour Johⁱ Chepman et Johⁱ Deneman her'bus et assig. suis Unam placeam terre cum suis pert^s in Yevelchestre jacentem in fine Venelle vocate Abbey Lane ex opposito modo Domui Fratrum Predicatorum ejusdem ville Que placea continet in longitudine sexaginta et sex pedes Et in latitudine viginti et duos pedes Dedi eciam prefatis Alexandro Will° &c., toftum et curtil'um unius burgagii in eadem villa jacentis inter predictam placeam et tenuram quam Thomas Broune de Tyntenhulle de me tenet Et que Joh^{es} Worme de prefato Thoma Cole dum vixit aliquando tenuit Hab. et Ten . . . Hiis Test. Nich° Coker Joh^e Mascalle Will° Trut Roberto Pypere Joh^e Smythe de Northovere Joh^e Lemman Henrico Gryndelle qui cartam istam scripsit Data nono die Mensis Maii ann. reg. Reg. Henrici Sexti post conq^m secundo.

———

John Abbot, cousin and heir of Thomas Cole of Yevelchester, to Alexander de la Lynde and others—A plot of ground with appurtenants, in Yevelchester; lying at the end of Venella, called Abbey Lane. nearly opposite to the House of the Preaching Friars in the same town. The plot 66 feet long, and 22 feet wide. Also, to the same Alexander and others, a site and curtill. of a burgage in the same town, situate between the aforesaid plot and the tenem^t which Thomas Broune of Tyntenhulle held of him (Abbot) . . . Nich^{as} Coker, Henry Gryndelle who wrote this Deed—and others. May 9. 2d year, Hen. VI.

———

No. 116. Henry VI. 1424. May 9.

Sci. pres. et fut. quod ego Robertus Veel dedi . . . . Alexandro de la Lynde Will° Walkedene Ric° Cerle Henrico Havegod Johⁱ Glainville David Hawys Thome Drapere Thome Saymour Johⁱ Chepman et Johⁱ Deneman her'bus et assig. suis omnia burg'a mea terras ten'ta redd's serv'a et rever'es cum suis pert^s Que nuper cum Johanne Lane habui ex dono et feoff'to Johannis Kyngestone alias dicti Joh^{is} Brys in Yevelchestre et Northovere in Com. Somers. Hab. et Ten. . . . . In cujus rei testim. Sigil. meum pre'bus apposui Hiis test. Nich° Coker Joh^e Mascalle Will° Trut Roberto Pypere Joh^e Smythe de Northovere Joh^e Lemman Henrico Gryndelle qui cartam istam scripsit Et aliis Data nono die Mensis Maii ann. reg. Reg. Henrici Sexti post conq^m secundo.

Robert Veel to Alexander de la Lynde and others—All my lands and tenements which I lately held with John Lane by grant of John Kyngeston, otherwise called John Brys, in Yevelchester and Northover. May 9. 2d year of Henry VI.

No. 117. Henry VI. 1426. February 1.

Om'bus Xti Fid . . . . . Joh^{es} Fauntleroy Hugo Deverelle Thomas Frome et Ric^{us} Wrynge Sal. in Dno. Cum quidam Will^{us} Martyn filius et heres Joh^{is} Martyn de Stokelynche nuper seisitus fuisset in Dominico suo Videlicet de feodo de certis terris et ten'tis in Stokelynche Ostryzer vocatis Hilcombes Que eidem Will^o et her'bus suis jure hereditario descendebant per mortem ejusdem Joh^{is} Martyn patris sui Et idem Will^{us} sic inde seisitus eadem terras et ten'ta cum pert^s per cartam suam dedisset et conc'set Davidi Persone Ecclesie de Southcadebury Johⁱ Venables Will^o Pontone et Thome Mere her'bus et assig. suis imperp. Virtute quorum doni et conc'is iidem David Joh^{es} Venables, &c., de tali statu inde seisiti extitissent Et iidem David Joh^{es} &c., sic inde seisiti per cartam suam eadem terras et ten'ta cum pert^s dedissent et conc'nt Roberto Veel et nobis ante dictis Johⁱ Fauntleroy Hugoni Thome Frome et Ric^o. Ac quibusdam Will^o Haukeforde Militi Will^o Kyngstone et Roberto Walsham jam defunctis her'bus et assig. nostris imperp. prout in cartis pred'is super premissis inde confectis plenius poterit apparere Virtute quorum doni et conc'nis Nos predicti Joh^{es} Fauntleroy. &c., conjunctim cum eodem Roberto Veel de et in eisdem terris et ten'tis pred'is cum pert^s in Dominico nostro Videlicet de feodo seisiti existimus in presenti Noveritis nos ante dictos Joh^{em} Fauntleroy, &c., remisisse . . . . . Roberto Veel Totum jus nostrum , ... Hiis Test. Egidio Dauboney Thoma Beauchampe Militibus Nich^o Reed Will^o Poulet de Bere Alexandro de la Lynde Ric^o More Joh^e Bolour Will^o Muredene

Ric° Serle Et aliis Data primo die Februarii ann. reg. Reg. Henrici Sexti post conq^m Quarto.

John Fauntleroy Hugh Deverelle, &c., wish health in the Lord. Whereas Willm Martyn, by hereditary right, was recently seised in fee of certain lands in Stokelynche Ostryzer, called Hilcombes; and the same Willm did make over those lands by deed, to David, Parson of South Cadbury and others, for ever—Whereas also, by virtue of this disposal, David and his co-proprietors did, by deed, make grant of the same property to Robert Veel and to us (with others now deceased) Know, that we do hereby yield up to Robert Veel all our right . . . . Witnesses, Giles Dauboney, Thomas Beauchamp, knights; William Poulet of Bere, Alexander de la Lynde, and others. February 1. in the 4th year of Henry VI,

---

No. 118. Henry VI. 1426. March 3.

Sciant pres. et fut. quod Nos Joh^es Fauntleroy et Joh^es Lovelle dimisimus . . . . . Roberto Veel Manerium Nostrum de Stokelynche cum pert^s suis Quod Manerium simul cum Joh^e Wadham Milite Will^o Haukeforde Milite Henrico Fulleforde Roberto Hulle filio Joh^is Hulle Edmundo Elyot clerico et Joh^e Lopenforde jam defunctis nuper habuimus de dono et concessione Willielmi Ekerdone clerici Nichi Yonge clerici Will^i Coventre Petri Blount et predicti Roberti Veel Et Ricardus Cloptone frater et heres Walteri Cloptone Militis postea totum jus suum et clameum Que habuit in eodem Manerio . . . . Hab. et ten. totum predictum Manerium cum pert^s suis eidem Roberto Veel her'bus et assig. suis de Capitali Domino Feodi illius Hiis test. Will^o Boneville Egidio Daubeneye Thoma Beauchampe Militibus Nich^o Reede Alexandro de la Lynde Will^o Poulet de Bere Joh^e Bolour Will^o Muredene Edwardo Muttelbury Ric^o Huwet Philippo

Bradone Et aliis Data tercio die Marcii ann. reg. Reg. Henrici Sexti post conq^m Quarto.

John Fauntleroy and John Lovelle, to Robert Veel— The Manor of Stokelynche. Which Manor we held, with John Wadham kn^t, Willm Haukeforde kn^t, Henry Fulleforde, Robert Hulle, Edmund Elyot clerk, and John Lopenforde, (all now deceased)—by gift of Willm Ekerdone, clerk, Nicholas Yonge, clerk, the aforesaid Robert Veel, and others . . . . Witnesses—Willm Boneville, Giles Daubeneye, Thoma Beauchampe, knights, Alexander de la Lynde, Willm Poulet of Bere, and others. Dated March 3. in the 4th year of Henry sixth.

No. 119. Henry VI. 1426. March 3.

Noverint univ. per pres. Nos Joh^em Fauntleroy et Joh^em Lovelle attornasse et loco nostro posuisse dilectos nobis Johannem Croftere et Henricum Havegode conjunc. et divis. ad lib'dum pro nobis et nomine nostro Roberto Veel plen'am seisinam in et de Manerio de Stokelynche cum pert^s Quod eidem Roberto her'bus et assig. suis concessimus Hab. et Ten. . . . . Data tercio die Marcii ann. reg. Reg. Henrici sexti post conq^m Quarto.

John Fauntleroy and John Lovelle, appoint John Croftere and Henry Havegode their Attorneys, to give full possession to Robert Veel of the Manor of Stokelynche . . . . . March 3. in the 4th year of Henry VI.

No. 120. Henry VI. 1426. March 3.

Sciant pres. et fut. quod Nos Joh^es Fauntleroy et Joh^es Lovelle dimisimus . . . . Et Ric^us Cloptone frater et heres Walteri Cloptone militis postea totum jus suum et clameum que habuit in eodem manerio nobis in seisina nostra inde ad tunc existentibus . . . . This Deed, the counterpart of No. 118. supra.

No. 121, Henry VI, 1426. Monday after March 12.

DEED OF FOUNDATION OF ILCHESTER ALMSHOUSE.

Sciant presentes et futuri quod Ego Robertus Veel dedi concessi et hac presenti carta mea confirmavi Will'mo Boneville Egidio Daubeney Thome Beauchampe Militibus Joh¹ Stourtone Alexandro de la Lynde Nich'o Yonge clerico Joh¹ Boef Joh'i Gregory Joh'i Bolour Edwardo Coleforde Will'o Walkedene Joh'i Baret Joh'i Guldene Hugoni Kene Will'o Shourt Henrico Grey Joh'i Pupulpenne Ric'o Serle Henrico Havegod et Joh'i Glainville Manerium meum de Stokelynche Maudeleyne cum pertinenciis Nec non omnia alia mea terras tenementa redditus servicia et reversiones cum pert's in eadem villa et in villis de Stokelynche Ostrizer Yevelchestre Sook Lymyngtone Northovere Somertone Erleighe et in Parochia de Somertone in Comitatu Somerset. Advocacione Ecclesie Beate Marie Magdalene de Stokelynche Maudeleyne predicta dumtaxat excepta Habendum et Tenendum omnia predicta Manerium terras ten'ta redd'us serv'a et rever'es cum pert's Prefatis Will'mo Egidio, &c. . . . heredibus et assignatis suis de Capitalibus Dominis feodorum illorum per servicia inde debita et de jure consueta imperpetuum Sub modo forma et condicione subsequentibus Videlicet quod predicti Will'us Egidius, &c. . . . . heredes et assig. sui aut aliquis eorundem per quinquaginta annos proximos sequentes post datam presentium cum et de exitibus et proficuis omnium predictorum terrarum et ten'orum cum pert's in quantum medietas valoris inde annuatim se extendit annuatim sustentabunt seu sustentari facient ant faciet secundum ordinationem meam inde ut subsequitur conficiendum Quinque ad minus Sex vel Septem pauperes homines debiles senio confractos et ad laborandum impotentes in Quadam Domo de novo per me pred'm Robertum Veel in Yevelchestre ex opposito Porte Orientalis Fratrum Predicatorum ibidem pro Habitacione dictorum Pauperum constructa commoraturorum Et alteram medietatem valoris inde conservent aut conservet sub salva custodia in Abbathia de Muchelnye aut in Prioratu de Mountagu per tempus predictum custodiendam ad illum finem et effectum quod iidem Will'us Egidius, &c. . . . . heredes et assig. sui aut eorum aliquis perquirere possint aut possit Licenciam de Domino Rege et aliis secundum legis exigenciam in ea parte necessariam ad Amortizandum omnia predicta terras et ten'ta cum pert's Ballivis Domini Regis Ville sue de Yevelchestre et successoribus suis Ballivis ejusdem ville imperpetuum Ad usum dictorum pauperum in auxilium sustentacionis eorumdem temporibus futuris imperpet. duraturis Nisi dicta Amortizatio cum dicta altera medietate exituum et proficuorum pred'orum infra idem tempus citius fieri poterit Et si terre et ten'ta pred'a cum pert's ut prefertur Amortizentur Quod ex tunc omni tempore tunc futuro imperpetuum exitus et proficua de dictis terris et ten'tis proveniencia ad usum dictorum pauperum ibidem pro tempore existencium convertentur per bonam et discretam gubernacionem dictorum Ballivorum ejusdem ville Qui quidem Ballivi et Successores Sui predicti omnes dictos pauperes et eorum quemlibet in eadem Domo caritative commoraturos de tempore in tempus quotiens indiguerit supervideant et gubernent Et si eos aut eorum aliquem in culpa mala gubernacione aut defectu invenerint tunc ipsos et eorum quemlibet in tali culpa mala gubernacione aut defectu existentes aut existentem primo secundo et tercio debite corrigendum reformandum et puniendum Et quarta vice si noluerint vel noluerit emendari Ab eadem Domo totaliter expelli et amoveri faciant eos vel eum sic in culpa existentes vel existentem Alios vel alium loco eorum vel ejus ibidem de novo majus caritative eligendum et imponendum Et insuper iidem Ballivi et Successores sui predicti omnia terras et ten'ta pre'ta cum pert's toto posse suo gubernabunt Ac exitus et proficua inde proveniencia levabunt et de recepcionibus et solucionibus suis in hac parte factis et habitis reddent iidem Ballivi et successores sui predicti Fidelem Compotum coram Coronatore Constabulario et Sex Hominibus magis discretioribus Communitatis ejusdem ville de Yevelchestre ibidem annuatim in Festo Animarum imperpetuum Et iidem Ballivi et successores sui pred'i ex causis pred'is habebunt et percipient de exitibus et proficuis predictis tresdecim solidos quatuor denarios annuatim imperp'm. Et si contingat quod dicta Amortizatio modo forma et intencione meis pred'is infra dictos quinquaginta annos effectualiter ut predictum est fieri non possit Quod tunc iidem Will'us Egidius, &c., ... he'des et assig. sui aut eorum aliquis ad eorum instantiam cum dicta medietate exituum et proficuorum remanente superius in custodia per Licenciam Domini Regis in hac parte perquirendam concedent vel concedet Ballivis Ville de Yevelchestre pre'ta ad tunc pro tempore existentibus et successoribus suis Ballivis ejusdem ville imperpetuum quendam annualem Redditum quatuordecim Marcarum Habendum percipiendum et levandum in et de omnibus terris et ten'tis pre'tis cum pert's Ad usum d'orum Pauperum in auxilium sustentacionis eorum et Domus p'dicte ad quatuor anni terminos principales equis porcionibus sub debita forma in scriptis inde sufficienter conficiendis cum clausula ad distringendum super terras et ten'ta pre'ta pro defectu solucionis redditus p'dicti totiens quotieus contiguerit dic'm redditum a retro fore ad aliquem terminum non solutum Et si idem redditus quatuordecim Marcarum in forma pre'ta debite Amortizari poterit Tunc iidem Ballivi et successores sui pre'ti dictos pauperes et eorum quemlibet in omnibus ut predictum est gubernabunt et reformabunt ac dictum annualem redditum levabunt capiendum inde ad usum suum proprium annuatim tresdecim solidos quatuor

denarios ex causis prescriptis Residuumque inde eisdem pauperibus in auxilium sustentacionis eorundem et Domus pre'te
temporibus congruis fideliter persolvent Ceteraque omnia et
singula facient sic ut si terre et ten'ta illa Amortizarentur in
o'bus sicut superius declaratum existit Et interim consimilem
gubernacionem faciant et habeant supradicti feoffati mei heredes et assig. sui in et de om'bus et singulis gubernacionibus
suprascriptis si unanimi assensu eorum concordare possint
alioquin per eorum majorem partem quousque aliqua Amortizatio terrarum et ten'orum pre'orum aut ejusdem annui
redditus ut superius annotatum est in omnibus perimpleatur Et
si dictus annualis redditus quatuor decim Marcarum eisdem
Ballivis et suc' oribus suis pre'is per dictos feof'os meos heredes
et as'os suos aut eorum aliquem per Licenciam Regiam secundum formam et effectum pred'a sit pro perpetuo Amor-
tizatus et iidem Ballivi in plena seisina ejusdem redditus
existant Quod tunc iidem Will^{us} Egidius, &c., heredes et assig.
sui infra dimidium annum ex tunc proxime sequentem post
seisinam ejusdem redditus in forma pre'ta plene habitam
Feoffabunt heredem meum vel heredes mei predicti Roberti
Veel quem vel quos superstitem vel superstites ad tunc fore
contigerit in et de omnibus pre'is terris et ten'tis cum pert's
Habendum sibi her'bus et as'tis suis imperpet'm Supportando
onus pred'm et faciendum inde omnia alia onera et servicia
inde debita et consueta Et si ita contingat quod talis concessio
dicti annualis redditus quatuordecim marcarum per Licenciam
Regiam modo et forma pre'is fieri non poterit ullo modo Quod
tunc iidem Will^{us} Egidius, &c., heredes et as'ti sui aut eorum
aliquis feoffabunt feoffabit her'em vel he'des mei pr'ti Roberti
Veel quem vel quos superstitem vel sup'tes ad tunc fore
contigerit de om'us terris et ten'tis pre'is cum pert's Habendum
sibi her'bus et as'tis suis imperp. Si idem heres vel he'des
super liberationem seisine ei vel eis inde facte quadraginta
libras legalis monete Anglie prefatis Will'mo, &c. her'bus et

as'tis suis aut saltem ei qui liberationem seisine inde in forma pr'ta debite fecerit solverint solverit aut solvi fecerit aut fecerint cum affectu Absque qua solucione pre'tarum quadraginta librarum sicut prefertur facta dicti Will'us, &c., her'es aut as'ti sui aut eorum aliquis aliquod feof'tum inde ut premittitur alicui heredum meorum non facient nec faciet ullo modo Sed tunc feoffati mei pre'ti he'des et as'ti sui aut eorum aliquis feof'ntum inde facient aut faciet in feodo simplici illi aut illis qui pro hujusmodi feoff'nto inde sibi her'bus et as'tis suis imper'm habendo maximam pecunie summam solvere voluerint vel voluerit malo ingenio in eodem contractu penitus proculpulso Ita quod omnes denarii ex eodem contractu et quacunque venditione inde provenientes per manus dictorum Ballivorum aut successorum suorum dicte ville de Yevelchestre Ballivorum aliorumve sufficiencium hominum per bonam securitatem ex parte ipsorum qui dictam pecuniam receperint super recepcione ejusdem pecunie dictis Abbati et Priori aut eorum alteri qui pro tempore fuerint aut fuerit faciendam In auxilium sustentacionis dictorum pauperum qui pro tempore illo ibidem ad tunc fore contigerit totaliter sine fraude convertantur Proviso semper quod nullus heredum meorum nec aliquis alius nomine suo post mortem meam aliquo tempore tunc futuro in Eadem terras seu ten'ta cum pert's neque in aliquam parcellam eorundem per aliquem defectum aut negligenciam pre'orum feof'orum meorum he'dum seu as'torum suorum aut eorum alicujus aut Ballivorum pre'orum seu suc'orum suorum in gubernacione premissorum ex quacunque causa intrare presumat aut intret clamando aliquod liberum ten'tum seu juris titulum aliquem inde Dumtamen iidem Feoffati heredes aut as'ti sui aut Ballivi predicti aut eorum successores aut eorum aliquis per ad tunc heredem meum in presentia fide dignorum requisitiaut requisitus ad defectum illum seu negligenciam si indiguerit debite reformandum Et ipsi aut eorum aliquis hujusmodi defectum infra duos annos post hujusmodi requisicionem proximos subsequentes rationabiliter secundum suum posse corrigi emendari et reformari fecerint aut fecerit per supervisum sex hominum de valioribus ejusdem ville ad intentionem meam ut prefertur in quantum honeste fieri poterit perimplendam Proviso etiam semper Quod si aliqua obscuritas ambiguitas defectus superfluitas omissio difficultas aui aliquod minus stricte aut minus large aut aliquod aliud in premissorum aliquo quod reformatione indigeat in futurum reperiatur per dictos feoffatos meos heredes aut as'tos suos aut majorem partem eorundem corrigatur emendetur et effectualiter reformetur premissorum substantia (ad meam intencionem in premissis respectu habito) in omnibus semper salva Et ego vero predictus Robertus Veel et heredes mei Omnia predicta Manerium terras ten'ta redditus servicia et reversiones cum pert's prefatis Will'mo Egidio, &c., ... her'bus et ass'tis suis modo forma condicionibus et intentione predictis contra omnes gentes Warantizabimus imperpetuum perpresentes In cujus rei testimonium Sigillum meum presentibus apposui Hiis Testibus Hugone Lutrelle, Thoma Broke, Thoma Stawelle, Militibus; Nicholao Reede, Joh^e Speeke, Joh^e Jerarde, Joh^e Lyte, Roberto Geffrey, Will'mo Murcdene, Will'mo Balsham, Nicholao Caas, · Henrico Gryndelle, Joh^e Brymptone, Joh^e Mascalle, David Hawes, Et aliis. Datum apud Stokelynche die Lune proximo post Festum Sancti Gregorii Pape Anno Regni Regis Henrici Sexti post Conquestum Quarto.*

Endorsed. De Stokelynch et alibi concessio pro Pauperibus in Domo apud Yevelchestre.

DEED OF FOUNDATION—ABSTRACT.

Be it known to all men, present and future, that I, Robert Veel have granted, and by this my present Deed have con-

* Although I have gone through the Foundation Deed in its turn with the others, independently; I must not omit to mention, that the credit of *first* transcribing this Document, and also Swanne's Indenture, is due to F. H. Dickinson, Esq. W. B.

firmed, to William Boneville, Giles Daubeney, Thos Beau-champe, knights; John Stourtone, Alexander de la Lynde (and other Trustees named) My Manor of Stokelynche Maudeleyne, with appurtenants. Also all other my lands, tenements, rents, services and reversions in the same vill, and in the vills of Stokelynche Ostriser, Yevelchester, Sook, Lymyngtone, Northover, Somerton Erleighe, and in the Parish of Somertone, in the County of Somerset; The Advowson of the Church of the Blessed Mary Magdalene, of Stokelynche Maudeleyne, alone excepted: To have and to hold . . . . subject to these terms and conditions. 1. The said Trustees, their heirs or assigns, or any one of them, for the period of Fifty years following the execution of this Deed, shall expend one Moiety of the Rents and profits of all the Lands specified, in the support of FIVE, SIX, or SEVEN Poor Men, infirm, broken down with old age, and unable to work; who shall dwell together in a certain House re-built by me, Robert Veel, in Yevelchester, opposite to the East Gate of the Preaching Friars of the same town, as a place of Residence for the said Poor men. 2. The other Moiety of rents and profits, the Trustees were to lay by in safe keeping in the Abbey of Muchelney, or the Priory of Montacute; to accumulate during that term of Fifty years, in order to meet the expenses of Amortizement. At the expiration of this term, the Trustees, or the survivors of them, were to take proper legal measures to obtain the King's Licence for the amortizement of the Charity Lands—which legal process having been duly effected, the property would become vested in "the Bailiffs of our Lord the King's Ville of Yevelchester," and their successors the Bailiffs of that Ville, for ever. 3. In trust, however, for the benefit of the said poor men; in aid of their maintenance, in all future times for ever. The Licence of Mortmain obtained, thenceforth the whole of the proceeds of the property to be applied to the use of the poor men, under the management and Superintendence of the Bailiffs. 4. The Bailiffs to have the supervision and government of the Almsmen; with power to punish the inmates for bad conduct, or misbehaviour; even to expel an offender as incorrigible for a fourth offence, ond to appoint another person in his room. 5. Bailiffs to render an account of Receipts and Expenditure every year, at the Feast of all Souls, before the Coroner, the Constable, and six of the most respectable inhabitants of the Town of Yevelchester. And to reserve to themselves out of the rents every year, the sum of 13s. and 4d.

[The rest of the Deed is occupied with Instructions and Provisos, in the event of the Licence of Mortmain not being obtained after Fifty years, or possibly not being obtainable at all. As the Royal Licence was, in fact, granted in due time by the reigning Monarch, Edward the Fourth; and the intentions of the Founder in this respect were fully carried out, it is unneccessary to quote the "contingent remainder] In testimony whereof, I have set my seal to these presents, before these Witnesses—Hugh Lutrelle, Thomas Broke, Thomas Stawelle, knights. John Speeke, John Lyte (and others named.) Given at Stokelynche on Monday next after the Feast of Pope St. Gregory; in the fourth year of the Reign of King Henry the Sixth after Conquest.

No. 122. Henry VI. 1427. Wednesday, October 29.

Sciant pres. et fut. quod ego Will'us Gosse dedi . . . Roberto Veel unum burgagium cum perts. in Yevelchestre quondam Joh'is Cole de Briggewatere situatum in Alto Vico in parte bori. unius bur'ii Joh'is Mascalle in quo David Hawes modo inhabitat Ex opposito Cruci juxta les Shameles Et quod bur'm nuper simul cum Stephano Coke Capellano inter alia terras et ten'ta habui de dono et concess. pre'ti Joh'is Cole factis nobis her'bus et as'tis nostris imper'm Qui quidem

Stephanus Coke in possessione mea Totum jus suum et clameum postea de se et her'bus suis michi antedicto Will'mo et her'bus meis remisit et relaxavit per scriptum suum imperp'm Hab. et Ten . . . . . Hiis Test. Jacobo atte Welle Ric'o Trubelas, Ballivis ville de Yevelchestre, Joh'e Lyte Edmundo Dommer Nich'o Coker Joh'e Peny David Hawes Joh'e Chepman Thoma Folky, Will'o Baker, Gilb'to Bouche. Johe' Glainville Et aliis Data die Mercurii in Crastino Apostolorum Simonis et Jude ann. reg. Reg. Henrici Sexti post conq'm Sexto.

William Gosse to Robert Veel—a burgage in Yevelchester, once belonging to Thomas Cole of Bridgwater; in High Street, north of a burg. of John Mascalle, where David Hawes lives, opposite to the Cross near the Shambles . . . . James Atte Welle and Richd Trubelas, Bailiffs of Yevelchester, John Lyte, Edmund Dommer, Nich^{as} Coker, and others . . . Wednesday, the Morrow of the Apostles Simon and Jude. In the 6th year of Henry VI.

No. 123, Henry VI. 1427. Thursday after October 28.

Noverint universi per presentes me Will'um Gosse attornasse et loco meo posuisse dilectos mihi Joh'm Glainville et Joh'm Deneman conjunctim et divisim ad liberandum pro me et nomine meo Roberto Veel plenariam seisinam in et de uno burg'o cum perts, in Yevelchestre quondam Joh'is Cole de Bruggewatere situato in Alto Vico in par. bori. unius burg'ii Joh'is Mascalle in quo David Hawes modo inhabitat ex opposito Cruci juxta les Shameles Quod quidem burg'um eidem Roberto her'bus, &c., ... Data die Jovis prox. post Fest. Apostolorum Simonis et Jude ann. reg. Reg. Henrici Sexti post conq^m sexto.

Willm Gosse empowers John Deneman, to put Robert

Veel into possession of a burgage in Yevelchester, once the property of John Cole of Bridgwater; in the High Street, north of John Mascalle's burg. where David Hawes is now living, opposite the Cross, near the Shambles. . . . . Thursday after the Feast of the Apostles, Simon and Jude. In the 6th year of Henry VI.

No. 124. Henry VI. 1427. Saturday after Novr 11.

Sciant pres. et fut. quod Ego Robertus Veel dedi . . . . Will'mo Boneville Egidio Dauboney Thome Beauchampe Militibus Joh'i Stourtone Alexandro de la Lynde Nicho' Yonge clerico Joh'i Beof Joh'i Gregory Joh'i Bolour Edwardo Coleforde Joh'i Baret Joh'i Guldene Hugoni Kene Will'o Shourt Henrico Grey Joh'i Pupelpenne Ric'o Serle Henrico Havegode et Joh'i Glainville duo Mesuagia cum perts, in Yevelchestre situ. in Alto Vico ejusdem Ville ex par. bori. et occid. Quorum Mesuagiorum unum jacet inter ten'um quod Thomas Fauconer modo tenet et ten'um Joh'is Taillour Et quod Mesuagium nuper cum aliis personis habui de dono et concess. Will'i Whittoke Et quod idem Will'us prius perquisivit sibi et her'bus suis de Joh e Fysshe Et aliud mesuagium jacet in par. bori. ten'ti Joh'is Mascalle in quo David Hawes modo inhabitat ex opposito Cruci in Mercato juxta les Shameles ejusdem ville Et quod mesuagium nuper habui de dono . . . . . Will'i Gosse Et quod ipse prius habuit de dono . . . . . Joh'is Cole de Bruggewater Dedi etiam . . . . . unum mes'm in Mountagu quod quondam cum aliis personis habui de dono pred'i Will'i Whyttoke Habendum, &c., Hiis test. Joh'e Wynforde, Edmundo Dommere, Joh'e Mascalle. Joh'e Chepman, Will'o Salesbury, Joh'e Cole, Ric'o Helyere, Et aliis Data die Sabbati prox. post Fest. S'ci Martini Episcopi in Yeme. Ann. reg. Henrici Sexti post conq^m Sexto.

Robert Veel to Willm Boneville, Giles Dauboney, Thomas Beauchampe, knights; John Stourtone, Alexander de la Lynde and others; Two Messuages in the High Street of Yevelchester, in the North West quarter of the street; one of them bought of William Whyttoke, the other to the North of the house occupied by David Hawes, opposite the Cross in the Market Place, near the Shambles . . . . Richard Helyere, and others. Saturday after the Feast of St. Martin, Bishop, in the Winter. 6th year of Henry VI.

No. 125. Henry VI. 1428. March 12.

Sciant pres. et fut. quod ego Nicholaus Moleyns filius et heres Joh'is Moleyns dedi . . . . Will'o Boneville Egidio Dauboney Thome Beauchampe, Militibus; Joh'i Stourtone, Alexandro de la Lynde, Nich'o Yonge clerico, Joh'i Beoff, Joh'i Gregory, Joh'i Bolour, Edwardo Coleforde, Joh'i Baret, Joh'i Guldene, Hugoni Kene, Will'o Shourt, Henrico Grey, Joh'i Pupelpenne. Ric'o Serle, Henrico Havegode, et Joh'i Glainville, unam denaratam annui redditus quam Joh'es Drapere, de Yevelchestre et Isabella Shortes michi annuatim reddere consueverunt pro uno mesuagio et uno curtill'o cum perts in Yevelchestre situato in Chepstrete, &c. . . . Pro hac autem concess. Robertus Veel, solvit mihi duas marcas Hiis Test. Edmundo Dommere, Johanne Lyte, Joh'e Peny, David Hawes, Joh'e Chepman, Joh'e Corteys, Joh'e Denman, Thoma Faukener, Data. apud Yevelchestre duodecimo die Mensis Marcii ann. reg. Reg. Henrici Sexti post conq^m Anglie Sexto.

Nicholas Moleyns, son and heir of John Moleyns, to Willm Boneville, knight, and others—a yearly rent of one penny, now paid to me by John Draper and Isabella Shortes, for a tenement in Chepstrete. For this grant, Robert Veel has paid to me two marks . . . . Edmund Dommer. John Lyte, and others.   March 12; in 6th year of Henry VI.

No. 126. Henry VI.

Memorandum quod postquam Johannes Draper et Johanna uxor ejus et Isabella Shortes filia Lucie Sororis predicti Joh'is perquisierant ten'tum in Indentura inter ipsos et Nicholaum Moleyns contentum Dicta Johanna obiit et dictus Johannes dictum ten'tum concessit Thome Couche in Maritagium cum dicta Isabella Qui Thomas Couche apud Yevelchestre postea dictum ten'tum concessit prefate Lucie Matri ejusdem Isabelle durante vita ejusdem Lucie cujus statum eadem Lucia concessit feoffatis nominatis in dicta carta ejusdem Nicholai pro quo statu Robertus Veel die Martis in Quarta Septimana Quadragesime anno sexto Regis Henrici Sexti Solvit eidem Lucie apud Yevelchestre vi^s viii^d Et tamen quod idem Thomas concessit statum suum inde eidem Lucie durante vita ejusdem Lucie Idem Thomas statum suum inde foris fecit, &c.

Memorandum—That after John Draper and his wife Johanna, and Isabella Shortes, daughter of Lucy, sister of John, had acquired the tenement conveyed in the Indenture between them and Nicholas Moleyns, the said Johanna died; and John gave up the tenement to Thomas Couche on his Marriage with Isabella. This Thomas Couche, afterwards, at Yevelchester, made over the same tenement to Lucy, the mother of Isabella, for her life. This, Lucy resigned her interest to the Feoffees named in the Deed of Nicholas Moleyns. For which life interest, Robert Veel, on Tuesday, in the fourth week in Lent, in the 6th year of King Henry VI. paid to the same Lucy, at Yevelchester. vi^s viii^d.

No. 127. Henry VI. 1428. Monday after Augt 29.

Omn. Xti Fid . . . . Robertus Veel Sal. in Dno.

Nover. me tradidisse . . . . Will⁰ Neutone unum burg'm cum perts, in Yevelchestre situa, inter ten'tum Willⁱ Trut ex par, una Et ten'tum quod Thoˢ Faukoner modo tenet ex par altera Quod quidem burg'm idem Willᵘˢ nuper habuit ex concess. Marci Whyttoke Cujus eciam burg'ii idem Will'us statum suum michi prefato Roberto concessit et sursum reddidit Hab. et Ten . . . . In cujus rei testim. Uni parti hujus scripti penes prefatum Will'um remanenti Ego pref'us Robertus Sigillum meum apposui Alteri vero parti hujus Scripti penes me pref'um Robertum remanenti Idem Will'us Sigillum suum apposuit Hiis Test. Joh'e Chepman, Joh'e Glainville, Ballivis ville de Yevelchestre, Will'o Balsham, David Hawes, Waltero Boucher Datum die Lune prox. post Fest. Decollacionis S'ci Joh'is Baptiste ann. reg. Reg. Henrici Sexti post conqᵐ Anglie Sexto.

Robert Veel to Willᵐ Neutone, a burgage in Yevelchester, formerly belonging to Marcus Whyttoke . . . . John Chepman, John Glainville, Bailiffs of Yevelchester . . . . Monday after the Feast of the Beheading of St. John Baptist. 6th year of Henry VI.

No. 128. Henry VI. 1429. Saturday after Janʸ 13.

Noverint Universi per presentes me Stephanum Isaak alias vocatum Stephanum Hulle Vicarium Ecclesie de Tolre Porcorum in Com. Dorset. Attornasse constituisse et loco meo posuisse dilectos michi Ricardum Slade David Hawes et Henricum Martyn conj. et div. ad lib'dum pro me et nomine meo Will'o Boneville, Egidio Daubeney, Thome Beauchampe, Militibus Joh'i Stourtone Alexandro de la Lynde, Rob'to Veel, Nich'o Yonge, cl'ico, Joh'i Beoff, Joh'i Gregory, Joh'i Bolour, Edw'do Coleford, Joh'i Baret, Joh'i Guldene, Hugoni Kene, Will'o Shourt, Henrico Grey, Joh'i Pupelpenne, Ric'o Serle,

Henrico Havegode, et Joh'i Glainville her'bus et as'tis suis plenam et pacif'm seisinam in et de omnibus et singulis terris ten'tis. &c., Que sibi her'bus et as'tis suis imperp'm per Cartam meam dedi et concessi in Chilterne Dom, Chilt. Vagge Ocle et Hulle juxta Yevelchestre in Com. Somers. ac in o'bus aliis villis et locis infra Parochiam de Chilt. Dom. pre'am Hab. et Ten. eisdem Will'o Egidio, &c., her'bus et as'tis suis imperp. secundum vim formam et effectum carte mee pred'e sibi inde confecte Ratum et gratum habens et habiturus quicquid predicti Ric'us Slade, David et Henricus Martyn, fecerint aut unus eorum fecerit nomine meo in premissis et quolibet premissorum In cujus rei testim. Sigill. meum pres'bus apposui Datum apud Dorchestre in Com. Dorset. die Sabbati prox. post Fest. S'ci Hillarii Episcopi ann reg. Reg. Henrici Sexti post conq^m Anglie Septimo.

Stephen Isaak, otherwise called Stephen Hylle, vicar of the Church of Tolre Porcorum in the Co. of Dorset, appoints Richard Slade, and others, to deliver to Willm Boneville, knight and others, possession of all the lands which he has made over to them by Deed, for ever, in Chilt. Dom. Chilte. Vagge, Oakley, and Hylle, near Yevelchester, in the Co. of Somerset; and in all other places within the parish of Chiltern Dommer. At Dorchester, in Co. Dorset. Saturday after the Feast of St Hillary, Bishop. 7th year of Henry VI.

No. 129. Henry VI. 1429. March 6.

Sci. pres. et fut. quod Ego Will'us Borde de Badecombe in Com. Somers. dedi . . . . . Will'o Boneville Egidio Daubeneye Thome Beauchampe, Militibus Joh'i Stourtone, Alex'o de la Lynde, Roberto Veel, Nich'o Yonge, cl'co, Johi Beoff, Joh'i Gregory, Joh'i Bolour Edw'do Coleforde, Joh'i Baret, Joh'i Guldene, Hugoni Kene, Will'o Shourt, Henrico

Grey, Joh'i Pupelpenne, Ric'o Serle, Henrico Havegode, et Joh'i Glainville, Unum burg'm ad presens non edificatum in Yevelchestre prope Locum Mercati ejusdem ville modo usitati jacens inter ten'tum Priorisse Albe Aule ejusdem ville in quo Will'us Tancarde modo inhabitat ex par. bori. et tentum quondam Joh'is Cole de Bruggewater ex par. occid. in quo Gaola Prisonn' ab antiquo esse solebat Hab. et Ten . . . . Hiis Test. Ric'o Purye Thoma Seymour tunc Ballivis ejusdem ville, Edmundo Dommere Nich'o Coker, David Hawes, et multis aliis Datum apud Yevelchestre sexto die Marcii ann. reg. Reg. Henrici Sexti Septimo.

Will'm Borde of Badecombe, in the Co. of Somerset, to Will'm Boneville. kn', and others; a burgage at present not built upon, in Yevelchester, near the Market Place; between a tenement of the Prioress of White Hall, occupied by Will'm Tancarde on the North, and a ten' once belonging to John Cole of Bridgewater to the West, in which the Gaol for Prisoners was wont to be of old . . . . Rich'd Purye, Tho' Seymour, Bailiffs for the time being of the same town, Edmund Dommer, and many others. March, 6th, 7th year of Henry VI.

No. 130. Henry VI. 1429. March 7.

Nover. univ. per pres. me Will'm Borde de Badecombe in Com. Somers. attornasse . . . . dilectos michi Davidem Hawes et Joh'em Denman conj. et div. ad lib'dum pro me et nom. meo Will'o Boneville Egidio Daubeneye Thome Beauchampe militibus . . . . plen'am seisinam in et de uno burg'o cum perts. ad pres. non edificato in Yevelchestre prope Locum Mercati ejusdem ville modo usitati jacente inter ten'tum Priorisse Albe Aule ejusdem ville in quo Will'us Tancarde modo inhabitat ex par. bori. et ten'tum quondam Joh'is Cole de Bruggewater ex par. occid. In Quo Gaola Prisonn' ab antiquo esse solebat Hab, &c. Datum septimo die Marcii ann. reg. reg. Henrici sexti septimo.

Willm Borde of Badecombe, appoints David Hawes and John Denman to deliver to Willm Boneville kn^t, and others, full possession of a burgage at present not built upon, near the Market Place, in Yevelchester, between a burg. of the Prioress of White Hall, on the North, and a former tenement of John Cole's of Bridgwater to the West, in which the Gaol for Prisoners used to be of old.   March 7.

No. 131. Henry VI. 1429.   March 2.

Sci. pres. et fut. quod Nos Robertus Veel et Joh'es Lane dedimus . , . . Johanni Lyte filio et heredi Edmundi Lyte unum bur'gm ad presens non edificatum in Yevelchestre jacens in Alto Vico ejusdem ville inter ten'tum Priorisse Albe Aule ejusdem ville in quo Margeria Carpotteres modo inhabitat ex par. orien. Et Domum vocatum Almeshous ex par. austr. ex opposito quasi Porte Fratrum Predicatorum ejusdem ville Quod quidem burg'm nuper habuimus de dono et concess. Joh'is Kyngestone aliter vocati Brice Hab. &c., Hiis Test. Ric'o Purye Thoma Seymour tunc Ballivis dicte ville de Yevelchestre Nich'o Coker, Joh'e Chepman, David Hawes, Thoma Ffelpot. Jacobo Attewelle, Joh'e Denman, et aliis Datum apud Yevelchestre secundo die Marcii ann. reg. Reg. Henrici Sexti post conq^m Anglie Septimo.

Robert Veel and John Lane to John Lyte, son and heir of Edmund Lyte, a burgage at present not built upon, in Yevelchester, in the High Street, between a tenement of the Prioress of White Hall on the East, where Margery Carpotteres lives, and the house called Almshouse on the South, opposite as it were to the Gate of the Preaching Friars

. . . . Richard Purye, Tho⁵ Seymour, then Bailiffs of Yevelch. and others. March 2. 7th of Henry Sixth.

AN INTERVAL OF 47 YEARS. 1429—1476.

No. 132. Edward the Fourth, 1476 December 10.

Sci. pres. et fut. quod ego Robertus Grey, filius et heres Henrici Grey, dedi concessi et hac pre'ti carta mea confirmavi Magistro Ricardo Swanne. Canonico Ecclesie Cathedralis Wellensis, Thome Tremaylle, Will° Dodesham, Thome Larder, Joh'i Bevyne, Thome Baker, Roberto Northe, et Waltero Yartecombe, Manerium meum de Stokelynche Maudeleyne cum pert's Necnon omnia terras et ten'ta redd's serv'a et rever'es cum suis pert's in eadem villa et in villis de Stoke- lynche Ostryser, Yevelchestre, Lymyngtone, Northovere. Somertone Erleyghe, et in Parochia de Somertone in Com. rever'es cum suis pert's in eadem villa et in villis de Stoke- lynche Ostryser Yevelchestre, Lmyngtone, Northovere, Somertone Erleyghe, et in Parochia de Somertone. in Com. Somers. Que quondam fuerunt Roberti Veel Et que pred's Henricus pater meus simul cum aliis quos idem Henricus supervixit nuper habuit ex dono et feof'nto pred'i Roberti Veel sub certa forma et condicione ut in quadam carta inde indentata rimis data *est* apud Stokelynche die Lune prox. post Fest. S'ci Gregorii Pape ann. reg. Reg. Henrici Sexti post conq'm Quarto plenius apparet Hab. et Ten. omnia pred'a Manerium terras ten'ta et alia premissa cum pert'iis prefatis Ricardo, &c., . . . herbus et as'tis suis imperp. Tenendum de Capitalibus Dominis Feodi illius per servicia inde debita et consueta juxta formam et condicionem pred'as et ad volun- tatem dicti Roberti Veel perimplendam Et ego vero pred s Robertus Grey, et her'es mei pred'a Manerium terras et ten'ta ac alia premissa cum perts. pref'is Ricardo, &c., herbus et as'tis suis contra JOHANNEM ABBATEM GLASTONBURIENSEM et successores suos Warantizabimus imperp' um Ac eciam attornavi et in loco meo posui dilectos mihi Joh'em Chaffy et Joh'em Vyalle meos attornatos conj. et div. ad intrandum pro me, &c., Hiis test. Will'o Paulet, milite, Joh'e Hugyne Henrico Burnelle, Armigeris, Et multis aliis Data decimo die Decembris ann. reg. Reg. Edwardi Quarti post conq'm Anglie Sexto decimo,

Endorsed. A feofment from the survyving feoffee to Swanne and others.

Robert Grey, son and heir of Henry Grey, to Master Richard Swanne, Canon of the Cathedral Church of Wells. Thoˢ Tremaylle, &c. My Manor of Stokelynche Maudeleyne, together with all lands, &c in the same ville, and in the villes of Stokelynche Ostryser, &c., which formerly belonged to Robert Veel, and which Henry, my Father, together with his Co-Trustees, whom the same Henry outlived, lately possessed. by grant of Robert Veel, under certain conditions (No. 121) . . . . And I, Robert Grey, will guarantee * the same Manor, lands, and tenements, to Richard Swanne, &c., *against. John Abbot of Glastonbury* and his Successors for ever. And also I have appointed John Chaffy, and John Vyalle, my attorneys, &c. Witn. William Paulet, knᵗ; John Hugyne, Henry Burnelle, Esquires; and others. December 10. In 16 year of Edward the Fourth. 1476.

No. 133. Edward IV. 1477. January 22.

Omn. Xti Fid. ad quos pres. scri'm pervenerit Will'us

* This Guarantee, which carries a touch of sarcasm with it, supplies another incidental proof of the arbitary authority claimed, and where possible exerted, by the Mitred Heads of the Great Abbey over their weaker Brethren, the Abbots of Muchelney, the Priors of Montacute, and the Superiors of other smaller Religious Communities that lay within the grasp of their power. The undertaking of Robert Grey, the Grantor, which seems to imply no great compliment to Abbot John and his successors, was no doubt a necessary precaution; since certain sums of money accumulated out of the property here transferred, had been placed for safe custody (No. 121) in the Abbey of Muchelney, and in Montacute Priory; in compliance with a special Proviso of the Deed of Foundation.

Paulet Miles Sal. in Dno Sempit'am Noveritis me concessisse
et licenciam dedisse quantum in me est dilectis michi Magistro
Ricardo Swanne Canonico Ecclesie Cathedralis Wellensis
Will'o Dodesham Thome Tremaylle Thome Larder Joh'i
Bevyne Thome Baker Rob'to Northe et Waltero Yartecombe
Quod ipsi Manerium de Stokelynche Maudeleyne cum pert'iis
ac unum mes'um quadraginta acras terre quatuor acras prati
et tres acras pasture cum pert'iis in Stokelynche Ostryser,
in Com. Somers. Que de me tenent per certa servicia per
annum Dare possint et concedere Ballivis Ville de Yevilchestre et Burgensibus ejusdem ville Hab. et Ten. sibi et successoribus suis imperp'm Et eisdem Ballivis et Burgensibus
quod ipsi Mesuagia terras ten'ta prata et pasturas predicta
cum pert'iis a prefatis Magistro Ric'o, &c., recipere possint et
tenere sibi et successoribus suis imperp'm. Silicet licenciam
dedisse per presentes pro sustentacione pauperum et aliis
omnibus per ipsos supportandis juxta ordinacionem pred'orum
Magistri Ric'i, &c., absque impeticione impedimento moles-
tacione seu gravamine mei vel her'dum meorum aut alicujus
alterius pro nobis aut nomine nostro Salvis michi et her'bus
meis annuatim redd'bus et serv'iis inde nobis debitis et consuetis
In cujus rei testim. Huic pres'i scr'o meo Sigill. meum apposui
Datum apud Yevilchestre vicesimo secundo die Januarii ann.
reg. Reg. Edwardi Quarti post conq'm Sexto decimo.

———

Willm Paulet, kn^t, authorises (so far as his power extends)
Master Richard Swanne Canon of the Cathedral Church of
Wells, and others, to make over the Manor of Stokelynche
Maudeleyne, and lands in Stokelynche Ostryser, which they
held of him by certain yearly services, to the Bailiffs and
Burgesses of Yevelchester; for the maintenance of the poor
men; and for the carrying out by the said Bailiffs of all other
needful measures, according to the appointment of Richard
Swanne and his fellow Trustees. Jany 22. 16th year of Edw. IV.

No. 134. Edward IV. 1477. January 22.

Omn. Xti Fid . . . . Will'us Paulet Miles Sal. in
Dno. Noveritis me prefatum Will'm remisisse . . . .
Magistro Ric'o Swanne, &c., totum jus meum titulum clameum
et demandam que habui habeo seu quovismodo in futuro habere
potero de et in Manerio de Stokelynche Maudeleyne ac om'bus
terris et ten'tis redd'bus serv'iis et revers'bus cum pert's in
eadem villa et in villis de Yevilchestre, Lymyngtone, Northovere, Somertone Erleyghe, et in Parochia de Somertone in
Com. Somers. Que nuper fuerunt Roberti Veel Ita quod nec
ego pred's Will'us Paulet &c., . . . set ab omni accione
jure titulo et demanda inde totaliter simus exclusi per presentes
Salvis michi et her'bus meis redd'bus et serv'iis ab antiquo
debitis et consuetis In cujus rei testim . . . . Datum
apud Yevilchestram pred'am Vicesimo secundo die Januarii
ann. reg. Reg. Edwardi Quarti post conq'm sexto decimo.

William Paulet, kn^t, to Master Richard Swanne, &c.,
All his right and title in the Manor of Stokelynche Maudeleyne, and in all lands, &c., in the same ville, and in the villes
of Yevilchester, Lymyngtone, Northovere, Somertone Erleyghe, and in the Parish of Somerton, in the Co. of Somerset,
which formerly belonged to Robert Veel. Jany 22, 16th year
of Edward IV.

No. 135. Edward IV. 1477. January 25.

Thys Bylle endented made the XXV day of Januar' the
XVI yere of the Reygne of Kyng Edward the iiij after conquest Wytnessyt that Thomas Baker off Yevylcestre ye man
hathe receyved the day and the yere aforeseyde of M. Ryc'
Swan Chanon off the Cathedralle Chyrche off Welles VI li.
XIII s. IIIId to the entent to Morteys or to be Morteysed
to ye Almyshowse in Yevylcestre the Man' of Stokelynche

Maudelyn w^t the purtynence And all londes, tenementes, rentes, s'rvice and reversyones w^t ther p'tinents in the same Paryshe the wyche were late Robard Veel's before the Ffest of Seynt Gregory next folovyng the Date of thys present wryting. And yff so be, as God forbede, that the seyde Mortysment be not doon pformed and stabelyshed w^t in the t'me aboveseyde Y foreseyde Thomas Baker bynde me my eyres and my executores to pay in the Ffeste of the Annucyacon of our Lady next foloving the date of thys present wryting to the seyde M. Ryc' Swan or to hys assygnes eyres or executores VI li. XIII s. iiij d. by thys present Wrytinge In wytnesse where of Y the seyde Thomas Baker to the pte Remaynyng in the hands of the seyde M. Ric' have put to my Seeale Gvyuen the day and the yere aforeseyde.

No. 136. Edward IV. 1477. Hilary Term. January.

BILL OF EXPENSES FOR THE AMORTISEMENT OF THE ALMSHOUSE LANDS.

Termino Hilarii Anno regni Regis Edwardi iiij XVI Thomas Baker recepit et habuit ad Mortizandam domum Pauperum de Yevelchestre Videlicet.

De Magistro Ric'o Swanne	. .	VI li. xiijs. iiijd.
De Roberto Northe	. .	VI xiij iiij.
De ipso Thoma Baker ex donacione sua propria . . .	}	XX. — —
De Waltero Yartecombe	. .	— XL —
De Edwardo Dole	. .	. — XXVI viij

Summa Recepta **XXXVI Xiij iiij**

De quibus solvit dicto Regi quidem pro Licencia habenda ad Mortizandum quidem pro Sigillo harum Patentium Amortizacionis . . . XLVIII li. —
Et scriptura dictarum harum Patentium. . xiijs. iiijd.

Et pro le *lace** dicti Sigilli. . . — XX

Et viridi Sero . . . — . — . viij d

Et Irrotulatione ejusdem ^{harum patentium (sic)} — . X . viij

Et clerico vocato Cecretario Regis pro Waranto, &c. . xxx . x

Et pro breve privati Sygilli . . — . xvi . viij

Et tum pro breve quidem inter * concionem placiti
et judicii (or *indic.*) ejusdem . . . . } vi. . —
Will'm Poulet* . . . . .

Et Ricardo Lane pro Scriptura evidenciarum — . — . xx

Et Ric'o Ffovler ad laborandum Regia (Curia) }
pro Amortizacione predicta . . } xli . —

Et Thome Tremaylle tum pro consilio ad faciend*um*
et ordinand*um* omnia premissa ac quidem labore } XL —
suo ad perimplend*um*, &c. .

Et clerico pro scriptura dictorum premissorum . VI . viij

Et Christoforo Coke ad essendum de consilio cum }
dicta materia . . . . } xiij . iiij

Et Ric'o Pygot Servienti Domini Regis ad }
essendum de consilio cum dicta materia } iij . iiij

Et in expensis dicti Thome Baker tum . . — . — XL

Per Ipsum solutis Termino Michaelis pro dicta }
materia . . . . } — . xxiii . iiij

Et insolutis Johanni Bevyne ad equitandum a }
Crukerne versus Dorchestre pro dicta materia } (iiij · * vic')

Quidem pro expensis Thome Tremaylle et }
Christofori Coke apud Londinium Termino } — . viij . —
Michaelis pro dicta materia. . }

Summa soluta Lviii li. XVIs. ij d.

Et Summa remanens Solvendum Thome Baker.
XXij li. ijs Xd.

BILL OF EXPENSES FOR THE AMORTISEMENT OF THE
ALMSHOUSE LANDS.

In Hilary Term, in the 16th year of the Reign of King

* This word is blotted in the Original, and partly illegible. Other passages which cannot be satisfactorily deciphered are likewise marked by an
asterisk. This is a very difficult MS. to decipher, as it is written in the cursive
form and in a cramp hand. Hence, the items summed up do not quite
balance with the Sum Total.

Edward the Fourth, Thomas Baker received and had for the Mortisement of the House of the Poor Men at Yevelchester—namely :—

	£	s.	d.
Of Master Richard Swanne . .	6	13	4
Of Robert Northe	6	13	4
Of Thomas Baker himself, by his own private gift	20	0	0
Of Walter Yartecombe . .	2	0	0
Of Edward Dole . . .	1	6	8
Amount received . . £36	13	4

Out of which † he paid—To the said King, for instance, for the procuring of a Licence for Mortisement ; also for the Seal to these Patents of Amortization. . . . . — 48 0 0

And for a Copy of these said Patents .	0	13	4
And for the setting * of the said Seal .	0	1	8
And for green Wax . . .	0	0	8
And for the Enrolment of the same of these patents (sic)	0	10	8
And to the clerk called the King's Secretary for Warrant, &c. . . .	1	10	10
And for writ of Privy Seal . .	0	16	8
And also for writ * between the hearing of the Plea and Judgment of the same versus* William Poulet . . .	0	6	0
And to Richard Lane for a Copy of the evidence	0	1	8
And to Richard Fowler for work done in the King's Court for the aforesaid Amortization	2	1	0
And to Thomas Tremaylle also, for his advice in determining & settling all the Premisses, & also for his labour in fully carrying out &c.	2	0	0
And to Clerk for Copy of said Premisses	0	6	8

† Or rather, perhaps, " In respect of which matters " (the business of the Mortisement.)

* The rendering of the passages marked with asterisks is doubtful.

And to Christopher Coke for attending consultation on the said subject .	0	13	4
And to Richard Pygot, Serjeant of our Lord the King, for being present at consultation on the said subject . . .	0	3	4
And for expenses of said Thomas Baker on that occasion . . .	0	3	4
Expenses paid by him in Michaelmas Term on behalf of this matter . .	1	3	4
And unpaid to John Bevyne for riding from Crewkerne to Dorchester on said business	*	4	*
Also for expenses of Thomas Tremaylle and Christopher Coke in London in Michaelmas Term about the said business .	0	8	0
Amount disbursed . . .	58	16	2
And Balance remaining to be paid to Thomas Baker . . .	22	2	10

No. 137. Edward IV. 1477. February 6.

Omn. Xti Fid . . . . Magister Ric'us Swanne Canonicus Ecclesie Cathedralis Wellensis, Will'us Dodesham, Thomas Tremaylle, Thomas Larder, Joh'es Bevyne, Thomas Baker, Rob'us Northe, et Walterus Yartecombe, Sal. in Dno. semp'am Noveritis nos prefatos Magis'm Ric'um, &c., dedisse et per pres. concess. Will'o Poulet Militi, Joh'i Porter, Joh'i Bevyne jun^d et Edw'o Dole quendam annualem redditum octo librarum exeuntem de Manerio de Stokelynche Maudeleyne cum pert'iis Nec non de om'bus terris et ten'tis redd'bus ser'iis et revers'bus cum pert's in cadem villa et in villis de Stokelynche Ostryser Yevilchestre, Lymyngtone, Northovere, Somerton Erleighe et in Parochia de Somertone cum pert's in Com. Somers. Que nuper fuerunt Roberti Veel Hab. percipi'um et levandum pred'm annualem redditum de et in Manerio terris, &c., Will'o Poulet Joh'i Porter, &c., per manus

Ffirmariorum prepositorum tenentium et aliorum occupatorum eorundem pro tempore existentium ad Festa Pasche, &c., ad inveniendum et sustentandum imperp'm de eodem redditu secundum ordinacionem et voluntatem predicti Roberti Veel Quinque ad minus Sex vel Septem pauperes homines debiles Senio confractos et ad laborandum impotentes in quadam Domo de novo per ipsum Robertum Veel in Yevilchestre pred'a ex opposito Porte Orientali Fratrum Predicatorum ibidem pro habitacione dictorum pauperum constructa commoraturorum Et quod pred'i Will'us Poulet, &c., omnes dictos pauperes et eorum quemlibet in eadem domo caritative commoraturos de tempore in tempus quotiens indiguerit supervideant et gubernant Et si eos aut eorum aliquem in culpa mala gubernacione aut defectu existentes aut existentem primo secunda et tertio debite corrigendum reform'dm et puni'um Et quarta vice si noluerint vel noluerit emendari ab eadem Domo totaliter expelli et amoveri faciant eos vel eum sic in culpa existentes vel existentem Alium vel alios loco eorum vel ejus ibidem de novo magis caritative eligend. et imponend. Etsi contingat pred'm redditum octo librarum a retro fore in parte vel in toto post aliquod Festum quo solvi debeat Nos pred'i Magister Ric'us. &c., volumus et concedimus per pres. Quod tunc bene licebit pref'is Will'o Poulet, &c., in pred'is Manerio terris et ten'tis cum pert'iis intrare et pro redditu sic a retro distringere Et districtiones sic captas abducere fugare asportare et penes se retinere quousque de pred'o redditu illo sibi plenarie fuerit satisfactum et persolutum In cujus rei testim. pres'bus sigil. nostra apposu*erunt* Data sexto die Ffebruarii ann. reg. Reg. Edwardi Quarti post conq'm Sexto decimo.

Master Richard Swanne, Canon of the Cathedral Church of Wells, aud others; to Willm Poulet, kn^t, &c., a certain yearly rent of £8; issuing out of the Manor of Stokelynche

Maudeleyne, and of all the lands, &c in the same vill, and in the vills of Stokelynche Ostriser, Yevilchester, Lymyngton, Northover, Somerton Erleighe, and in the Parish of Somerton; which formerly belonged to Robert Veel . . . . to seek out and maintain for ever out of the same rent, according to the appointment and will of the late Robert Veel, Five at least, Six or Seven poor men, infirm, broken down with old age, and unable to work; in a certain House lately rebuilt by Robert Veel himself, in Yevilchester, opposite to the East Gate of the Preaching Friars of the same Town, as a Residence for the said poor men to abide in, &c., (as in No. 121.) Feb[y] 6. 16th year of Edward IV.

No. 138. Edward IV. 1477. February 6.

Omn. Xti Fid . . . . . Magister Ric'us Swanne, &c., Noveritis Nos dedisse et per presentes concessisse Priori et Conventui Domus et Ecclesie de Mountacu quendam annualem redditum, &c., ... Prefatis Priori et Conventui et successoribus suis . . . . Datum sexto die Ffebruarii ann. reg. Reg Edwardi Quarti post conq'm sexto decimo. A counterpart of No. 137. Mutatis Mutandis.

Master Richard Swanne, Canon, &c., to the Prior and Convent of the House and Church of Montacute, a certain yearly Rent of £8. (No. 137) Feb[y] 6. 16th year of Edward IV.

No. 139. Edward IV. 1477. February 12.
Swanne's Indenture to the Bailiffs and Burgesses of Ilchester.

Hec Indentura facta inter Magistrum Ricardum Swanne Canonicum Ecclesie Cathedralis Wellensis, Will'um Dodesham, Thomam Tremayle, Thomam Larder, Joh'em Bevyne, Thomam Baker, Rob'm Northe et Walterum Yartecombe ex una parte Et Robertum Aughte, et Walterum Wale

Ballivos ville de Yevilchestra et Burgenses ejusdem ville ex altera parte Testatur Quod pred'i Magister Ric'us Will'us Thomas Thomas Job'es Thomas Rob'tus et Walterus Yartecombe juxta intencionem et voluntatem Roberti Veel Et in complementum ejusdem Licencia Regia optenta tradiderunt dimiserunt et per presentes confirmaverunt prefatis Roberto Aughte et Waltero Wale Ballivis et Burgensibus ville pred'e Manerium de Stokelynche Maudeleyne cum pert's Necnon novem Mesuagia Quadraginta et octo acras terre Viginti acras prati Sex acras pasture Tres Solidat' redditus Ac redditus unius libre et dimid' piperis et unius libre cumini cum pert's in villis de Stokelynche Maudeleyne pred'a Stokelynche Ostryser, Yevilchestre, Lymyngtone, Northovere, Somertone, Erleighe et in Parochia de Somertone cum pert's in Com. Somers. Que nuper fuerunt dicti Roberti Veel Habendum et Tenendum Manerium terras et ten'ta pred'a ac alia premissa cum pert's Prefatis Ballivis et Burgensibus et successoribus suis De Capitalibus Dominis Feodi illius per servicia inde debita et consueta imperp'm Ad inveniend' et sustendand' imper'm de exitibus et proficuis Manerii terrarum et ten'orum pred'rum cum pert's Secundum ordinacionem et voluntatem pred'i Roberti Veel Quinque ad minus Sex vel Septem pauperes homines debiles senio confractos et ad laborandum impotentes in quadam Domo de novo per ipsum Robertum Veel in Yevilchestre pred'a ex opposito Porte Orientali Fratrum Predicatorum ibidem pro habitacione dictorum pauperum constructa commoraturos Et quod omni tempore futuro imperp'm exitus et proficua de eisdem Manerio terris et ten'tis et aliis premissis proveniencia ad usum dictorum pauperum ibidem pro tempore existentium juxta modum et formam subscript' convertentur per bonam et discretam gubernacionem dictorum Ballivorum et successorum suorum Ballivorum ejusdem ville Ac iidem. Ballivi et successores sui omnes dictos pauperes et eorum quemlibet in

Eadem Domo caritative commoraturos de tempore in tempus quociens indiguerit supervideant et gubernent Et si eos aut eorum aliquem in culpa mala gubernacione aut defectu invenerint Tunc ipsos et eorum quemlibet in tali culpa mala gubernacione aut defectu existentes aut existentem primo secundo et tercio debite corrigend' et reformand' et puniend' Et quarta vice si noluerint vel noluerit emendari ab eadem Domo totaliter expelli et ammoveri faciant eos vel cum sic in culpa existentes vel existentem Alium vel alios loco eorum vel ejus ibidem de novo magis caritative eligend' et imponend' Et insuper Iidem Ballivi et successores sui omnia terras et ten'ta pred'a cum pert's toto posse suo gubernabunt ac exitus et proficua inde proveniencia levabunt et de recepcionibus et solucionibus suis in hac parte factis et habitis Reddant Fidelem Compotum coram Coronatore Constabulario et sex hominibus magis discrecioribus communitatis ejusdem ville de Yevilchestr' ibidem annuatim in Festo Animarum imperp'm Et iidem Ballivi et Burgenses et successores sui ex causis pred'is habeant et percipiant de exitibus et proficuis Manerii terrarum et ten'orum pre'orum tresdecim solidos et quatuor denarios annuatim imperp'm. In cujus rei testim. Partes pred'e Hiis Indent'is Sigil. sua alternatim apposuerunt. Datum duodecimo die Mensis Februarii ann. reg. Reg. Edwardi Quarti sexto decimo.

Endorsed, at three different times, in different hand-writings. "The Indenture showing the uses of the Lands" "made by Swanne and others according to the first Ffoundation" to the Bailyffs and Burgesses."

Swanne's Indenture to the Bailiffs and Burgesses of Ilchester. This Indenture, made between Master Richard Swanne, Canon of the Cathedral Church of Wells, &c., on the one part; and Robert Aughte and Walter Wale, Bailiffs of the town of Yevilchester, and the Burgesses of the same town,

on the other part—Witnesseth; That the aforesaid Master
Richard, &c., according to the intention and will of Robert
Veel, and in fulfilment of the same (the King's Licence
having already been obtained) have delivered up, and do now
confirm to the aforesaid Robert Aughte and Walter Wale,
Bailiffs, and to the Burgesses of the said Town, The Manor of
Stokelynche Maudeleyne; also nine messuages, 48 acres of
Arable, 20 acres of meadow, six acres of Pasture, a Rent of
three, shillings, and a Rent of one pound and a half of pepper
and one pound of cummin, in the vills of Stokel. Maude.
Stokel. Ostry. Yevilches. Lymyngt. Northo. Somer. Erleighe,
and in the Parish of Somerton, in the Co. of Somerset. Which
lately belonged to Robert Veel. To Have and to Hold the
said manor, lands, and tenements, to the aforesaid Bailiffs and
Burgesses and their successors, of the Head lords of that Fee,
by services thence due and customary, for ever. To seek out
and to support, for ever, out of the rents and profits of the
said Manor . . . . according to the appointment and
will of the said Robert Veel, Five at least, Six or Seven poor
men, &c. See 121, 137. February 12. 16th year of Edward IV.

No. 140, Edward IV, 1477. February 12.

Noverint universi per presentes Nos Mag'um Ric'm
Swanne Canonicum Ecclesie Cathedralis Wellensis Will'um
Dodesham, Thomam Tremaylle, Thomam Larder, Johem
Bevyne, Thomam Baker, Robertum Northe, et Walterum
Yartecombe Attornasse et in loco nostro posuisse dilectos
.nobis in Christo Joh'em Vyalle Rob'tum Palmer et Nich'um
Taylloure nostros Attornatos conj'm et div'm ad Intrand' pro
Nobis et nomine Nostro in Manerium de Stokelynche Maude-
leyne, cum pert'iis Nec non novem Messuagia Quadraginta et
octo acras terre Viginti acras prati Sex acras pasture Tres
solidatus redd'us Ac redd'm unius libre et dimid' piperis et
unius libre cumini cum perts. in villis de Stokelynche Ostryser,

Yevilchestre, Lymyngtone, Northovere, Somertone Erleyghe, et in Parochia de Somertone, cum pert's in Com. Somers. Que nuper fuerunt Roberti Veel Et plenam possessionem inde capiendum Seisinaque et possessione inde sic capta ad plenam seisinam inde pro Nobis et nomine Nostro Roberto Aughte et Waltero Wale Ballivis ville de Yevilchestre et Burgensibus ejusdem ville Liberandum juxta vim formam et effectum quarumdam Indenturarum inde inter Nos ex una parte et pred'os Ballivos et Burgenses ex altera parte de dato presencium factarum Ratum et gratum habentes et habituri quicquid pred'ti Attornaii nostri fecerint vel unus eorum fecerit pro nobis aut nomine nostro in premissis per presentes In cujus rei testim. pres'bus Sigil. nostra apposuimus Data duodecimo die Mensis Februarii ann. reg. Reg. Edwardi Quarti Sexto decimo.

Endorsed. A L'r of Attorney for seisen of Stocklinch to the Baylifs of Ilchester, from the Feoffees.

Master Richd Swanne, Canon, &c., and others, appoint John Vyalle and two more, as their Attorneys, to give full possession of the Manor of Stocklinch and all the other lands, &c., before named, once belonging to Robert Veel, to the then Bailiffs and Burgesses of Ilchester. Feby 12. 16th of Edw. IV.

No. 141. Henry the Seventh. 1486. September 22.

Omn. Xti Fid . . . . Walterus Yartecombe Sal. in Dno Cum ego pred's Walterus nuper de novo construxissem et edificassem ad custos meos proprios Quoddam Molendinum Bladi in et super quodam porciunculo soli parcella gardini sive Pomarii Domus Elimosinarie in Yevelchester jacentis in Orientali parte ejusdem Domus Scilicet in longitudine viginti trium pedum Et in latitudine viginti duorum pedum Quod quidem porciunculum soli inter alia Ego predictus Walterus

Magister Ric'us Swanne clericus Canonicus Ecclesie Cathedralis Wellensis et Thomas Trcmaylle nuper simul habuimus conjunctim cum Will'o Dodesham, Thoma Larder, Joh'e Bevyne, Thoma Baker, et Roberto Northe, jam defunctis Noveritis me pref'm Walt'm remisisse relax. et omnino pro me et her'bus meis quietum clamasse prefatis Mag'o Ric'o Swanne et Thome Tremaylle in plena possessione sua existent' et her'bus suis totum jus meum titulum clameum et demandam que habui habeo seu quovis modo habere potero de et in pred'o porciunculo soli ac Molendino pred'o cum pert's imperp'm Ita quod nec Ego pred's Walt's nec heredes mei nec aliquis alius pro nobis aut nomine nostro aliquod jus titulum clameum seu demandam in pred'o porciunculo et Molendino exigere vel vendicare poterimus Sed ab omni accione jure titulo clameo interesse et demanda inde simus exclusi per presentes In cujus rei testim. pres'bus Sigil. meum apposui. Datum vicesimo secundo die Septembris ann. reg. Reg. Henrici Septimi post conq'm Anglie Secundo.

Walter Yartecombe, having lately built, at his own expense, a Corn Mill, on a piece of ground, forming a part of the Garden or Orchard, on the East side of the Almshouse in Yevelchester, 23 feet long and 22 feet wide; this piece having been lately held with other land by Walter himself, Richard Swanne, Canon of Wells, and Thomas Tremaylle, conjointly with Willm Dodesham, Thomas Larder, John Bevyne, Thos Baker, and Robert North, now deceased—Walter, by this Deed gives up all his right and title to the piece of ground and the Mill erected thereon to his co-Tenants, Richard Swanne and Thos Tremaylle. Septr 22. In 2d year of King Henry the Seventh after conq^t of England.

No. 142. Henry VII. 1486. September 23.
Omn. Xti Fid . . . . . Mag'r Ric's Swanne clericus

Canonicus Ecclesie Cathedralis Wellen' et Tho's Tremaylle
Sal. in Dno Noveritis Nos pref'os Ric'm et Tho'm tradidisse
dimisisse et per pres. concess. Waltero Yartecombe et Johanne
uxori ejus Illud Molendinum Bladi cum pert's in Yevelchester
situat. in Orientali parte Domus Elimosinarie ibidem super
quodam porciunculo soli parcella Gardini sive Pomarii dicte
Domus Elimosinarie Quod quidem Molendinum idem Walterus
nuper de novo ad custos suos proprios construxit et edificavit
Hab. et Ten. idem Molendinum cum pert's pref'is Waltero
et Johanne ad terminum vite eorum et unius eorum diutius
viventis Reddendo inde annuatim nobis her'bus et as'tis nostris
durante vita sua unam rosam rubiam ad Festum Nativ'is S'ci
Joh'is Baptiste si petatur Et post decessum pred'orum Walteri
et Johanne volumus et concedimus per pres. Quod pred'm
Molendinum cum pert's integre remaneat Roberto Yartecombe
et Joh'i Yartecombe ad terminum vite eorum et alterius eorum
diucius viventis Reddendo inde annuatim post mortem sive
sursum reddicionem pred'orum Walteri et Johanne nobis her'bus
et as'tis nostris Sex Solidos et octo denarios Legalis Monete
Anglie ad Festum Pasche Nativ'is S'ci Joh'is Baptiste S'ci
Mich'is Archangeli et Natalis Domini per equales porciones
Et pred'i Walterus et Johanna in vita sua Ac pred'i Rob'tus
et Joh'es post mortem sive sursum reddicionem pred'orum
Walteri et Johanne pred'm Molendinum et domum ejusdem
in omnibus bene et sufficienter quociens necesse fuerit repara-
bunt sustentabunt et manutenebunt custibus suis propriis Et
si contingat pred'm redditum a retro fore in parte vel in toto
per sex Septimanas post aliquod Festum quo solvi debeat et
nulla sufficiens districtio pro redditu illo sic a retro existente
in Molendino et Domo pred'a inveniri poterit Quod ex tunc
bene licebit nobis her'bus et as'tis nostris in pred'm Molendinum re intrare et in pristinum statum nostrum inde resumere
Ac dictos Rob'tum et Joh'em et quoscunque alios inde ex-
pellere et amovere Hac dimissione non obstante In cujus rei

testim. tam nos pred'i Ric'us et Thomas quam pred'i Walterus Johanna Robtus et Joh'es pres'bus Sigil. nostra apposuimus Datum vicesimo tercio die Septembris ann. reg. Reg. Henrici Septimi post conq^m secundo.

Richard Swanne, clerk, Canon of Wells, and Tho' Tremaylle, make over to Walter Yartecombe and Johanna his wife, the Corn Mill, erected on a part of the Garden or Orchard at the East end of the Almshouse, in Yevilchester: the Mill having been recently rebuilt by Walter, at his own expense: To be held for the term of their lives. After the death of Walter and Joan, Robert and John Yartecombe, to have the reversion of the property for the term of their lives: To pay a yearly rent of six shillings and eight pence, lawful money of England, at Easter, Midsummer, Michaelmas, and Christmas; and to keep the premises in good repair. Septr 23. 2d year of Henry VII.

INTERVAL OF 52 YEARS. 1486—1538.

No. 143. Henry the Eighth. 1538. August 31.

Omn. Xti Fid . . . . . Joh'es Cuffe Constabularius ville Yevelchestre ac Supervisor omnium terre et ten'torum pertinencium Domo Elimozinarie in Yevelchestre pred'a Ac Thomas Hawkere Capitalis Seneschallus ejusdem Domus Necnon Will'us Raymonde Ballivus Dicte Domus Et tota Communitas ejusdem ville Salutem in Domino sempiternam Noveritis Nos pref'os Joh'em Thomam Will'um ac tota Communitas pred'a Unanimi assensu consensu et pari voluntate nostris concessisse Will'o Hogges unum Mesuagium sive Burg'm cum duabus acris terre jacentibus in Lymyngtone Fylde Et cum duabus acris prati in Fotemede modo in tenura Thome Coke Ac eciam tria burg'ia insimul jacentia juxta mesuag'm pred'm nondum edificata cum suis curtillagiis in Yevelchestra pred'a in Com. Somers. Hab et Ten. Prefato

Will'o Hogges et as'tis suis a die confectionis pres'ium usque
ad finem Termini Septuaginta annorum tunc proxime sequen-
tium plenarie complend' Reddendo inde annuatim Ballivo
dicte Domus Elimozinarie qui pro tempore fuerit ad usum
dicte Domus Quindecim solidos legalis Monete Anglie ad
Quatuor Anni Terminos ibidem usuales solvendos equis
porcionibus ac Secta Curie per racionabilem summam bis per
annum Quod si contingat pred'm redd'um quindecim solidorum
a retro fore in parte vel in toto per dimidiam unius anni post
aliquem terminum terminorum pre'orum quo solvi debeat
Quod tunc bene licebit nobis pref'is Joh'i Thome et Will'o ac
Communitati ville pred'e et successoribus nostris in omnia
pred'a Mes'a Bur'a terras et prata cum suis pert's reintrare
et reseisire et ut in pristino statu nostro illa retinere Presentibus Indenturis in aliquo non obstantibus Et pre'us Will'us
Hogges convenit cum pre'is Joh'e Thoma et Will'o ac cum
tota comunitate et successoribus suis modo et forma sequenti-
bus—viz.   That he the sayde Will'm or Assignez shalle newe
make a Howse with stone walles & cover the same with
Tyle upon the sayde iii Burg' nowe at the makynge hereof
not byldyde contanynge yn the same a Halle with a Chymney
A Kechene with a Chymney & to Chambours over them with
to Chymneys Withyn the space of ij yeres next commyng
And to kepe uppe repare & mayntayne as welle the sayde
newe Howse as all the other Messuag' & other premissiz at
hys propere costes charges & expences And towarde the
byldynge of the same to receve of the sayde Will'm Raymonde
VI li. xiijs. iiijd.   Of the wych I know myselfe welle & truly
to be contentyde & payde by thes presentes In cujus rei testim.
uni parti harum Indenturarum penes pred'm Will'm Hogges
remanenti Prefati Joh'es Cuffe Thomas Hawkere Will'us
Raymonde et dicta Tota Communitas pred'e ville de Yevelchestre Communem Sigillum ville pred'e in hac parte usitatum
apposuerunt Alteri vero parti earum Ind' arum penes pref'os

Joh'em Cuffe Thomam Will'um Raymonde ac Communitatem pre'am remanenti pre'us Will'us Hogges sigilla sua apposuit Datum apud Yevelchestre pre'am ultimo die Augusti ann. reg. Reg. Henrici Octavi tricesimo. P me Thomam Hawker Sen'll'.

Endorsed. This p'nt Indenture is surrendred into the hands of Mr. William Hodges the younger, gent, bayleif of the landes within mentioned to the use of the Comynaltie & feoffees of the Almes Howse landes the first daie of October, in the xxx4th yere of the raigne of o^r Soveraigne Ladye Quene Elizabeth in p'sence of such persons whose names are sub-scribed—George Raymonde, Hieram Bushop and Henry Woude, under Steward. A.D. 1592.

No. 143². Henry VIII. 1540. Novr 8.

Stockelynche Mawdelyne. Ad Curiam Manerii tent' ib'm viii° die Novembris ann. reg. Reg Henrici Octavi xxxij^mo sic irro' Ad istam ven. Robertus Breynter, &c., ... nuper in tenura Elizab' Andros, &c., ... That the seid Robert shalle doo the Kynge o^u' Soveraine lorde his servis by mony . . . . for the tyme beynge of the Officers of the seid Manor & binde such as he shall lymytt for the Kynge, &c.

No 144. Henry VIII. 1544. April 17.

A remembrance. Be yt known to all men that I Robert Coker of Mapowdder, Squyer, have recevyd of the burgeses of Ylchester & for the Almeshowse the xvij day of Ap'll in the XXXV yere of the Raygne of o^r Sov'ayne Lorde, Kyng Henry the viij^th Sup' hede of the Churche of Yglande xxxvi polles of Evydens w^t y bynde me my heres to bryng forth at al tymes for the p'fyt & surtey of Ylchester and Almeshowse In Wytnes wherof y have subscribyd my name w^t my o'n hand the daye and yere abowe seyde. R' by me Roberte Cokere.

No. 145. Queen Elizabeth. 1566. October 1.

This Indenture made the first daie of October in the eighth yeare of the reigne of o^r Soveraigne Ladie Elizabeth by the Grace of God, Quene of Inglonde, Fraunce & Irelond defendo^r of the feithe, &c. Betwene Henry Lyte of Lyte's Cary, in the Countie of Somerset, Esquier, and Frauncys his Wiffe of th'one p'tie and John Fryday th'elder of Yevelton in the said Countie of Som. husbondman, and Robert Fryday the sonne of John Fryday the younger, decessyd, and John Lockyer, the son of Robert Lockyer of Yevelton aforsaid, of th'other p'tie Witnessith that the said Henry and Frauncys In considerac'on of the some of LXVIs. viijd. of lawfull money of Inglond to them by the said John Fryday th'elder, before th'ensealing of these presents Well & trulye contentid & paid, Have Graunted dymysed & to ferme letten & by these presents do graunt dymyse & to ferme let unto the said John Frydaye th'elder Robert Fryday & John Lockyer all theire twoo closes of arrable land or pasture called Sondrushe contaynyng by estimac'on fortene acres lyeng & being within the Parishe of Yevelton aforsaid and now in the tenure or occupac'on of the said John Fryday th'elder or of his assignes To Have and to Hold, &c., ... And it is covenaunted & agreyd betwene the said p'ties that the said John Fridaie th'elder, Robert Fridaie & John Lockyer and any of them that shall happen to dye possessyd & seisyd of & in the premisses shall paie a Heryet of his or theire best cattaile unto the said Henry and Frauncys or to th'eires of the said Henry after the decesse of any of them so dyeng possessid or seasyd of the premyssys, &c. . . . . Per me Henricu' Lyte. 1566 Frances Lyte.

Endorsed. Seled & delyvered in the presence of John Sayntabyn, Thomas Harres, and Wyllyam Colle, John Master, Thomas Wyttenstalle w^t otherse   John Stroude.

No. 146. Counterpart of above. 1566.

Henry Lyte of Lyte's Cary, Esquier and ffrauncys his Wiffe, to John Fryday th'elder of Yeveltone, husbondman . . . and John Lockyer of Yevelton. Close called Sondrushe fortene acres lyeng & being in the Parishe of Yevelton aforsayd. Per me Henricum Lyte 1566 frances Lyte. John Edhams. Endorsed as above. 145.

No. 147. Elizabeth. 1576. February 12.

Noverint universi . . . . , me Thomam Jeffrey de Ivelchester in Com. Somers. Taylor Teneri et firmiter obligari Henrico Hodges modo Ballivo Domus Elimosyne de Ivelchester in octo libris bone et legalis monete Anglie., &c. Datum duodecimo die Februarii ann. reg. Elizabethe Dei Gracia Anglie Ffrauncie et Hibernie Regine Fidei Defensoris, &c., decimo octavo. 1575. The condycyon of this obligacyon is suche that yf th'above bounden Thomas Jeffrey his executors or assignes doe shall & will well & truly contente and paye or cause to be well & truly contented & payd to th'above named Henrye Hodges, &c. . . . . , To th'use & behouf of the Almeshowse and Almes people of Ivelchester above rehersed the some of fower poundes of lawfull money of Englond in manner and forme followinge Too wcete At the Feaste of All Sainctes whiche shal be in the yeare of our Lorde God a thousand fyve hundred three score and eightene Fortye shillinges And at the Feaste of All Sainctes nexte after whiche shall be in the yeare of o' lorde God a thousand fyve hundred three score and nyntene other fortie shillinges in full paymente of the said fower poundes without anye collusion guile fraude or deceipte That then this oblygacyon to be voyd and of none effecte or els to stand and be in full power strengthe and vertue signed, sealed, and delivered in the presence of George Raymond, John Phelipps & Jerr' Byshopp.

No. 148. 1582. Elizabeth.   Easter.

Hec est Finalis Concordia facta in Curia Domine Regine apud Westmon' a die Pasche in quindecim dies anno regnorum Elizabeth Dei gratia Anglie Francie et Hibernie Regine Fidei Defensoris et a conqu' vicesimo quarto Coram Ed'o Andersone Thoma Meade Francisco Wyndame et Will'o Peryam Justic' et aliis Domine Regine fidelibus tunc ibi presentibus Inter Georgium Raymonde et Joh'em Fathers Querentes Et Henricum Lyte Armigerum et Franciscam uxorem ejus Deforc' de uno mesuagio Quatuordecim acris terre et Sex acris pasture cum pert's in Ilchester, Iveltone West Charletone et Charletone Mackerelle Unde placitum, &c.

No. 149. Elizabeth. 1587. May 1.

Omn. Xti Fid . . . . Joh'es Fathers de Ivelchester in Com. Somers. Mercer Sal. in Duo sempit'm Noveritis me pref'm Joh'em tam pro quadam pecunie summa mihi per Egidium Fathers de Ivelchester in dicto Com. Somers. Generosum soluta quam pro aliis bonis causis et consideracyonibus me ad hoc specialiter moventibus dedisse concess. et hoc pres'i scr'o meo indentato confirmasse pref'o Egidio et her'bus suis Totam illam Medietatem meam unius Burg'ii sive ten't; cum pert's in Ivelchester pred'a modo vel nuper in tenura sive occupacione Joh'is Gill vel as'torum suorum jacentis et existentis in quodam Vico ibidem vocato West Streete inter Burg'm mei pref'i Joh'is ex par. austr. et Burg'm modo vel nuper in tenura sive occupacione cujusdam Joh'is Sherlock ex par. bori. Ac eciamtotam illam Medietatem meam unius clausi terre et unius clausi pasture continentem per estimacionem IX acras jacentes apud Sandrushe infra Maner' de Lyte's Carye in dicto Com. Somers. modo vel nuper in tenura sive occupacione cujusdam Rob'ti Fryday vel as'torum su'm Ac eciam unius clausi pasture ibidem vocati Longeclose continentis per estimacionem VI acras modo vel nuper in tenura . . . Joh'is Gill vel as'torum su'm Ac eciam totum jus statum titulum interesse clameum demandam, &c., ... Hab. et Ten . . . . Noveritis insuper me pref'm Joh'em Fathers attornasse, &c., dilectos mihi in Xto Thomam Fathers et Gregorium Raynoldes meos veros et legitimos Attornatos, &c. . . . Datum primo die Maii ann. reg. Domine Elizabethe Dei Gratia Anglie Francie et Hibernie Regine Fidei Defensoris, &c., Vicesimo nono. Signat. Sigillat et deliberat. in presencia Thome Fathers Ambrosii Baskett et Ric'i Powell. Peter Hawkins, Willm Noiris and Robert Bartlet.

N° 150. James 1. 1604.

We, Sir Mychaell Stanhope and Sir Edward Stanhope of London, knightes. Will'm Hodges and Gyles Phelpes, gentle-men. Romane Sprackline. Called Whegehouse and Phillipe's house, situate in Ivelchester. Richd Coopper, Morris Michille, Edmund Littleworthe, Cleophas Bakon. (Signed) Mich Stan-hope. On the back. The letter of Attorney from Stanhopp and Stanhopp. Wegens and Phillipp's house in Ilchester. To the within named Romane Spracklyne in one ten't called Wheggen's house.

No. 151, James 1. 1604.

Indenture between George Raymond of Ivelchester, Gentleman, and Gyles, Father of Weston, Dorset. Gentleman, on one part; and John Lokyer of Ivelchester, Merchaunte, of the other part. Whereas the said John Lokyer now hath and holdeth for the terme of the lyfe of Jone Sugge, the wife of Tristram Sugg. All that house or burgage sett lyeng and being within the Borough of Ivelchester aforesaid, between a burg. belonging to the Allmeshouse of Ivelchester on the

South parte and a ten't belonging to Whitehall on the North parte togeather with one close of pasture called Longeclose, about six acres, lyeng and being within the mannour of Lyte's Cary, that is to saye betwixt the ferches on the South parte and Cary Moor on the North parte . . . . Sandhill . . . The force way (Fossway)   Wm Raymonde   Thos Gould   John Browne.

No. 152. James 1. April 5, 1621.

The Bailiff and Burgesses of the Borough of Ivelchester let to Andrew Belly all that close of meadow and pasture called Twenty Acres lying and being in Ivelchester aforesaid; for a term of three years, at a yearly Rent of £14 13s. 4d. Signed . . . in presence of   ⎫   Andrew ——— Bellie John Rauens—Rector de Ilchester   ⎬   his marke John Wyllys.   ⎭

No 153. James 1. Septr 27. 1623.

Noverint universi . . . . Nos Joh'em Lokyer de Ivelchester in com. Somers. Mercer, Joh'em Hucker de ville et com. pred'is Vitler, Will'm Beaton de eisdem vill. et com. pred'is Yeoman, et Edwardus Fathers de vill. et com. pred'is Yeoman Teneri et firmiter obligari Zach'io Crabbe de Upotry in Com Devon. Yeoman in centum et viginti libris bone et legalis monete Anglie., &c. . . . . Signed—John Lokyer, John Hucker, Wm Beaton Ed. Fathers.   In presence of John Wyllys, John Paulle, Robart Jerferery.   Datum xxvij die Septembr. ann, reg. Domini nostri Jacobi Dei gracia Anglie Ffrancie et Hibernie Regis Fidei Defensor' &c., xxj° Et Scotie Lvj°.

No 154. James 1. 1623.

Peter Vyle de Bemister in Co. Dorset, Tayler. is firmly

bound to the Bailiff and Burgesses of the Borough of Ivelchester in £40 . . . . Signed, Peter Viell. In presence of John Ford The marke of (R) Robert Quicke. Thomas Farnam of Puckington in Co. Somerset, Peter Vyle. Signed Peter Viell, Wᵐ Cary, John Wyllys Iⁿ Fford. 1623.

No. 155. 1727. Last year of George I.

Man' de Stocklinch Magdalin. In Curia Baron' Manerii predicti ib'm tent' pro Ballivo et Burgen' Burgi de Ivelchester in Com. Somerset D'nis Maner' predicti Decimo nono die Junii anno r'ni D'ni Georgii nunc Regis, &c., *(sic)* decimo tertio Annoque D'ni 1727 tempore Tho. Lockyer Ball'i Ad hanc Curiam venit Johes' Dabbynot, &c. 11 Apr' 1729 Jone Dabinet Wid' of John Dabinet is admitted tenᵗ for her widowhood to the premisses.

J. LOCKYER, Senʳ Ib'm

𝔈𝔫𝔡 𝔬𝔣 𝔇𝔢𝔢𝔡𝔰.

𝔑𝔞𝔪𝔢𝔰 𝔬𝔣 𝔓𝔢𝔯𝔰𝔬𝔫𝔰 𝔞𝔫𝔡 𝔓𝔩𝔞𝔠𝔢𝔰 𝔬𝔠𝔠𝔲𝔯𝔯𝔦𝔫𝔤 𝔦𝔫 𝔱𝔥𝔢 𝔣𝔬𝔯𝔢𝔤𝔬𝔦𝔫𝔤 𝔇𝔢𝔢𝔡𝔰.

Abbey Lane, Yevelchestre. 1424.
Abbey of Muchelnye. 1426.
Abbot (John) of Glastonbury. 1476.
Acle, 1329. Ocle 1365. Oakley, Chilthorn Domer.
Aclere, William de   Edw. I.
Aisshlonde, Willᵐ de 1336. Asshelonde John 1400.
Albe John, de Ivelcestre   Henry III.
Albe Aule, in Ivelcestra. Whitehall. 1304—1429.
Alicia wife of Robert Veel. 1396.
Almeshous 1429. Ye Almyshowse in Yevylcestra 1477.

Alfford Robert. 1364.

Amianus, Parson of Crihg (Crick?) Edw. I.

Arundelle Roger, 1391. He gave Halse with its appurtenances. to the Priory of Mynchyn Buckland, 1374. (Hugo.)

Arderne Henry de Ed. I.

Attebroke John 1346. Atte Castel John 1346.

Atteforde John 1330.

Attewelle James, Bailiff of Yevelchester 1427.

Atte Yerde Robert, Ivelcester. 1366.—John 1391.

Atte Water—watre Reginald, of West Cammel. 1404.

Aughte Robert, Bailiff of Yevelchester 1477.

Axstild Willm, Ed. I. Axtil Thomas 1304.

Aysshwyke John, Master of the House of the Hospital of St. John the Baptist at Bath, 1386.

Bailiffs of Yevelchester. 1427—1477.

Burgesses of Yevelchester. 1405—1477.

Bailiff of the Almshouse 1538.

Badecombe—Somerset. 1429.

Bakere D'ns Will'm Chaplain 1369.

Baker Willm 1409. Baker Thos of Yevelchester 1476.

Baret John 1341. 1427.

Barrye John de 1340.

Basset Robert 1363.

Bastard Willm. Hen. III. Bastard Henry. Edw. I.

Bat Adam, 1369. Bat Philip, of Mountagu 1373.

Bath Archdeacon of 1346.

Bath, Hospital of St. John Baptist 1386.

Beauchamp John de. 1279.

Beauchampe Will'm de, knight. Edw. III.

Beauchampe, Sir John de, of Somerset, knight, and Lord of Hatche. 1336.

Beauchampe John de, knight, of Lillesdone. 1366.

Beauchampe Thomas de, Earl of Warwick. 1370.

Beauchampe Thomas, knight. 1426.

Bere, Peter le, de Ivelcestra. Edw. I.

Bermundesie, Bermundusye Prior of, 1307.

Bevyn John, 1389. Bevyne John 1476.

Bischepistone, Byschepestone, Bisshopestone. Montacute.
   1362. 1373.

Blounte Peter. 1400.

Bolevyle, Bolevylle Nicholas de, knight. 1347.

Bonevyle, Boneville William, knight. 1409 1426.

Boure Robert le 1365.

Boucher William 1369. Bouchere Gilbert 1423.

Bradepole 1363.

Brayles Co. of Warwick 1362.

Bridiport Ed. I. Brideporte Brudeporte 1362.

Breuere John 1369.

Brice, Bryce Richard, Clerk. 1369.

Brice, Bryce John, de Yerde. Ivelcester. 1390.

Bruggewater, Briggewater 1370 1391.

Bristoll Bristolle, 1346.

Broke atte, John 1346.

Broke Thomas de 1349. Broke William 1358.

Broke Daniel 1358. Broke Thomas, knight. 1429.

Bromlyghe Stephen de. Hen. III.

Bruton Prior of 1340.

Burntone, Burtone Willm de. knight. Justice. 1279. & Ed. III.

Burnelle Henry, Esquire. 1476.

Busshup William Hen. III.

Byngham William de 1360.

Cammele West 1369.

Cantelo William de 1329.

Canterbrugia Thomas de 1346. Cambridge.

Carter Henry, Hen. III. Cartere Willm le, Notary. 1304.

Cary Walter 1362. Cary William 1623.

Cary John, de Blundyshey, knight. Blundelshay, Dorset.
Castle of Montacute 1367.

Cayllewey Nicholas. Edw. I.

Chalener Robert le. 1346.

Charletone, Chorletone Willm de. John de 1371. 1391.

Charltone, West, Charletone Mackerelle 1581

Chaplain Thomas, Lord of Cilterne. Edw. I.

Chaffy John 1476.

Charter howse Prior of. 1404.

Chedyngtone 1418.

Chepstrete in Ivelcester. Hen. III. 1346. 1428.

Cirencester Thomas de. King John.

Cilterne Dummere. Ed. I. Chilterne Vagge, Fagge. 1323, 1330.

Chilterne Dommere, Rector of the Church of, 1314. Vicar
of the Church of, 1358. Perpetual Vicar of, 1362.

Chiltone John de 1311.

Chitterne John de. 1307.

Church of the Blessed Mary at Lymyntone Edw. I.

Church of St Mary Minor in la Chepstret, Ivelcest. 1346.

Church of the Blessed Mary (minor) Yevelcester 1370.

Church of the Blessed Mary Major Ievelchest. 1403.

Church of the Blessed Mary Magdalene of Stokelynche
Maudeleyne.

Cloptone Walter de, and Alianor his wife 1364.—(This Sir
Walter was Chief Justice of the King's Bench 1388—1400.)

Cloptone Richard 1400. (Brother and heir of Walter Cloptone)

Clyvedone Sir John de, knight. 1346.

Coke Stephen, Chaplain. 1427.

Coke Christopher 1477. Coke Thomas 1538.

Coker Nicholas 1428. Cokere Roberte Squyer of Mapowdder.
1544—(Great great grandson of Eleanor dau. of Robert Veel.)

Cole Thomas, Edw. 1. Cole Walter, de Ivelcester 1304.

Cole William, Mercer de Ievelchestre. 1403.

Coleforde Edward. 1427.

Cinnoke John de, Edw. 1. Chinnock.

Colswayn John, Ed. I. Colsweyn Peter 1329.

Comelonde John 1402. (Married Joan Sexpenn, half sister of Alice wife of Robert Veel.)

Combe Kaygnes 1423.

Conndenham John de 1341. Corton Denham.

Constable of Yevelchestre. Coroner. 1426. 1477.

Cuffe John, Constable of Yevelchestre, and Superintendant of the Almshouse property. 1538.

Corn Mill in the Almshouse Garden 1486.

Court at Westminster (King's Bench) 1279. 1767.

Courtenay Sir Peter de, knight. 1389.

Coventre William 1400.

Crawecumbe Roger de Edw. I.

Craddoke Richard, Parson of the Church of Cury Malet. Edw. III.

Crihg. Crick, Cricket. Edw. I.

Cristina Prioress of Whitehall, Yevelchester. 1423.

Cross in the Church of St Mary at Lymyntone. Edw. I.

Cross of St Peter in Chepstrete, Yevilchester. 1405.

Cross in the Market Place, near the Shambles. 1427.

Crukerne John de 1323. Crukerne 1364. 1477.

Crukerne John Croukerne J. 1406. 1418.

Cumptone Walter de 1311.

Cury Malet Edw. III.

Dacus (Dacres?) William, and Gilbert. King John.

Dakham William de 1279.

Darri Luke de 1323.

Daubeny Willm Hen. III. Daubeney Giles, knight. 1426.

Deghere, Dezare Thomas le 1307.

Degare Osmund le—de Northover 1346.

Deneman, Denman John 1424.

Deverelle Hugh 1412. (of Combe Deverelle, Dorset)

Devon County of. Edw. III.

Dommere, Dummere Dominus John de, Miles. Dommer John de, Armiger (Esquire) 1317. 1330,

Dummere Stephen de, Edw. I. Dommer Edmund 1427.

Dommere, Dummere Edmund, Knight. 1362.

Dorchestre 1429. 1477.

Draycote Peter de, clerk, Lymyntone. Ed. I.

Draycote Hugh de 1307. Draycote John 1370.

Duket Jordan. Durre William. Ed. I.

Dylyngtone Richard de 1341. John de 1366.

Dynyngtone Nicholas 1362.

East Gate of the Friars Preachers, Yevelch. 1426. 1477.

Ekerdone William, Chaplain. 1391.

Elizabeth' our Soveraigne Ladye Quene 1592.

Elizabeth "by the grace of God of England France and
   Ireland Queen Defender of the Faith, &c." 1575.

Engelbi—by Thomas de 1304.

Eltone John de Ed. I. The Priest of Elton Coombe Chapel
   at Hendford in Yeovil.

Erleghe John de 1370. Somerton.

Est lang broke 1341. East lambrook.

Estyntone John de Ed. I.

Eustace the Carpenter, Stoke. Ed. I.

Faber Willm. Fageht Thos. Faget Ralf. Ed. I.

Fagge, Fag John. Fagge Mermeduke 1314. 1355.

Fagge's Chilterne. 1311.

Fauconer John le 1340. Faukenor Thos 1427.

Fauntleroy John 1402.

Filzjamys James 1389.

Fitz Payn Elias 1392.

Fletchere Walter 1369.

Folquy Rich^d 1351. Folkey, Folqui Thos 1403.

Forde atte, John. Forde Robert 1340 1360.

Forneaux Sir Simon de, knight. 1346.

Furneus Mathew de, knight. Edw. I.

Frampton Richard, Bailiff of Ilchester 1753.

Friars Preachers House of, Yevelch. 1424. 1477.

Fromme Walter 1307. Frome Tho' 1412.

Fulleforde Henry 1402.

Fyssche, Fysshe John, of Ievelch. 1369.

Gascoigne William 1421.

Gaol in Yevelch. 1429.

Gate North, Ivelcester. Hen. III. Gate, West. 1387.

Gedding Willm de. King John. [Gidding, in Huntingdon, and in Suffolk.]

Glastonbury, John Abbot of, 1476.

Glebe in Soke Deneys, belonging to Rector of Ivelcester. 1307.

Glainville John, Bailiff of Yevelchestre 1428.

Godewyne Stephen. 1362.

Goldsmith Luke the, Ivelcester. Edw. I.

Golafre Nicholas, knight. Edw. III.

Grey Robert 1476. Grey Henry 1427.

Grigory Dominus Richard, Chaplain. 1362.

Gryndelle Henry, Notary. 1424.

Gyldene Roger le 1311.

Gyldene John 1416. Guldene John 1427.

Gylebert, clerk. Hen. III.

Gyot Johanna. Guyotesplace 1362. Montacute.

Gyverney Richard de, knight. 1329. Gournay. Gurney.

Hardyngtone Maundevylle 1360.

Hatche Beauchampe Edw. I. 1336.

Haukeforde William, Knight. 1402.

Hawkere Tho', Head Steward of the Almshouse. 1583.

Helyere Richard 1427.

Helym Walter de 1279.

Hewenebere Heunebere, Geoffry de Edw. I.

Hewenebere Willm de Edw. I. Hewingbeer, a hamlet or Farmhouse between Hardington and North Perrott. Vide Ordn. Map.

Henry VIII. "our Soverayne Lorde Kynge, Supreme hede of the Church of Yglande."

Herward. King John.

Herward "Ralph son of" Hen. III.

Herward "John son of Ralph" Edw. I.

Hilcumbe John de 1341.

Hockedies. 1346. This feast of Hockday was held on the 2ᵈ Tuesday after Easter.

Hogges William 1538. "Hodges, Mr. Willᵐ the younger Gent. Baylief of the Almshouse Lands" 1592.

Hodges Henry, Bailiff of the Almshouse. 1575.

Hontelegh Davyd de 1346. Honteley Thoˢ de 1351.

Hunteleghe Thomas de, knight. Edw. I.

Hoper, the Countryman (Paganus) king John. Hoper Nichˢ 1402.

Hospitale Geoffry de, King John.

Hospital of St. John Baptist at Bath 1386.

Hugyne John, Esquire (Armiger) 1476. ·

Huchyn John 1358.

Hulle "near Chilt. Dom." 1319. "near Yevelchest." 1429. "in the Parish of Chylt. Dom." [Now Chilthorne Hill.]

Huldebrond John 1346.

Hurdecote John 1380.

Hyde in la, in Byschepestone. Montacute.

Isaac Walter, de Hulle. 1314.

Ysaac Master Walter, de Hulle, Archdeacon of Bath. 1346.

Isaak Stephen, "otherwise called Stephen Hulle," Vicar of the church of Tolre Porcorum. 1429.

Ivelcester Rector of 1307.

Yvelchester 1409. Ivelchester 1604. Ilchester 1621.

Iveltone 1581. Ive John 1346.

Kayrhays John de Perpetual vicar of the Church of Combe Kaygnes 1323.

Kene Hugh 1427. Keu Willᵐ le, de Lymyntone. Hen. III.

Knoel Thoˢ 1389. Koker John de. Edw. I.

Landaff Dean of, 1346.

Laueranz John 1323. Lemman John 1424.

Leonard Altar of S^t, in Lymyntone Church. Edw. I.

Leyc Roger de, Justice. 1279.

Leyghe William 1418. Lidiarde John 1387.

Lillesdone 1366. Lodelawe John de, Chaplain. 1346.

Lockyer John, of Yevelton 1566. Lokyer John, merchaunte. 1604.

Lokyer John, of Ivelchester, Mercer. 1623.

Lockyer Thomas, Bailiff of Ivelchester. 1727.

London 1346. Longh John 1364.

Lopenforde John 1402. Love John 1304.

Lovelle Philip, Parson of Tintenell. 1304. Luvell.

Lovetot John de, Justice 1279.

Lutrelle Hugh, Knight. 1429.

Lumyntone, Lymyntone Hen. III. church of the Blessed Mary.

Lymintone, Lymyngtone, Manor of 1304.

Lynde Alexander de la 1426.

Lyscwys Adam de 1279.

Lyte Edmund 1391. Lyte John 1428. Lyte Henry " of
Lyte's Cary Esquier, & Fraunceys his Wiffe." 1566.

Machum Thos le Edw. I Machun Ralf le, de Bridiport

Malerbe Willm 1311. Maloisel John 1336.

Mannyngford John 1389.

Mapowdder Dorset. 1544.

Mareschal Ralf de, de Chilterne 1346.

Market Place of Yevelchester 1429.

Martyn John, de Stokelynche 1366. Martyn Henry 1429.

Mary Prioress of Newhall (Whitehall) Ivelcester 1370.

Mascalys Isabella, Mascalle, Maschal John 1366. 1426.

Masson (Mason) John le 1341. Middelsex Edw. I.

Middeltone John de 1311.

Mill the New, Ivelcester 1349.

Mill the Corn, in the Almshouse Garden 1486.

Milton John de 1323.

Miltone Walter de, of North peret 1362.

Moltone John de, knight. 1366.

Molyns Henry de 1341. Moleyns Nicholas 1423.

Modeforde William de 1362.

Mone Henry le 1314.

Montacute Prior and Convent of Edw. I. (Montis Acuti)

Montacute Castle of 1367.

Montagu, Mountagu 1367 Mountagu John 1412.

Mountagu Priory of, 1426. Mountacu Prior and Brotherhood of the House and Church of, 1477.

More Luke de la. More Ralf de la Edw. I.

Muchelnye Abbey of 1426.

Mulewarde Walter called the, of Southwark 1311. (Millward)

Mullewarde Thomas, of Northover. 1404.

Mullewey, at Stokclynche 1416.

Muttelbury Edward. 1426.

Neutone, Nywetone, Newtone Willm 1408, 1416.

Newhall (Nywehalle) Yevelch. 1370.

Nicholas D'nus, Rector of the Church of Stoke Gyffard 1380.

Nicholas Revd Father in Christ, by the Grace of God, Lord Bishop of Bath and Wells. 1410.

Northovere. Northovere fields, Northfield Southfield. Edw. I.

Northovere { Geoffry de, Chaplain. | Osebert de, Miller. | Turstan de, Goldsmith | Walter de, Clerk } Edw. I. 1346.

Northperet 1362. Nyenhude (Nynehead) 1402.

Nortone Robert de 1304.

Ocle 1365, 1429. Acle 1329. Oakley, Chilt, Domer.

Oseborne Walter, de Stokelynche Magdalene 1336.

Otery Richard 1404.

Page Roger 1307. Payn William 1367.

Payvot Roger Hen. III. Peck Walter, de Northovere Edw. I.

Penne 1314. Penne Richard de 1360 (Pendomer)

Peny John 1367. Peryam William, Justice, 1581.

Peyto William de 1362. Peystour Robert 1367.

Phelypes Willm, and Nicholas 1366.

Phelipps John 1575. Phelipps E. 1727.

Phelpes Gyles, Gent. 1604.

Phillipe's House—Ivelchester. 1604.

Pigaz John, Roger Edw. I. Pygaz Robert 1314.

Pygatz Stephen, vicar of the church of Chilterne Dummere 1358.

Pingeho, Pynghou, Pighow Edw. I. 1323.

Porta John de 1314. Porter John 1477.

Poulet Nicholas 1389. Poulet Willm, de Bere 1426.

Paulet William, knight. 1476.

Puckington, Somers. 1623.

Pypere Robert 1424. Pygott Richard 1477.

Pypelpenne Henry de 1314. Pipelpenne Thos de 1329.

Pupelpenne John 1427. Pipplepen, a hamlet near South Perrot. Ordn. Map.

Raffe William. King John.

Rat Robert le. Lumyntone. Hen. III.

Rauens John Rector de Ilchester. 1621.

Raymonde Willm Bailiff of the Almshouse 1538.

Raymonde George 1592. Raymond George 1727.

Remmysbury Thomas de 1314. Remmesbury Thos de 1330.

Richeman Richard, of Northover Edw. I. Rycheman Willm 1380.

Rodeny Richard de 1311.

Rokebourne John de 1340. Rokkeborne Sarah 1365.

Romfray William 1346.

Romesye Henry de 1314. Romesye Sir Walter de, Kn^t 1314.

Romesye 1319. Romesie Sir John de, Kn^t 1330.

Rus Hugh le. Rus Adam le. Hen. III.

Rus Peter le, Stephen le. William le. Edw. I.

Roucetre Willm 1402. Ryponne, Rypon John 1327. 1346.

Salisbury John 1362. Salesbury Willm 1427.

Sayntabyn John 1566.

Schordiche Robert de 1346.

Schephurde, Schepert John 1402.

Scheptone Robert de, clerk, 1304.

Sepere Roger le Edw. 1.

Seymour, Saymour Walter 1362.

Seymour, Thomas, Bailiff of Yevelch. 1429.

Seynlowe John de, knight. Edw. III. (S^t Lo.)

Shambles in Market Place, Yevelch. 1427.

Sherlock John 1581.

Soke Deneys near Ivelcester, Manor of 1307.

Soke Deneys Manor of 1386. Socke Lord of 1307.

Somerset—Sumerset. Edw. I. 1311.

Somertone Robert de 1336. Somertone 1370.

Somertone Erleghe 1370. Erleigh 1426. Erleyghe 1476.

Southmor near Ivelcester 1370 (in Somerton Erleigh.)

South Cadebury, David Parson of the Church of 1412.

Speek John 1426.

Spegeton H. de, King John. Speketone Willm de 1304.
    (Speckington, in Yeovilton Par.

Speketone Thomas de, son and heir of Henry de Speketone.
    1304.

Spicer, Spycer Andrew le 1327.

Stafford Hugh de, Earl of Stafford. 1380.

Stafford Humfry, knight. 1400.

St John Richard de 1346.

Stanhope Sir Mychaell, kn^t. Stanhope Sir Edwd kn^t. 1604.

Stawell Thomas, knight. 1426.

Steward Chief, of the Almshouse. 1538,

Stoford, South Strete in, 1367,

Stoke, Osbert of Edw. I.

Stoke Gyffard   1380.

Stoke South (sub) Hamedone   1371.

Stokelinche Manor of   1279.

Stokelynche—linche, Roger de 1336.

Stokelynche Magdalene. Sto. Ostrizer. 1336. 1366.

Stokelynche Maudeleyne Manor of 1402. 1426.

Stourtone John 1427. (Afterwards Lord Stourton.)

Strecche John 1409. (Strachey?)

Stylard Richard, Chaplain, 1383. Suell Willm 1314.

Sugge Joan, Sugge Tristram 1604.

Swan Stephen 1362. Swanne Master Richard, Canon of
    the Cathedral Church of Wells. 1476.

Sylveyn John 1341.—Roger 1366. Sylveyns Alicia, Stoke-
    lynche. 1416.

Tantoune Gilbert de Edw. I. (was Almoner of Glastonbury
    1274. From Hugo.)

Teissun Willm, clerk, Hen. III. Tessun Willm de Ivelcestra
    Edw. I.

Terel. Torel Roger. 1355. 1374.

Thorne Coffyne 1404. Thorne ditch (fossata) Edw. I.

Tintenell, Tintenull Richard de, clerk, Edw. I.

Tyntenhulle. 1366. 1424.

Tolre porcorum. 1429. Torellyscourt, in Yevelch. 1396.

Trenet-Thomas kn^t Edw. III. Trente Roger de 1307. Trenet
    John 1389.

Tremaylle Thos 1476. Triz, Tryz Robert. King John and
    Hen. III.

Trubelas Richard, Bailiff of Yevelch. 1427.

Turke John Edw. I. Torke, Turke John 1323. 1340. of
    Chilt. Dom.

Turburvyle Cecilia 1373.

Tyssebury John, clerk, Commissary General of Nicholas,
    Bishop of Bath and Wells. 1410.

Twenty acres—meadow land in Ivelchester. 1621.

Upotry, Devon. 1623. Vagge Chilterne 1323.

Vagge, Vag John. 1340. Valeze Hugh de. Edw. I.

Veel Robert. Octr 28. 1386. Veele Robert. July 1387.

Veel Robert " who wrote this " deed. 1399.

Vele Robert 1410. Veel Robert Senr March 5, 6. 1416.

Veel Robert 1426. Founded Ilchester Almshouse in this year.

Veel Robard 1477. Veel Robert 1477.

Venele Hugh de la, Hen III. Venella. Abbey Lane. 1424.

Vyngnur Willm le, Hen. III. Vysshere, Fysshere John, of Ievelch. 1370.

Wadham John, knight. 1402. Waltham Adam de 1330.

Wale Walter, Bailiff of Yevelch. 1477.

Warmwelle W. de, Rich^d de. 1346. Warmwelle Roger 1362. (In 1349 one Roger de Warmwille of Ievele was adjudged to do penance for various offences in the church of Ievele. From Hugo.)

Warre Richard 1400. Warr.' Warwick Edw III.

atte Watre, de la Watere, Reginald, of West Cammele. 1369. 1404.

Wayforde Thomas de 1314. Welde Willm 1346.

Welde D'nus William, Chaplain, 1380. Welde Willm Vicar in the Cathedral Church of Wells. 1383.

Weleham Eustace de Edw. I. Welham's Mill, near Stoke sub Hamb.

Welesleghe Willm de. Welleslegh Walter de, clerk. Edw. I.

Welonde Thomas, Justice. 1279. Waleslegh 1330.

Wells Cathedral Church of 1410. 1477.

Westminster Court at 1279. 1767.

Westone near Brayles, in Co. Warwick 1362.

West Cammele 1369. West Strete Ivelcester 1369. 1581.

White Hall, Ivelcester. 1304—1604. Prioress of 1340. 1429.

Whittoke, Whyttoke, Wyttok, Whittok Willm. of Ivelcester. 1386. 1391.

Whyttokes Johanna, Nun of Whitehall, 1423 Whittoke Marcus. 1416.

Wilmot John Eardley, Justice. 1767.

atte Will, atte Welle John 1370. atte Welle James 1427.

Woxbregge Roger de 1346. Uxbridge.

Wynforde John 1404. 1427. Wyndame Francis, Justice. 1581.

Wytbryd Walter Hen. III. Wyttenstalle Thomas 1556.

Yartecombe Walter 1476. Yevele Webbe 1409.

Yeveltone 1402. 1566. Iveltone 1581.

atte Yerde, Robert 1366. Yerde in Ievelchester 1390.

Yerde, John Brice de, Atte Yerde John, alias Brice. 1391.

Yonge Robert, Vicar of the Church of Bradepole 1362.

Yonge Nicholas, clerk. 1400.

APPENDIX:

Some brief Notices Topographical and Historical of Mediæbal Ilchester.

The substance of these Notes is derived chiefly from the foregoing Deeds; in part, from local tradition and personal investigation; and in some instances, recourse has been had to the
Archæological researches of others.

The Antiquarian gleanings thus brought together, though
of minor importance, may yet serve as a slight contribution to
the meagre Topography of this now decayed, but ancient and
once celebrated place.

In the time of the earlier Norman Kings, the name of this
Town was written IVELCESTER; an euphonious appellation which
was afterwards corrupted into Yevel, or Yevil-chester. This
again, was subsequently improved into Ivelchester; and finally,
by an awkward contraction of the first two syllables, the word
settled down into Ilchester; the name by which the Town and
Parish are now designated.

1. THE ROADS AND STREETS OF IVELCESTER.

Among the most permanent features of a District, or a
Town, may be reckoned its public Roads and Thoroughfares;
and we find, that the lapse of six centuries has effected no
material change in the course of the principal Thoroughfares
of Ilchester. From a very Early Period, the Streets of the
Town have been, as they now are, Five in number. 1. Chepstrete (Deeds, Hen. III. to 1428.) now Church Street. 2.
West Strete (1369) also called High Street (1390) The former

name yet survives. 3. La Venele. Venella (Hen. III. to 1424) afterwards Abbey Lane; now Almshouse Lane. 4. La Lane (Hen. III.); called Back Lane, and terminating with Free Street. 5. A Street, no otherwise distinguished in the Deed which refers to it, than as the " Public Road on the South side of the Church of the Blessed St Mary Major." 1402. At that date, it was strictly a street within the Town Wall, but is now the commencement of the Road to Limington.

1. CHEPSTRETE. This Street began at the Bridge, and the North Gate; passing over the Roman road, or Fosse way, for the first sixty yards. Then making a turn to the left, it curved in a southerly direction towards Chilthorne and Yeovil, and terminated at the South Gate. Near the North Gate, on the West side of Chepstrete, was the Nunnery called White Hall; on the opposite side of the Road stood the church of St. Mary Minor; and considerably further down the Street, on the same side, was St. Mary Major, the present Parish Church; and the sole existing Church in Ilchester.

In Chepstrete much of the trade of the Town was carried on, in the Shops and Stalls with which it was lined. This was by far the longest, and probably the most populous and busy thoroughfare of Ivelcester. Houses extended on either side of it, from the North Gate at the Bridge, to the South Gate, which crossed the Yeovil Road at a spot somewhere near the present Turnpike bar. The orchard on the left, and the Rectory garden on the right, were then covered with dwellings. At no great distance from the South Gate, in Chepstrete, and just within the Town Wall, must have stood the Church of St. Peter. No manuscript indeed, makes special mention of St. Peter's *Church;* but the *Cross* of St. Peter is distinctly assigned to this precise locality; and the Church, it may naturally be presumed, was not far removed from the Cross.

2. WEST STRETE. 1369. West Street is a part of the ancient Roman Road, or Fosse-way; and beginning at the

junction with Chepstrete, near the Market Cross, continues its course South West in the direction of Ilminster and Exeter. The West Gate of the Town was the boundary of the Street in that direction. From the undeviating straightness of the Fosseway until it touched the Wall, the position of this Gate might be distinctly seen from the North Gate at the Bridge : and thus, the eye could take in at a single glance, a view of the Street throughout. In early times, the ancient Prison, or Common Gaol, stood near the Market Place, but withdrawn from the road; and was approached by the County Path, or "Shire Path Lane" At the other extremity of West Strete was the House of the Friars Preachers, having its Eastern Gate opening into the Road. Opposite to this Gate of the Friary was erected, in 1426, the Almshouse; at the North West corner of the Lane Venella, which led from West Street into Chepstrete. The diversified aspect of this interesting Street in those early days, would contrast strangely with its present deteriorated appearance— with its long array of mean cottages, stretching from end to end in ugly uniformity. On the one side, the Precincts of the Friary extended from the West Gate for a considerable distance, presenting a handsome frontage towards the Street. From the Friary Northwards, the houses, built in blocks, or detached, disclosed glimpses at intervals of the Town Wall behind. While, near the Market Place, where the population congregated more closely, the dwellings doubled back from the street; to which they had access by an outlet or lane, opening opposite to the West end of the Guildhall. This outlet is called by Dr. Stukeley Shirepath Lane ; and as such it continued to be known, until its final disappearance some fifty years ago, when the Street was remodelled after its present homely fashion. At the end of Shirepath, under the Town Wall Westward, ran another lane, leading to a place called The Yard, and hence deriving its name of *Yard Lane.* The exact locality of "The Yard" is doubtful, and no trace is left to de-note the kind of trade carried on there. The business, what-ever its nature, was no doubt important and thriving; and in some of the Deeds the name of the *place*, after the manner of the time, was frequently substituted for the surname of the occupier. Thus, John Brice de Yerde, is commonly described as John atte Yerde, or John Yerde. The special business of the tenant, was most probably combined with Farming; to judge from the circumstance, that the names of "Great Yard" and "Long Yard" still attach to two large fields, comprising together forty three acres of the richest pasture land in the Parish. This fine tract of land lay close outside the Western wall, being bounded to the North by the Ivel, on the South by "Langport Way" or Pill Bridge Lane. In two of the earlier Deeds (Hen. III. Ed. III.) allusion is made to small sums paid annually out of certain tenements in Ivelcester, to "the Farm of the Town"—Firme Ville Ivelcestre. I think it very probable, that this Town Farm and the Yard were identical. Among several significations of the word *Yard*, formerly in use, was one now obsolete, applying to the measure of land. A yard of land was computed generally at about *forty* acres: but the measurement varied in different counties, from twenty acres or less, to forty acres.

Nor was the other side of West Street deficient in in-teresting features. From the West Gate to the cross street Venella, the space was covered by the Manor House and grounds, possibly the abode of Hugh de Venele in the reign of Henry the Third. Several centuries later, a large Mansion was erected on the spot by one of the Lockyers', then become the wealthiest and most influential family in Ivelchester. A portion of this edifice, comprising the two Eastern gables, was taken down many years ago: the remainder was converted into the Manor Farm House. Crossing Venella, the next object of interest was the Almshouse, founded by Robert

Veel in 1426—a building we may imagine to have been constructed in the substantial and picturesque style of the Architecture of that period. Nearer to the Market Place was another handsome Mansion, in which the Lion-hearted king, as tradition reports, once held his Court, during a Royal Progress through the Western Counties. In reality, perhaps, this house belonged to the old family of the Cordelyons', who died out in the last century.* A curious fragment of this building, forming part of the stables of the Dolphin Inn, was destroyed by fire about twenty years ago.

Facing the Market Place the Ancient Guildhall would form a conspicuous and attractive object. This old building gave way to the Sessions House of later times; which in its turn, has long been superseded by the modern plain and unpretending Town Hall. The Public Shambles, which, in 1428, were placed in the vicinity of the Cross, made up the grouping of the Market Place. The positions of two of the Churches of Ivelcester are as yet unaccounted for. In the absence of proof to the contrary, there is room for reasonable conjecture, that these sacred edifices, dedicated one to St. Michael the Archangel, the other to St John the Evangelist,† adorned and added interest to this Street—the principal thoroughfare of the then County Town. On the whole then, it may be fairly presumed, that West Street, the ancient High Street of Ivelcester, in the days of the Edwards and Henries, would offer to the eye of the spectator a highly picturesque and attractive view as he entered the old Town by it's North or it's West Gate.

3. LA VENELE, Venella, or Abbey Lane. Hen. III—1424.

* The following entries appear in the Parish Register. Burialls Anno 1700. Mary Cordelio' was buryed Aprill ye 13th. John Cordelio' was buryed Apr. ye 14th. To these entries is appended this remark by another hand; Descendants of Richard Cœur de Lion.

† The Advowson of St. John's Church was in the patronage of the Abbots of Muchelney. Hugo's Much. Abb.

This road, running nearly East and West, joined Chepstrete to West Strete. Directly opposite to the end of the Lane, in West Street, stood the House of the Preaching Friars. Hence doubtless, the later appellation of *Abbey Lane* given to this cross street communicating with the Friary. 1424. One Hugh de la Venele was an attesting witness to a Deed in the time of Henry III: and two hundred years later, this street continued to be known by the name of Venella.* Here, in the reign of Henry VII. was a Corn Mill, built on a part of the Garden or Orchard belonging to the Almshouse, on the East Side of the House. Originally, the course of this Lane was in a slanting direction, to the South of East, under the Garden wall of the Manor House; and then across the yard of the present Rectory House, to its junction with the Yeovil Road (chepstrete), opposite one of the inlets to Borough Green. When the dwellings near the Green were removed some fifty years since, and the waste ground was taken into the fields on each side of the Limington Road, it became necessary to change the course of Almshouse Lane by a curve to the left, in order to make a convenient approach to the narrowed entrance of the Road to Limington.

4 LA LANE, Back Lane. In an undated Deed; temp. Hen, III., this by-way is called La Lane; and is afterwards mentioned, 1349, as "the road leading towards the New Mill." The entrance to Back Lane is facing the North East corner of the Market Place. At its further end, the Lane branches off right and left: the turn to the left leads to the River, and to the field path towards Limington and Yeovilton. This same turning led formerly to the New Mill; which was just outside the Town Wall, in the Kingsham field. The New Mill was in existence when Dr. Stukeley published his Itinerary in 1723, but was destroyed in the early part of the present century. In Stukeley's Plan of Ischalis, the New Mill Stream is shewn

* Venella. viculus, angiportus, via strictior. A narrow alley. *Du Cange.*

running parallel with the Old Yeo River as far as the main stream of the Yeo; into which it discharged itself between the Weir and the Mill at Hainbury. The bed of this ancient Mill Stream may be traced through the Kingsham Fields, by a deep channel reaching to the River at the point above indicated; although here and there the hollow has been partially filled up. At the place where the field path strikes off on the left towards Limington, Back Lane itself takes a turn to the right, and joins at it's extremity the Limington Road. This part of the Lane is now known as Free Street—a row of neat Cottages built many years since on the Rectory glebe, for Borough purposes, and acquiring it's name during the feverish crisis of some hotly contested Election—Anciently, this lane was lined throughout with tenements, sheltering a numerous population.

5. The PUBLIC ROAD on the South side of the Church of St. Mary Major.   Between the South Gate of the Town and the Church of St. Mary Major, a turning to the East out of Chepstrete, led to a maze of lanes and habitations. The entrance to what is now called the Limington Road was a wide gorge, but at the distance of a few paces, contracted into two narrow streets, by the interposition of a block of buildings, with their gardens, filling up the centre of the space. Into the channel on the left, opened out a thoroughfare (now Free Street) which passed behind Sᵗ Mary's Church; and on both sides of the central block were scattered dwellings as far as the East Gate; which was the limit of the Town at that point. The East Gate crossed the Road about 200 feet to the West of the Brook which separates the Parishes of Limington and Ilchester; and outside the point of section was then the actual commencement of the Road to Limington. The name by which this part of the Parish was known, before Dr. Stukeley's visit at the beginning of the last century, and also subsequently, was Borough Green. The whole of this

quarter of the town has been swept away: and Kingshams House is now the solitary occupant of a locality once closely built over, and teeming with population.

II. THE WALL AND GATES.

Traces of the greater portion of the course of the Wall are still discernible. Stukeley's Plan represents the place as enclosed within an oblong fence or Wall, of regular proportions; and the Author states, that he "traced out the manifest vestigia thereof quite round." Whatever may have been the exact shape or figure of the *enceinte*, there can be no question that when the Civil Wars broke out, Ilchester was a walled and regulated fortified town. Like Bridgwater, Langport, and other strong holds in the West, it was at first garrisoned by Royalist troops. But one after another in quick succession, the Western fortresses fell into the hands of the Parliamentary Generals; and in their turn the Walls and Fortifications of Ilchester, after a stubborn defence, were stormed and captured by the gallant Blake.

The line of the Wall may yet be tracked across the pasture lands at the South and East of the Town. A remnant of the Wall itself is said to have been standing fifty years ago, in the garden of a house, now the King William Inn, within the recollection of the present owner. Just where the Inn joins on to the next house beyond, West Street (thus far quite straight) makes a bend to the right, towards the Mead. At the point where this bend occurs, the street was formerly spanned by the West Gate. From thence, the line of the Wall followed a South easterly direction, through the Manor-Farm Barton, and Waggon House, across the Paddock and the lower end of the Rectory Garden; emerging at length into the Yeovil Road, near the site of the present Turnpike House. Here, the South Gate guarded the entrance to the Town; and the Wall continued its South-easterly route though the Orchard, along the left bank of the brook, up to the spot where the latter abruptly deviates from its straight course. Then, leaving the stream, the track runs obliquely across the Orchard, North East, to the Limington Road, where the East Gate commanded the approach to the Town. From this Gate the Wall resumed its North easterly course for a short distance in the Kingsham field; then turned to the North West, and pursued that route through the same field, until it touched the River. Thus far, the line of the enclosure may even now, be more or less distinctly traced, by the peculiar configuration of the ground. Along the whole extent of track just described, the land slopes gently down towards the old moat of the fortifications; the site of the town being slightly raised above the level of the surrounding fields: but this formation of the ground is less perceptible on the Western side. On touching the River, the Wall was carried along the left bank,* to the Bridge and the North Gate. Beyond the Gate, it continued to skirt the River bank as far as the Barton now extends, and then made an angle, to the South West. Near the Bridge, and on the West of the town, all undoubted traces of the boundary have disappeared. It is almost certain, that its site is, for the most part, now included within the gardens that stretch out to a considerable length behind the houses on that side of West Street: and thus, every sign of prior occupation of the soil has been gradually, but effectually obliterated by the constant action of the Spade. A remnant of an earth work which must have run nearly parallel with the Town Wall, but outside, may still be seen in Great Yard, near the Farm buildings; having a sharply defined outline, with a steep descent into the trench. This may be a relic of the " bastions and modern fortifications of the time of King Charles I," observed by Dr. Stukeley "in the northern angle, beyond the old ditch of the city, towards the River."

In the Manuscripts, mention is made of two Gates. 1. The

* Here, between the River and the Bridge, Dr. Stukeley found the "track of the Roman wall."

North Gate, guarding the Bridge, where Chepstrete began. "A tenement near the North Gate, to the South of White Hall." 1304. 2. The West Gate, at the extremity of West Street, beyond the Friary. "A messuage, situate outside the West Gate of the town of Yevelchestre." 1387. The South and East Gates, it has been observed, commanded respectively, the roads to Yeovil and Limington; traversing them at the points where the line of enclosure breaks off—as shewn in the Plan.   Camden, in his "Britannia," (first published in 1586) says of Ilchester—"It appears by the ruins to have been anciently large, and surrounded with a double wall. At the Norman Conquest it was populous, and had 107 Burgesses. It was then a place of strength, and well fortified. For A.D. 1088, when the English lords had formed a wicked design to cut off William Rufus, to make his brother Robert, Duke of Normandy, King—Robert Moubray, a great warrior, after burning Bath vigorously assaulted this place, but without success. But what he could not do, time has in some measure effected."

III. THE BRIDGE.   The Bridge is only once mentioned in the Deeds: "A tenement in Northover, over against the Bridge of Ievelcester, bounded by the River on the South, &c., 1369. There are no data to shew, what description of bridge this was: whether it was constructed of stone or of timber; adapted for foot passengers only, or built sufficiently wide for purposes of general traffic. The River when not swollen by floods, was easily forded; and Stukeley draws attention to "a pavement across the River," on the Western side of the Bridge. This pavement is not visible now, if it is still in existence. It was no doubt a relic of the Roman passage—the connecting link of the Fosse way—across the bed of the Ivel; and continued to be used, so long as the necessity lasted for fording the stream. There is still to be seen on the Western flank of the Bridge, a narrow roadway from the town, leading down to the water at the old Ford. The Ford, and this roadway to it, were in use until the Bridge which now spans the Ivel took the place, in 1809, of one narrow and inconvenient, and perhaps of no great antiquity. Leland, about 1540, thus describes the bridge, as he found it. "I enterid by South West, (i.e. *towards* the South West) into Ilchester, over a great stone bridge of seven arches, now one of two, yn the midle wherof were two little houses of stone, one of the right hand, wher the commune gaiol is for prisoners' yn Somersetshir. The other house is on the left hand. The lesser of booth seemed to me to have beene a chapelle. The toune of Ilchester hath beene a very large thyng, and one of the auncientest tounes yn al that quarter. At this tyme it is in wonderful decay, as a thing in a manner rasid with men of warre." Camden (1586) remarks upon this statement—"Leland's free Chapel by the Bridge, on the opposite side of the River, is still known by the name of Whitehall, now a weaving shop, anciently a hospital, and then a nunnery, and at last a Free Chapel. Near it was a house of lepers. If this be not Leland's house on the right hand of the Bridge, that is quite gone; but his Chapel on the left hand is still a dwelling house." There is some confusion in these descriptions, which it is not easy to reconcile. If Leland's account is to be taken literally; it would mean, that of the two little stone houses *in the midle* of the Bridge, the one on his right hand as he crossed into the town, was the Gaol, and the other on his left was the Chapel. But Camden's comment on this description rather perplexes than elucidates the meaning; for he seems to identify the right hand house *on* the Bridge, with Whitehall which, though close to the river, had no connexion with the Bridge. In Stukeley's map, the disused Chapel is placed near the water, *below* the Bridge, not *upon* it. These particulars are further alluded to elsewhere. IV. WHITEHALL. In one of the Earliest Manucripts (Hen III.) occurs the name of "Johannes Albe de Ivelcestra."

This John White appears to have been the owner of various messuages and tenements in the town. To another deed of about the same time, he was an attesting witness. On these two occasions only, does the name of Albe, or White, appear. He may possibly have been the last surviving male of his race; and in default of male issue, or (agreeably to the prevalent notion of the age) for his soul's welfare, may have bequeathed his house of residence and other property in Ivelcester, to the Church, for religious uses. For in another record, dated 1304, the first mention occurs in these deeds of a Religious House, or Nunnery, called Albe Aule, White Hall. And in subsequent agreements the Prioress of this Conventual House is frequently alluded to—1346 to 1429. Once she is designated Prioress of Nywehalle, New Hall; perhaps from the circumstance of her Convent having been recently enlarged or rebuilt. The Convent or Nunnery of Whitehall, occupied a narrow belt of ground extending from the River, parallel with the Road, as far as the present Farm House, formerly the well known Castle Inn. It's precincts must have been confined, and hemmed in on the North and West sides by the Town Wall. The front of the building was towards Chepstrete, facing the Church of St Mary the Less, on the opposite side of the street. When Dr. Stukeley wrote, in the first quarter of the last century, there no doubt remained some portion of the old Convent buildings; for little more than a century earlier, in 1604, a tenement is described as " belonging to Whitehall." In his Plan of Ivelchester, is depicted a house of some kind, standing on the angle of ground projecting towards the River (now used as a Rick Barton) which he miscalls Whitechapel. The genuine name White*hall*, however, has been faithfully handed down by tradition to this day; and is still familiar to the memory of many aged persons in the Parish. *

* An interesting History of this, and other Somersetshire Nunneries, is in preparation by the Revd. Thos. Hugo.

V. THE FRIARY. In West Strete, facing the Almshouse, was the East Gate of entrance to the House of the Franciscan or Gray Friars, otherwise called the Preaching Friars; and over against the end of the Lane which bounds the Almshouse on the South, stood the Friary itself. There is an accurate description of this locality given in the Deed of Foundation, and in some others, which mark out with precision the Almshouse premises. Stukeley was correct in his remark, that "the religious (meaning the Friars) had extended their bounds beyond the city"; for no doubt, the precincts of the Friary comprised that angle of ground beyond the Wall, shut in between Pill Bridge Lane and the high Road. Two quotations will suffice to determine the precise position of the Friary. In 1424, one John Abbot grants to Alexander de la Lynde and others, " a piece of ground in Yevelchester, situate at the end of Venella, otherwise Abbey Lane, just opposite the House of the Preaching Friars of the same place." Again, the position of the Almshouse is thus exactly described, "exopposito Portæ Orientali Fratrum Prædicatorum," over against the East Gate of the Friars Preachers. 1477. The East Gate, and the House to which it was the Portal, were consequently near to each other, and both within the Walls of the Town: though Dr Stukeley's Plan also exhibits some extra mural buildings in connexion with this Monastic Foundation. There are now no vestiges of The Friary existing above ground. But prior to the Reformation, it was no doubt a fine and striking pile of building. Camden leads us to infer as much when, alluding to this Monastery, he says—"the remains of the Priory Church, whose North Transept is used for spinning silk, shew it to have been magnificent. It belonged to a House of Friers Preachers, or Grey Friers, founded before the Eleventh of Edward the First." Leland's allusion to the Friary is very brief—"Ther was also a late a House of Freres yn this toune." At the Dissolution, the Friary shared the common fate of other

Religious Houses: the building was dismantled, and partially ruined, and the ground on which it stood was sold. "On the fourth day of July 1545, the King granted to William Hodgys of Myddelchynnock in the Co. of Somerset, and to William Hodgys of London, son of the former, and their heirs, for the sum of £695. 0. 5d. the site of the Monastery of the Grey Friars of Ivellchester, 29 Messuages in the Town of Bridgwater lately belonging to the Hospital of St John in that Town, &c. The property in Ivellchester was reckoned of the clear annual value of 13^s and 4^d." Hugo. Buckland Pri.

VI. THE CHURCHES OF IVELCESTER. There is a prevailing notion, that the town of Ivelcester was anciently crowded with a fabulous number of Churches. And even Collinson, adopting the previous "they say" of Stukeley, refers to the number *sixteen* as a not improbable quota. But no evidence whatever is produced in support of this exaggerated computation. If numerous Churches had been in reality erected and endowed there, and even afterwards demolished, some kind of record of the fact beyond mere tradition, must have survived their demolition. The *names* at least, would turn up in Ecclesiastical Terriers. Leland, in 1540, states—"there hath bene in hominum memoria four Paroche Chirchis yn the toune, whereof one yet is occupied. Tokens of the other two yet stond; and the fourth is clene yn ruine." He further says, "There is a fre *chapelle in the toune, the baksyde whereof cummith to the ryver syde, even hard bynethe the bridge, and ther joynith a right praty mansion house to this chapelle. I have hard that many yeres syns ther was a Nunry wher this chappelle is." Hence perhaps, Dr Stukeley derived the name of Whitechapel, which he gave to the building standing there in his time. Camden writes, some

* This was no doubt, the Chapel of the old Nunnery of Whitehall, converted into a Free Chapel after the Dissolution of that Foundation. I think too, that Camden must have reckoned this as one of his Six Churches.

fifty years after Leland, "†*There was not less than six Churches in this town.* The present Parish Church is very mean, but has an Octagon Tower and a North Chapel."

That there were *Five* Churches in Ivelcester during some part of the Middle Ages, may be proved satisfactorily from documents in the Muniment office at Wells. They will demonstrate this fact; that the Dues of Five Churches or Parishes are, even at the present time, chargeable in the shape of Procurations and Paschals upon the Rector of Ilchester. These five Churches are thus designated. 1. St Mary Major. 2. St Mary Minor. 3. St Michael. 4. St John. 5. St Peter.

1. St. Mary Major: Now the sole remaining, and the Parish Church. This appears to have been the case, as far back as the reign of Henry the Eight. The present Church was the only one "occupied" when Leland visited Ilchester; the others were in ruins. This Church is cited in two Deeds, dated 1402. 1403, as "the Church of the blessed St Mary Major." It is a small building of rather mean and dilapidated appearance. Indeed Camden, as we have just seen, denounced it as "very mean" nearly three hundred years ago: Perhaps he dealt uncharitably with the venerable Mother Church. Yet portions of it are of great Antiquity. The Tower is early English, and its date may certainly be carried back six hundred years, or more. It is an Octagon of solid proportions, supported by massive buttresses; devoid of ornament throughout; and in it's upper compartment pierced with simple lancet openings to admit light to the staircase and Belfry. But in the year 1611, it's South Side was grievously mutilated and disfigured, in order to provide a Staircase to a *Gallery*, then first erected in the Church. The Chancel is of early date, though less ancient than the Tower. The

† The words in Italics are not found in the Edition of 1789; but Camden there alludes to *four* and to *two* Churches, leading his readers to infer that there were Six.

East Window is pointed, has a narrow triple light, and three cusped openings over the triplet. Though a handsome interior window of its kind, there is yet observable a clumsy solidity in the piers and mullions, betokening an early period of transition from the severe to the more decorated style. This window, which had been filled up in two different stages, and then completely concealed inside by plaster, was reopened a few years since. The first blocking up, of the lower half, disclosed evidence of ruthless handling; the side pillars having been violently torn away, and broken up to help fill in the cavity; a memento, it may be, of the troublous era of the Commonwealth. The spring of the arch on either side, is decorated at the extremity of the moulding with the head of a king and a Bishop, in a good state of preservation. The North and South windows are later insertions; and the oak wainscotting lining the lower part of the walls, shows the date of 1673. The Nave has at some former period, anterior probably to the Reformation, undergone extensive alteration. This is apparent on a casual examination of the exterior walls. All the windows have the appearance of being after insertions, to judge from the vertical lines in the masonry. They are late perpendicular, of a very common character. The small North Transept is of the same late style, but contains some richly ornamented Canopied niches. This interior, however, was either left in an unfinished state, or the tracery must have been subjected heretofore to very extensive injury. The groined roof has entirely disappeared ; or possibly, the work was never carried up above the springs for the ribbed arches which still remain. It must be confessed, that this mean looking (Camdenice *very* mean) diminutive Church, reflects little credit on the old County Town, in these days of universal Church restoration. But in extenuation it may justly be pleaded, that the pecuniary difficulties besetting the question of its rebuilding are of more than ordinary magnitude.

2. St Mary Minor.　　　　　Opposite the Whitehall, in Chepstrete, and not far removed from the River, stood the Church of St Mary the Less. Dr Stukeley has certainly misapprehended the position of this edifice; which he calls Little St Mary's *Chapel;* and places (in his plan) on a small promontory thrown up by the action of the stream at the centre of the Bridge, on the East side: deeming it probably to have been a Way-side Chapel, similar in character to the beautiful Chantry on Wakefield Bridge. But the true site of this Church is very accurately determined in two of the Almshouse Deeds. It is "in Chepstrete"; "opposite to a certain tenement which adjoins the House of the Prioress of White Hall." 1346. And further, the same burgage is represented, in 1370, to be "in the public street of Yevelchester, over against the Church of the Blessed Mary, adjoining the burgage of Mary the Prioress of Nywehalle". We might now look for the site of St Mary Minor on the Lawn of Mr Harris's garden, somewhere between that gentleman's house and the River. A very fine Yew formerly grew near the spot, which from its large dimensions, might be supposed to represent the growth of several centuries; though bearing no outward impress of extreme antiquity. It is not a fanciful surmise, that this fine Yew tree may once have overshadowed the walls of Little St Mary's Church.

3. St Michael.　　　　　St Michael's Church is not alluded to in the Almshouse MSS. But Leland, in his quaint manner, gives this curious description of the sacred edifice. The greatest token of auncient building that I saw yn al the toune ys a stone gate archid and voltid, and a chapelle or Chirch of St Michael over it." If this is a true account of St Michael's Church at Ilchester, it was what is technically known as a Hanging Chapel; similar to the specimen which is still in existence at Langport: though in the latter instance, the Chapel was long ago diverted from its original purpose,

and·turned into a Free Grammar School. Leland gives no clue to guide his readers with respect to the situation of this Gate; but leaves them in doubt, whether it might be one of the four Wall Gates, or some arched and vaulted building more centrally placed within the town.

4. St John. Neither does the name of this Church occur in the Deeds. But it is well known that the advowson of St John's at Ivelcester, was in the patronage of the Abbots of Muchelney. The following entry appears in the Taxatio of Pope Nicholas IV. A.D. 1291. "Decanatus Ivelcestr.' Ivelcestr.' P'och' S'ci Joh'is." Deanery of Ivelcester. Ivel-cester, Parish of St John." (Hugo. Much. Abb.) It is not re-corded in what part of the Town this Church was placed.

5. St Peter. No express mention is made of the Church of St Peter. But one of the Deeds points out indirectly, though with a considerable degree of certainty, the former situation of this Church. It refers to the *Cross* of St Peter. The date is 1405, and the document runs thus; Cristiana Spensere to John Drapere, a piece of ground in Chepstrete in in the town of Yevilchester, formerly built upon, near the *Cross of St Peter*; being 18 feet long and 16 wide, *beneath the Walls*. Chepstrete terminated at the South Gate; and the Cross here designated, near which lay this piece of ground "beneath the Walls," must consequently have stood near the Wall Gate, either on the right or the left hand side of Chep-strete. The Church and the Cross would be close together, or at no great distance from each other. It may therefore be considered certain, that the site of the Cross, and consequently, of the *Church* of St Peter, if it lay on the West side of the street, was at the end of the present Rectory Garden; if it lay to the East, was in the Orchard on the opposite side of the road.

It appears then that there is proof more or less complete, of the existence of all the Five Churches the names of which are to be found in Diocesan records. If at some still earlier date, Churches flourished in greater abundance, they must have been utterly swept away, without leaving a trace or even a name behind.

VII. Some particulars relating to the RECTORY OF ILCHESTER. In two Deeds, dated in the first year of Edward the Second, A.D. 1307. allusions are made to a glebe field in the Manor of Soke Deneys, belonging to the Rector of Ilchester: "a meadow belonging to the Rector of the same ville on the East." And again—"between a field of the Parson on the East." (See Deeds 15, 16) This glebe has been long severed from the Rectory. It was most likely commuted ages ago, for the small yearly money-payment now payable to the Incumbents of Ilchester out of the Manor of Sock Dennis.

Extract from the Parish Register, relating to the Ilchester Glebe situate at Urgesay, in the Parish of West Camel. "1725. This year was finished the purchase of the Estate at Urgesay bought as an Augmentation to this Rectory of Ivelchester by the charitable munificence of the Lady Moyer of the City of London & ye Bounty of Queen Anne of blessed & glorious memory—Each contributing £200. George Hooper Bishop of the Diocess. Rid Harris Rect."

So recently as the year 1840, the old Rectory House stood within the Churchyard, and so close to the Tower at its North angle, as to leave only a narrow passage for access to the North side of the Church. In that year the Burial ground was considerably enlarged, the unsightly and obstructive glebe-house was taken down, and the ground on which it stood was included in the Churchyard.

RECTORS OF ILCHESTER.

John Rauens Rector de Ilchester. 1621. [He was witness to an Almshouse Deed, dated April 5. 1621.]

The following names are copied from the fly-leaf of the old Parish Register. 1690.

1. Mr. Richard Hody Rector was buryed ye 8th of Apr. 1690.
2. John Sweet was inducted into ye Rectory of Ilchester ye sixteenth day of September Anno 1690; was buryed August 17th 1713. And succeeded by
3. Ri. Harris; who died Jany 2nd was buried Jany 7th 1728-9 and was succeeded by
4. Thomas Frances; and Thos Francis who died April ye 4th 1730 was succeeded by
5. George Prowse, who died in the year 1776, and was succeeded by the Rev
6. Thomas Camplin, Lady Day 1776.
7. Evan Davies 1791.
8. Thomas Ebrey 1812.
9. Richard Thomas Whalley 1821.

CURATES OF ILCHESTER.

1. Mr. Ward was Curate when ye living was given to ye Rev^d Mr. Prowse.
2. Mr. French succeeded Mr. Ward.
3. Mr. Wm Gyllet succeeded Mr. Frence.
4. Charles Lockyer Maby succeeded Mr. Gyllet Machaelmas 1766.
5. Willm Domett succeeded Mr. Maby the First Sunday in Advent 1766.
6. Mr. Robert Edgar succeeded Mr. Domett Mich^ls 1774.
7. John Pester succeeded Mr. Edgar Lady Day 1775.
8. J. Farthing Curate 1776.
9. John Clothier Curate 1777.
10. John Pearson 1778. John Pearson Curate of this Town Anno Domini 1782.
11. Thomas Gwynne Rees was appointed Chaplain to the Jail and Curate of Ilchester March 25. 1789. (subsequent entry) Revd T. G. Rees appointed Curate September 29, 1804. (and held the Curacy until 1812.)
12. William Presgrave 1824.

VIII. CROSSES.   Only two are mentioned.
1. The Cross of St Peter, in Chepstrete. In 1405, Cristiana
Spensere grants to John Drapere a piece of ground in Chepstrete, near the Cross of St Peter *infra Muros*, under the
Walls. The approximate site of the Cross of St Peter, has
already been adverted to—Section VI. The condition of the
Tenure is specified thus—"by paying thenceforth yearly, to
the Burgesses of Yevilchester one farthing" at Christmas. This
is the earliest notice taken in these MSS. of the Burgesses of
Ivelcester.   2. The Cross in the
Market Place near the Shambles: Mesuagium . . . ex
opposito Cruci in Mercato juxta les Shameles ejusdem ville.
1427. It is almost needless to observe, that the existing
Cross, or rather, substitute for a Cross, is quite a modern
invention; and was not, I suspect, erected on the identical
spot at the junction of the streets, occupied by the ancient
Market Cross.

IX. THE ALMSHOUSE.   The Deed of Foundation
bears date March 12, 1426, the fourth year of King Henry
the Sixth. The Founder was Robert Veel; who vests in
certain Trustees named in the Deed, his Manor of Stokelynche Maudeleyne, and all his other lands and tenements in
Stokelynche Ostriser, Yevelchester, Sock, Lymyngton, Northover, Somerton Erleighe, and in the Parish of Somerton; to
endow. an Almshouse, lately erected by him at Yevelchester,
for the maintenance of "Five at least, Six or Seven poor men,
infirm, broken down with old age, and unable to work." For
a term of Fifty years, one Moiety of the Rents and profits
was to be set apart, and deposited either in the Abbey of
Muchelney, or the Priory of Montacute, to accumulate a
Fund for the Amortisement of the Charity Estates. At the
end of Fifty years, the Royal Licence of Mortmain having
been obtained, (or earlier, if that obligation were sooner ful-
filled) the Trustees, or the Survivors of them, were to transfer

their Trusteeship to the Bailiffs [and Burgesses] of Yevelchester. Accordingly, at the expiration of Fifty years, the Transfer
was duly effected to the Bailiffs and Burgesses, by Swanne's
Indenture dated February 12th in the sixteenth year of King
Edward the Fourth, 1477.   The name
of Robert Veel. is discovered first in a Deed dated 1386.
Subsequently, in 1398, he figures as an·attesting witness, and
Notary, Roberto Veel qui hoc scripsit—an addition that might
lead to the inference of his having been a *Scrivener* by occupation.   In the various and complex transactions connected with the acquisition of the Almshouse property, during
a period of more than forty years—from 1386 to 1429—appears the name of Robert Veel.   On two occasions,
March 5 and 6, 1416, the affix "Seniori" occurs after the
name Roberto Veel; an addition implying the existence of a
"Junior" of the same name; perhaps a son.   In which case,
it is quite possible, that the son may have been ultimately the
agent in carrying out the charitable intentions and will of his
Father.   There are however, no more tangible grounds that
I am aware of, for this supposition, than the length of time
over which these transfers of property extended, and the two-
fold occurrence of the epithet *Senior*.   The leading fact is
beyond question, namely, that Robert Veel either by his own
act and deed, or though the agency of his successor, was the
real and undoubted Benefactor to whom the Community of
Ilchester is indebted, for the munificent gift of their Almshouse Charity.   An impression of the Seal of Robert Veel is
attached to the Deed of Foundation, and to most of the other
deeds of this date.   The Symbol or Crest is a veritable *Calf*.
The Estate of the Ilchester Almshouse Charity consists of one
hundred and ninety seven acres, and seven perches, of rich
and valuable land; lying principally in the Parishes of Stocklinch Magdalen and Stocklinch Ottersey; but thirty six acres
lie scattered in five other Parishes.   Of these lands, 113 acres

are now in hand, and 84 acres leased out on lives.

	In hand.			On lives.		
	A.	R.	P.	A.	R.	P.
In Stocklinch Magdalen . .	63	0	7	58	2	6
Stocklinch Ottersey . .	31	0	9	7	1	34
Limington	1	1	36	—	—	—
Odcombe	—	—	—	15	0	10
Northover	2	0	7	3	0	0
Yeovilton	9	1	3	—	—	—
Charlton Mackerell . .	6	0	15	—	—	—
	£112.	3.	37	84.	0.	10

The present gross Income of the Charity is about £300 per annum. The Almshouse is a plain modern building, without the slightest pretension to good looks. It was rebuilt on the site of the former dilapidated House, in the year 1810. The number of Almsmen varies, according to the state of the Charity funds, from ten to eighteen. Besides lodging, clothing, and fuel, each Almsman receives four shillings weekly. The surplus Funds of the Charity are appropriated in the first instance to the maintenance of the National School; for which purpose a sum of Fifty pounds is set apart. After the payment of this special grant, any remaining surplus at some future time, is to be devoted to the advancement of Education generally, in the Parish of Ilchester.

X. THE CORPORATION. Ivelcester was a Corporate Town from very early times. Yet the Charters granted by successive sovereigns appear to have been forfeited on several occasions, through the poverty of the inhabitants, aggravated by destructive fires and other casualties, and the consequent inability of the Corporate body to pay their allotted Fine into the Royal Exchequer. The Preamble of the existing Charter, granted in the reign of Philip and Mary, points to these indigent circumstances, while referring to previous Charters and assigning the reasons of their lapse. The Corporation as now constituted, is composed of a Bailiff and twelve Capital Burgesses. Under previous Charters the Burgesses had been presided over by *two* Bailiffs—1427, 1477. The names of the Bailiffs who held office during the erection and endowment of the Almshouse, are preserved in some Deeds of that time.

BAILIFFS OF YEVELCHESTER.

1427. James Attewelle and Richard Trubelas.
1428. John Chepman and John Glainville.
1429. Richard Purye and Thomas Seymour.
1477. Robert Aughte and Walter Wale.

The last named, were the Bailiffs to whom Richard Swanne Canon of Wells, and his Co-Trustees, transferred the management of the Almshouse property. An Indenture of the time of Henry the Eight, 1538, opens with this enumeration of Civic Dignitaries—"To all Christs' Faithful . . . . John Cuffe, Constable of the Town of Yevelchester, and Superintendent of all the lands and tenements belonging to the Almshouse in Yevelchester aforesaid; and Thomas Hawkere Head Steward of the same House; also William Raymonde Bailiff of the said House; and the whole Community of the same Town . . . . wish health in the Lord, everlasting." Time has laid a heavy hand on the honours and privileges of this Venerable Body. The Reform Bill, at one fell blow reduced it to political nonentity; and the Corporation of Ilchester may now be said to be kept alive, solely by its relations with the noble bequest of Robert Veel.

In the year 1858, a material change was effected in the Trusteeship of the Ilchester Almshouse Charity. Under the auspices of Her Majesty's Attorney General, Nine additional Trustees, not being members of the Corporation, were nominated to act with the Bailiff and Burgesses. Together they constitute a Board of Trustees. The Bailiff, in virtue of his office, is Chairman, when present, at all meetings of the Board.

And the management and disposition of the Charity Property, are regulated in accordance with a Scheme propounded by the Master of the Rolls.

The Bailiffs and Burgesses of Ilchester, were the sole Trustees of this fine charity for the lengthened period of 381 years; from the 12th of February 1477, to the 5th of August 1858.

XI. THE GAOL. An old Prison is thus incidentally alluded to, in 1429. "William Borde to William Boneville Knt, Robert Veel," and others; "a burgage not at present built upon, in Yevelchester, near the spot now commonly used as the Market Place; situate between a tenement of the Prioress of Whitehall inhabited by William Tancarde on the North and a tenement once belonging to John Cole of Bruggewatere on the West, in which the Gaol for Prisoners was wont from ancient times to be." Witnessed by Richd Purye and Thomas Seymour, Bailiffs of the Town of Yevelchester. 1429. The County Gaol was subsequently removed to opposite side of the River. Leland's description of the Prison, is by no means clear. "I entered Ilchester (he says) over a great stone bridge of seven arches, in the middle whereof were two little houses of stone, one on the right hand where the Common Gaol is for Prisoners in Somersetshire; the other house is on the left hand; the lesser of both seemed to me to have been a Chapel." Did Leland intend these words "where the Common Gaol is for Prisoners" as a parenthesis? Meaning merely, that the Gaol was on his right hand as he crossed the Bridge—as it in fact would have appeared to him, if it were then removed to the North side of the River? The stone house on the Bridge could have been little more capacious than a modern lock-up; and quite inadequate to the requirements of the County prison. Camden evidently did not understand that the "little stone house" at the right, was intended by Leland as the *Gaol;* for he says—" Near it (Whitehall) was a house of lepers. If this be not Leland's *house on the right hand of the Bridge,* that is quite gone; but his Chapel on the left is still a dwelling house."

In 1843, the Prison establishment was transferred to Taunton; the building itself was sold, and the materials carried away; and a garden now covers the space which the once famed Ilchester Castle for centuries filled.

XII. HOSPITAL OF ST JOHN BAPTIST AT BATH.

This Brotherhood possessed lands and tenements in and near the Town of Ivelcester. A small field in Ilchester mead, adjoining the Glebe, is still the Freehold of the Bath Hospital, and is known as "The Bath Hospital Piece." It is held by Lease, under The Master Co-Brethren and Sisters of St John's Hospital, Bath, the Reversioners. Two larger fields adjacent to the Great mead, called the Great and Little Spital, probably belonged once to the same community.

In the 1386, John Aysshwyke master of the House of the Hospital (or Hospital-House) of St John the Baptist at Bath, and the assembled Brethren of the same House, appoint Robert Veel and John Churcheman their attorneys, to deliver full possession to William Whyttoke of a messuage in Yevel-chester. Ivvelchester Field, 1327. West Field, 1387. These names apply to the extensive tract of Meadow afterwards known as the Great Mead; which lay then and for centuries after, unenclosed. "Two acres of Meadow in the West Field of the same town, of the tenure of Socke Denys" 1387. Portions of it are thus distinguished, Bridemere; Godacre; Botes-mede or Fotemede—1327. The name of the last mentioned close of land still survives under the modification of Foots or Footmead.

The Hospital of St John possessed common rights in the West Field, or Great Mead; and when the enclosure of Ilchester Mead was effected by Lord Huntingtower in 1809, a portion of the enclosed Meadow was allotted in the customary way, to the Master and Co-Brethren, in lieu of those Common rights.

This is the Close already described as the "Bath Hospital Piece."

XIII. ANCIENT FAMILIES. HERWARD.

This name, which gives out a genuine Saxon ring, frequently occurs in the oldest of the Deeds; and first, in that supposed to be coeval with the reign of King John. The Herwards were a Family of considerable note in Ivelcester, in a Century (the 13th) when Ivelcester itself was the most important Town in the County. Succeeding generations of them became owners also of Estates in the adjacent Parishes of Lymyngton and Yevelton. The name appears often and prominently, in the earliest MSS. but at longer intervals in the 14th century. It disappears altogether after 1402. This Family can be traced in direct lineal succession from King John to Edward III.

(K. John)   Herward

|

(Hen. III.)   Ralph son of Herward

|

(Edw. I)   Ralph son of Ralph.
Married Matilda daughter of Wm le Keu of Lymynton and gr. d. of John Albe of Ivelcester.

|

(Ed. II. III.)   John son of Ralph and Matilda le Keu.
Matilda Herewarde de Yvelcestra—Widow. Ed. I. Cecillia Hereward de Ivelcestra, Widow. 1304. John Herewarde of Yevelton, son of Richard Herewarde of Lymynton, and Nephew of John Hereward of Ivelcestra (John Son of Ralph) 1387. 1402.
"To all Christs' faithful . . . John Herewarde de Yeveltone,

son and heir of Richard Herewarde de Lymyngtone the Brother of John Herewarde de Yevelchestre—Health in the Lord. Know, that I have made over to Robert Veel, all my right . . . . in all the lands and tenements . . . . which the same Robert Veel holds and occupies in Yevelchestre, Sooke Denys, and Lymyngtone . . . . And because my seal is unknown to very many, I have provided that the Seal of William Whyttoke of Yevelchestre, be affixed to these presents. And I the aforesaid William Whyttoke, at the Special request of the same John Herewarde of Yeveltone, have caused my Seal to be affixed in testimony of the premisses. In the presence of these witnesses. John Wike of Nynehead &c. (N° 86) April. 12. 1402. The Family had now sunk into obscurity; and this is the last occasion on which the name appears in these Deeds. This true Saxon name is not unknown in English History. The fugitive Saxons who, after the Norman invasion, betook themselves to the Fen district around the Isle of Ely, are said to have been led by a Hereward; and under the guidance of their brave fellow countryman, to have maintained for several years in that desolate country, a desperate but unavailing struggle for independence with their Norman foes.

2. SPEGETON, SPEKETONE.   Speckington.

The name of H. de Spegeton appears, with Herward's, in the oldest MS: but incidentally, as an owner of adjoining lands. The surname is found a second time with a slight variation in the spelling, in a deed of the 32^d of Edw. I. 1304. "To all the Faithful in Christ, Thomas de Speketone son and heir of Henry de Speketone, Health in the Lord . . · . . To Walter Cole of Ivelcester, a tenement in Ivelcester, situate towards the North Gate of the Town, to the East of Whitehall; which Thomas Axtil formerly occupied, and which was given to William surnamed le Cartere in Free Marriage with Matilda daughter of William de Speketone," &c. Speckington is a Tithing of the Parish of Yeovilton; and the Manor of Speckington belongs to the Bishops of Bath and Wells.

3. Names of other Ilchester Families, appearing in the Almshouse Deeds. Triz or Tryz, Albe, Cole, Tessun or Teissun, Carter, le Bere, le Broke, Ryponne, Seymour, Salisbury or Salesbury, Cuffe, Fletcher, Boucher, Fysshe, Bryce, Whyttoke, Mascalle, Baker, Newton, Draper, Trot or Trut, Curteys, Roucetre, Glainville, Hawes, Fauconer, Chepman, Tremaylle, Yartecombe, Raymonde, Hogges or Hodges, Lockyer. Frampton.

4. Robert Veel. The following particulars relating to Robert Veel and his Family, are to be found in Hutchins's History of Dorset; and were communicated to me by a friend. Robert Veel, or Veale, is styled "of Mapoudre." Of his origin and descent nothing is stated; but in the 40th Edw. III. 1367, John Russell of Mapoudre and Agnes his wife, gave by Charter to Robert Veel and his heirs, certain lands in Mapoudre and Melcombe. By a deed of the 6th of Henry IV. the land seems to have consisted of about 100 acres. In the 15th of Henry VI, one of the Family conveyed these lands to John Coker of Mapowder and his heirs. Robert Veel married Alice Muskett, of Frome Whitfield (See No. 81. 1396.) This Alice Muskett, was the only issue of the second marriage of her mother Joan, daughter and heir of Ralph and Joan Basset. By the first marriage, the said Joan had four children whose surname was Sexpenn. Henry and Nicholas Sexpenn died without issue, leaving their sisters Joan and Emmota their heirs. Emmota released all her right in the Frome Whitfield property to her half sister Alice Veel, in 1420. Joan Sexpenn married John Comeland. [His name appears as a witness, No. 86 1402]. By Alice Muskett, Robert Veel had one child and heiress,* Alianor or Eleanor. In a Roll of Court

* If this statement implies that Robert Veel at no time had more than this one child, it is of course conclusive against my supposition (Sec. IX.) that he might have had a son Robert, from whom he was distinguished by the addition of *Senior* to his name. The Founder of the Almshouse must have lived to a good old age,—for we gather from the above extracts, that he acquired land in 1367; and dating from this event to the probable time of his death in 1430, the long period of 63 years intervened.

Leet held at Frome Whitfield in 1431, she is said to be about
21 years old. She married John Coker de Worle, son of
Robert Coker de Bower, Esqr; the Founder of the Mapoudre
family of Coker. [Her great great grandson was " Roberte
Cokere Squyer of Mapowdder"; Deed 144. 1544.] In the
Roll of Court Leet, 1431, which states the age of Eleanor
Veel, it is also recited, that Alice who was Wife of Robert
Veel, held of the lord a tenement called Fippes place, and 18
acres of arable, and Eglisham Meadow, by Knight's service,
and rent of a pair of spurs yearly. And that Alianor, wife of
John Coker, was her daughter and heir. [Hence it appears,
that Robert Veel died before, or it might be in, the year 1431.]
In 1433, Robert and Alice Veel being both dead, John and
Joan Comelond sued John and Eleanor Coker at Shaftesbury
Assizes for the property of their maternal ancestor Joan
Basset. The Jury found for the Cokers, with seven marks
damages. And in the 24th of Henry VI. John and Eleanor
demise these lands, except Eglisham meadow, for nine years,
at a yearly rent of £10. On a view or survey, made of the
Coker lands, 1st of Richard III, in Frome Whitfield; it is
mentioned that Robert Veel at one time resided there. A
close, South of the Chantry, and a parrock where was his
kitchen, are described as being where he " lately dwelt." The
Arms of Robert Veel were Argent on a bend Sable 3 calves
passants of the first. They may be seen quartered with those of
Coker in Mapowder Church; and originally, might also have
been seen so quartered, over the principal Door of the Coker
Mansion at Mapowder; and in a window of the principal room.
XIV. MOUNDS and EARTH WORKS outside the Town.
1. In the fields to the right and left of the Yeovil Road, may be
seen some well defined remains of ancient Earthworks. Enter-
ing the first field at the right hand and following the foot path
towards Sock Dennis for fifty or sixty yards, the pedestrian
descends over the rim of one of these mounds on to the natural

level of the ground. These works, as they now appear, may be generally described as two rectangular platforms; following nearly the same straight line from North to South; of nearly equal height; and sloping down on their West and South sides into a shallow ditch, partially filled up in the lapse of ages. The first of these platforms commenced originally, I should suppose, at the Moat of the Town Wall. Now, it may be said to begin from the Cow Stalls just within the field; any traces beyond, being covered by these buildings. It is elevated some three feet or more, above the lower level of the land around, The height of the second platform is rather less. To the West. they face the meadows; the Road forms their boundary on the East. The breadth of the two is almost equal; and a ditch running East and West divides the one from the other.* From the buildings before mentioned to the opposite corner of the first platform, Southward, the distance is about one hundred and twenty five yards; its average width from West to East, about fifty yards.

The length of the second platform, in a continued Southerly direction, is fifty five yards, or thereabouts; its width to the road, from fifty to sixty. The Field is called " Heave Acre," with a reference doubtless to this peculiar upheaval of the soil in its North East quarter.

In the field called Prince's Pasture, on the opposite side of the road, there are two other quadrangular platforms corresponding with the two already described; but of some what inferior elevation. The North platform extends towards the town, sixty two yards to the brook; and is in breadth fifty four. The South mound, after a progress of sixty or seventy yards Southward, grows less distinct; though formerly, no

* Since this description was written (1862) the occupier has filled up these intersecting ditches between the platforms, on both sides of the road—ignorant perhaps, that he was defacing a work which had survived the injuries of Time for more than a thousand years.

doubt continuing its course parallel with the opposite mound in Heave Acre; with which it was probably connected, by a traverse across the road at right angles. The road here, it may be observed is hollow, being several feet lower than the platforms on either side. What may have been the origin, or the intention of these works, are questions not easy to be decided. They might possibly be relics of the Roman occupation: or they may have formed part of the double fortifications by which Ilchester was defended, previously to the Norman Conquest; as related by Camden. It is strange that Stukeley should not have detected and examined these remarkable elevations. His own quaint confession of the brief hours he devoted to the investigation of old Ischalis and its antiquities, may indeed amply account for the oversight. "These, he observes, were all the remarkables I met with at Ischalis, where I stayed but *half a day.*

A "*they say*" repeated by him, suggests a further question. Can these mounds be the foundations of buildings once constituting the "suburbs"? "They say here, that the suburbs extended Southwards, especially on the Yeovil Road, which formerly had a Gate." An assignment of these quadrilateral platforms to such traditional "suburbs," is however, open to reasonable objection. The site of a ruined Street or Village, usually presents a surface irregular and uneven. Here on the contrary, exist levelness, regularity, and every indication of an uniform plan. The Mounds on both sides of the road appear to have been systematically constructed, and carefully intersected by a regular trench. Such indications lead to the more probable opinion, that the ground in these parts was originally raised for some military purpose; if not by the Romans, at a subsequent period, by our own countrymen in turbulent times.
2. In a field called Great Yard, at the opposite quarter of the Town, North West, and bordered by the Ivel, are visible other extensive vestiges of Earthworks, or foundations.

But no portion of these inequalities appear to mark the course of the Town Wall. The works, whatever may have been their nature and intention, extend outside the old boundary, and fill up the centre of this large close of pasture. A long bank or *agger*, stretching East and West straight across the field, with a deep fosse; and flanked midway on the North side towards the River, by a circular mound and ditch—these are the chief features of the earth works in this quarter. There are also some remains of field fortifications nearer to the site of the Town Wall, and in the direction of the River; which are perhaps the fortifications pointed out by Stukeley, as having been thrown up by the army of King Charles the First.

It is to be regretted, that so keen and intelligent an antiquary as Dr Stukeley, should have neglected his opportunity of throwing a clearer light on the obscure history of ancient and mediœval Ilchester. For it is almost certain, that one hundred and fifty years ago, " the remarkables " of the place, which he dismissed so hastily in his brief visit, with a mere cursory glance, or neglected to observe at all, could neither have been few, nor quite unworthy of a more accurate research.

XV, MISCELLANEA. THE COMMUNION PLATE belonging to Ilchester Church, consists of a Chalice and two Patens, of silver. The Cup is of handsome shape. Its exterior is chased, around the upper and lower parts of its circumference, with leaf and scroll work enclosed within double bands or lines, divided by decorated bends into four equal compartments. A similar kind of ornament, without any division, is repeated round the under surface of the older Paten, which when reversed, fits on as a cover to the top of the Cup. On the stem of the Paten, which is the handle of the cover, appears in bold figures the date 1574, with the letters E C beneath. The other Paten is larger, and unornamented. An inscription on the rim proclaims it " The guifte of Anne Summers 1628."

Old Epitaphs in Ilchester Church.

Tablet in the Chancel. South Wall.

NEAR THIS PLACE LYETH Y^E BODY
OF MARY RAYMOND THE LATE WIFE OF
WILLIAM RAYMOND DECEASED OF THIS
TOWN OF IVELCHESTER AND DAUGHTER
OF JOHN EVERY ESQ SERVANT TO
KING HENRY THE 8TH AND SERVANT TO
EDWARD THE 6TH & SERVANT TO
QVEENE MARY & S^RIANT AT ARMES
TO QVEENE ELIZABETH
SHEE DIED Y^E SECOND DAY OF SEPTEM
B^R AN^O DNI 1639.
MORS MIHI LVCRVM EST.

Tablet in the Nave. North East corner.

Neere to t^s place lieth Bvried ye Body of William Raymond
of Ivelchester Gent: Who departed t^s Life ye 10th Day of
Septemb^r A^o: Dmi: 1625; Being in ye 56th yeare of his Age.
In whose Memorie Mary his Wife ye Daughter of John Every
of Charcombe in Co: of Somerset Esq: ye Sergeant at
Armes hath erected t^s Monvment.

On a flat stone, in the Nave.

Mors Nobis Lucrum.

Hic jacet in Tumulo Corpus Georgii Smith Senioris Qui obiit
octavo Die Maii Ano: Dom: 1660.

Prope Eundum Tumulum jacet Corpus Elizabethœ Uxoris
Georgii Smith prœdicti Quœ obiit Martii 3° Ano: Dom: 1657.

Necnon Corpus Georgii Filii prœdicti Georgii Smith Qui obiit Januar. 1º 1653. Et Corpus Mariœ Vxoris Georgii Smith Junioris Quœ obiit August. 5º 1641. Conceptio Culpa: Nasci Pœna.

XVI. Ischalis, 1velchester: And the Foss Way.

From Dr Stukeley' *Itinerarium Curiosum* Ed. 1723.

This Station of the Romans is scituate on the South side of the River Ivel or Yeovil, the Velox of Ravennas. Pillbridg a little lower seems to retain the name. It is the Uzella of Ptolomy. I perceiv'd immediately that this place had been originally encompass'd with a wall and ditch, and traced out the manifest vestigia thereof quite round. It was an oblong square 300 paces in length, 200 in breadth, standing upon the oblique points of the compass, conform to the Foss way, which passes through the town exactly from North East to South West. The N.E. side of the city lay against the River, where I saw foundations of the wall here and there, and took up several Roman bricks in searching for it in the gardens. The ditch on the N.W. side is become a road called Yard Lane,* as going behind the yards and gardens. Then it runs thro. the Friary Garden, (for the Religious had extended their bounds beyond the city,) and turned the road on the outside. Then it goes along the road† on the back of Mr Lockyer's garden. It is now visible between the Yeovil Road and the Southern angle: then runs thro another garden, being for the most part

* Here Dr. Stukeley has fallen into an error; probably never having heard of *The Yerde* so frequently mentioned in the Deeds, the Site of which must have been somewhere in the vicinity of this Lane.

† This road could only have been a temporary thoroughfare, since it has long disappeared in the Paddock of the Farm House. The channel of the Moat being unclaimed property, was at first used by the Public as a shorter means of communication, in those parts of it conveniently situated for the purpose.

levelled by the gardener, who shewed me the track of it and had by times in digging, taken up remainders of the wall with many coins, bricks, tiles, and other antiquities. I bought some coins of him; among which, the brass one of Antoninus Pius depicted in the Plate; on the Reverse, Britannia sitting on a Rock with a military ensign. Sir Philip Sydenham has a great quantity of coins, found here; and the Minister of the Parish gave many to the learned Mr. Coke of Norfolk. This gardener showed me many square paving bricks in the floor of his house, and told me he dug up a great brass coin as big as half a crown under the foundation of the wall, which doubtless would have discovered to us the era of it's building. Crossing the Sherborne and Limington road, we find the ditch again, turning up to the River side on the Eastern angle, conformable to the scheme; where it is again enclosed into gardens and pastures. The occupier of the gardens there, informed me too, that he had frequently dug up the like antiquities together with the foundations of the wall. The quickset hedge that fences in the garden, stands on the edge of the ditch, and observes its turn at that angle of the city. By the New Mill, it meets the River. In all the gardens hereabouts by the Borough Green, they find foundations of old houses, and some run across the present streets now visible above ground. This ditch, when perfect, admitted the water of the River quite round. Mr Lockyer's house is built upon Subterraneous Arches. They say, here have been Sixteen Parish Churches, and foundations are to be found all the town over; and that the suburbs extended southward, especially on the Yeovil Road, which formerly had a Gate, It is not to be doubted, but that there were Gates at the passage of all the other streets. They say, the Bishop of Bath & Wells has a manuscript relating to the ancient State of this town. They have the same tradition as in many other places, that the old city was set on fire by matches ty'd to the tayls of sparrows,

let fly from a place call'd Standard Cross Hill. As soon as I
came to the Inn, the Swan, I saw a great parcel of the little
stones of a tesselated pavement, found but two days before, in
a garden over the way near the River. A crowd of people
came immediately, out of curiosity to see it, and tore it up. I
saw some of the remainder *in situ*, about two foot deep, laid in
strong mortar upon a hard gravell'd floor. I made the Owner
melancholy, with informing him, what profit he might have
got by preserving it to shew to strangers. The Foss way re-
tains it's name, and makes the principal Street: the pavement
thereof, or the original Ford across the River, may be seen on
the West side of the Bridge, made with great flag stones.
Upon the Bridge is an old Chapel, called Little St Mary's.
At the foot of the Bridge, within the town, is another called
White Chapel, both converted into dwellings. Foundations of
houses, chimney pieces, and the like, have been dug up in the
meads on the West side of the town, and on both sides the
River, with stone coffins and funeral apparatus. The Head of
the Mayor's Staff,* or Mace, is a piece of great antiquity in
cast brass. There are four Niches with four images, two
Kings, a Queen, and an Angel. It seems to have been the
Crozier of some Religious House. Round the bottom is wrote,
in two lines,   † JESU DEDRUERIE.

† NEME DUNETMIE. In the Northern angle,
beyond the old ditch of the city, towards the River, have been
some bastions and modern fortifications of the time of King
Charles the First. Beyond the River is a Village adjoyning,
call'd Northover, with a Church. They talk of a Castle standing where now is the Gaol, and that the tide came formerly
up hither, tho· now it reaches not beyond Langport. These
were all the remarkables I met with at Ischalis, where I

---

* This Mace is still in existence, and is used at the annual Election of the
Bailiff. It was exhibited at Kensington, among other Corporation Maces, in
1863. The Inscription is in Lombardic letters, and has never been satisfactorily
construed.

stayed but half a day. Hence I continued my journey [towards Ham Hill] along the Foss, which I observed paved with the original work in many parts. It is composed of the flat quarry stones of the country, of good breadth, laid edgewise, and so close that it looks like the side of a wall fallen down, and thro. the current of so many ages is not worn thro.; a glorious and useful piece of industry, and to our shame not imitated, for a small reparation from time to time, would have preserved it entire, and where it is so much wanted in a dirty country. . . . . Here [on St Michael's Hill, Montacute] has been a Castle and Chapel at top, and below it a Religious House, built by the Earl of Moriton, in the time of William the Conqueror. Another Hill is near it, much of the same figure. Between them and the Foss, upon the same hilly ridge, is a Roman Camp called Hamden Hill, with a double ditch, to which leads a vicinal Roman way from the Foss thro. Stoke. The Foss is very plain and strait hither, and to Petherton Bridge near South Petherton, once the Palace of King Ina. . . . . . Beyond this the Foss grows intricate and obscure, from the many collateral roads made thro. the badness and want of reparation of the true one. Yet it seems to run thro. Donington, which stands on a very high hill. . .

. . I suppose this Foss went on the East side of Chard. and so by Axminster and Colyton to Seaton, or Moridunum; where properly it begins. Whence, if we measure its noble length to the Sea coast in Lincolnshire, at Grimsby or Salt fleet, where I imagine, it ends; it amounts to 250 Roman Miles, in a strait line from North East to South West.

Finis.

Index.

Sections   Page

I.   Roads and Streets of Ivelcester .   166—173.

II.   The Wall and Gates   .   .   173—175.

III.   The Bridge   .   .   .   175.

IV.   Whitehall   .   .   .   .   176.

V.   The Friary   .   .   .   178.

VI.   The Churches of Ivelcester   .   179—184.

VII.   The Rectory of Ilchester   ,   .   184.

VIII.   Crosses.   .   .   .   186.

IX.   The Almshouse   .   .   .   186.

X.   The Corporation   .   .   188.

XI.   The Gaol   .   .   ,   190.

XII.   The Hospital of St John the Baptist at Bath   191.

XIII.   Ancient Families   .   .   192.

XIV.   Mounds and Earthworks outside the Town   195.

XV.   Miscellanea   .   198.

XVI.   Extracts from Dr. Stukeley's Itinerary   200.

19 JY 66

ERRATA.

No. 16. line 17, *read* "faciendo."

No. 29. line 12, *read* "appertenaunces."

No. 34. line 2, after "omnino" *read* "in loco meo pono dilectum."

Page 49, line 6, *read* "dat etc."

Page 51, line 4, *read* "Edward III."

Page 69, line 6. *supply* "No. 65."

No. 67, line 3. *for* "ge" *read* "qe."

Page 81 line 2. *read* "habere."

No. 87, heading. *dele* "Eve."

No. 110, line 6. *read* "dono."

No. 110, line 11. after "Hiis test." *insert these names* "Will'o Nutone Will'o Balsham Joh'e Drapere Joh'e Curteys."

Page 116 line 6. *for* aui "aut."

Page 122, 7th line from bottom, *dele* the comma before "Lucy."

Page 128, Foot Note. *read* "arbitrary."

No. 143, line 7, *read* "ac totam communitatem pred'am."

Page 173 (Sect. II.) for "regulated fortified" *read* regularly fortified."

Page 177, 8th line from end, *read* "Convent buildings."

19 JY 66

IVELCESTER.
(From Stukeley's Plan of Ischalis.
S. at the end of a name 'Stukeley.'

Lightning Source UK Ltd.
Milton Keynes UK
UKOW07f1949261015

261430UK00004B/192/P